From My Kitchen To Yours

From My Kitchen

A Home Cook's Road To Success

To Yours

Betty Ann Litvak, CCP

With a Foreword by Shirley O. Corriher, CCP, author of *Cookwise* and *Bakewise*

Sunstone Press

SANTA FE

Sunstone books may be purchased for educational, business, or sales promotional use.
For information please write: Special Markets Department, Sunstone Press,
P.O. Box 2321, Santa Fe, New Mexico 87504-2321.

Book and Cover design › Vicki Ahl
Photograph on page 13 by Lisa Fox
Cover Photograph by Ron Litvak
Body typeface › Minion Pro
Printed on acid-free paper

Library of Congress Cataloging-in-Publication Data

Litvak, Betty Ann.
  From my kitchen to yours : a home cook's road to success / by Betty Ann Litvak, CCP ;
with a foreword by Shirley O. Corriher, CCP.
    pages cm
  Includes index.
  ISBN 978-0-86534-929-2 (softcover : alk. paper)
  1. Cooking, American. 2. Cooking--United States. I. Title.
  TX715.L7646 2013
  641.5973--dc23
                                    2013000802

WWW.SUNSTONEPRESS.COM
SUNSTONE PRESS / POST OFFICE BOX 2321 / SANTA FE, NM 87504-2321 /USA
(505) 988-4418 / ORDERS ONLY (800) 243-5644 / FAX (505) 988-1025

For my husband, Ron,
who has shared my table
for 52 years—with love.

Contents

Foreword

This cookbook is the work of a lifetime by a true food lover. You will love these recipes—everything from Aunt Evey's Mushroom Crescents to L' Armagnac's Cheesecake. Every time I tried to put the book down, I would run across something that I couldn't resist—super cheesy macaroni and cheese with the most unusual ingredients! And the mystery Bar B Q sauce—the best Bar B Q ribs that I have ever eaten were made with a sauce containing Coca-Cola. Betty Ann not only had the sauce recipe, but also the name of the famous Grilling Chef who originated it.

There are chapters on appetizers, desserts, and food gifts, but primarily the recipes are arranged in menus—nine additional chapters with five or six menus in each—over 250 recipes!—recipes for everything imaginable. From her days judging at the Ohio State Fair, Prize-Winning Peach Bars, and recipes with great histories. From The Best Crab Cakes, which the novelist Pat Conroy calls matrimonial crab cakes because after he prepared these for his girl friend (now wife), she instantly agreed to marry him to First Lady Mamie Eisenhower's Million Dollar Fudge.

I love these recipes. To me, Betty Ann's taste is superb. For example, her salad dressings are more subtle like European vinaigrettes than the sharply acidic, vinegary American dressings.

I went crazy over the food gifts chapter. Such totally different, wonderful ingredients in something that you thought was ordinary like Apricot Balls or Zesty Pretzel Nuggets. I had to stop everything and go to the store for ingredients to make them!

Betty Ann grew up in her mother's kitchen, raised her children cooking in her good kitchen, and when they were gone, she brought in students. She has literally spent a lifetime sharing the joy of great food. And now, in *From My Kitchen to Yours*, she makes these treasured recipes available to everyone. You are going to love this book!

—Shirley O. Corriher
Author of *CookWise* and *BakeWise*

Introduction

I am a "foodie!" I was a foodie before there was even a word to describe someone who loves and lives food, a term which fits me to a "T." When I'm not cooking, I'm planning our next meal or dinner party, reading a cookbook, or experimenting with a new recipe…you get the idea. It all started when I was a child. Coming from a large ethnic family that immigrated to the United States from the Ukraine during the Great Depression, I didn't realize that we were poor, as our table always overflowed with an abundance of good comfort food. The kitchen was the heart of our home, where wonderful aromas greeted me when I returned from school or work. My mother served us paprikash, a stew made of chicken wings and meatballs with a savory tomato-onion base, Swiss steak with roasted potatoes and thick slices of onion, beet borscht with boiled potatoes topped with sour cream, and my favorite—her melt-in-your-mouth cookies. I learned early on to equate love with food, and enjoyed not only cooking and eating, but also the warmth and companionship that I shared in my family's kitchen, where everyone gathered to share meals and each other's company. These childhood experiences made a huge impact on me and have been a part of my identity for as long as I can remember.

Teaching has been the other great career passion in my life. One of my first jobs in junior high school was working with inner city youths at a YWCA in Cleveland, Ohio, teaching them elementary cooking skills and how to put a nutritious meal on the table for their families. As a teen age camp counselor I loved taking my campers on overnights where I organized cook-outs, grilling chicken over a campfire under the stars. I found great satisfaction in sharing knowledge, and loved the excitement of the group dynamic. Having been inspired by outstanding teachers whom I admired in school, I found that my enthusiasm for whatever I was teaching was contagious and that I enjoyed being in a leadership role. When it came time to choose a career, it seemed natural to pick education. They say to find a way to get paid for doing what you love, and I was fortunate to do just that as a middle school French teacher in the early 1960s. Along with teaching the French language which I adored, I immersed my students in the culture, the art, and, of course, the food of France. At the end of every school year my students and I cooked a meal of classic French dishes. To this day I run into former students who still talk about the crème brûlée we cooked and the French songs we sang!

When I retired from teaching to raise my own family, I naturally recreated the atmosphere of my childhood kitchen in my own home, sharing my passion for cooking with family and friends. Our home became the entertainment hub for our circle. I am very lucky to have a husband who shares my spirit of adventure and willingness to try new foods. My husband and I started giving elaborate dinner parties, and I enjoyed baking cookies, making crêpes for my kids' sleepovers and cooking homemade pasta with them and their friends. This tradition continues today with fun sessions with my grandchildren, whether it is making gingerbread houses and OSU Buckeyes with my younger grandchildren, Courtney and Connor, or creating the fabulous Bûche de Noël (the French Yule Log), with my older grandsons Lee and Daniel, for their French classes or Croque Monsieur (glorious Ham and Cheese Sandwiches) for their French Club.

As I became more confident and adventurous, I expanded my repertoire to include many ethnic cuisines and new culinary techniques. The foods of the world have always been fascinating to me, and I love learning about various countries and regions and their cultures. I find that to study a region's food is to understand its culture. Cooking expanded my horizons at a time in my life when I couldn't afford to travel. Since those early days, my husband and I have had the good fortune to travel frequently and we love to try regional dishes in the US and abroad. Many of our travels are planned to expand our culinary experiences, seeking out destinations and adventures that increase our knowledge of food and wine. We have explored regions of France, Italy, Canada, and enjoy food on international cruises, tasting our way around the world. Every time I return from a trip I can't wait to begin cooking all of the new dishes I have sampled, and sharing my new knowledge with others.

As my children grew up and began to leave the nest, I felt the time was right to combine the two areas of my career that I valued most—cooking and teaching. After working at La Belle Pomme, a fine cooking school in downtown Columbus run by Director Betty Rosbottom, first as a volunteer and then as a culinary assistant and teacher, I opened Betty Ann's Kitchen Classes, my home-based cooking school, in 1987, and I knew right away that my focus would be to share my excitement and love of cooking with home cooks. I realized that many of my friends and acquaintances had the desire to cook interesting and new dishes, but lacked the exposure, experience and confidence to seek out new recipes and cuisines and to execute them. Inspired by watching the great Julia Child's television shows, which had awakened Americans to great French food and culture in the early 1960s, I patterned my presentations on Julia's enthusiasm and realistic, down-to-earth style. My cooking school's premise was to have small, intimate classes, where students participated in the preparation of dishes, discussions about the food, and shared the meal together when the cooking was completed. Classes brought together cooks of all ages, backgrounds, and culinary experiences and introduced them to new flavors, recipes, ways to organize shopping trips and prep work, helpful tips, and yes, even the inevitable mistakes and (near) disasters. This allowed students to become comfortable with every aspect of cooking, from making appetizers, preparing a family meal, to hosting an elegant dinner party. My philosophy for my school was to teach the tools not only to produce successful dishes, but also the ability to enjoy the process, a key for every successful home cook! I joined the International Association of Culinary Professionals and sat for the comprehensive examination, becoming a CCP, Certified Culinary Professional, to expand my culinary knowledge. I have attended IACP annual conferences for many years, taking classes taught by the leaders in my field, to inspire me and enhance my ability to bring the latest and most useful cooking information to my students. My goal for the past 24 years has been to empower home cooks to accomplish their goals in the kitchen. I gave them the ability to provide delicious meals for their families, exposed them to cutting edge ingredients, multicultural cuisines, and taught them the skills and techniques to inspire them to find the joy that I have always found in the kitchen.

After retiring, I knew that I wanted my next challenge to be to continue to share my knowledge and love of cooking, and thus this cookbook was born. This book is for the home cook, from young professionals and newlyweds to seasoned cooks who want to expand their knowledge. It contains a great variety of global recipes, from Asian Cuisine and American Regional Food to Italian and French Fare and beyond. You will find classic techniques such as *mise en place*, as well as important tips to enable you to become a better cook. I hope this cookbook will become your "go-to" book for all occasions.

In these pages you'll find easy, make-ahead recipes as well as more complex creations to challenge you. There is an icon with a *clock* ⏱ after the title of each recipe that has make-ahead components, and 1, 2 or 3 *chef's hat* 👨‍🍳 to indicate whether a recipe is

1 hat 👨‍🍳 Easy,

2 hats 👨‍🍳 👨‍🍳 of Medium difficulty,

and 3 hats 👨‍🍳 👨‍🍳 👨‍🍳 A Challenge but worth it.

Most chapters have five or six menus except for the Starters chapter, Desserts chapter, and Gifts from Your Kitchen chapter, each of which has 20 recipes.

Generally I do not list specific brands of products to use in your cooking, so if I do it means I feel they are products that are tried and true and will give consistently good results. Of course you are free to use your favorite brands, but for example, I recommend *More Than Gourmet* "pucks" of beef, veal and chicken broth which have no chemicals or additives, have low salt content and are very low fat, but have wonderful true flavor. I really believe solid *Crisco* does a better job of deep frying, and is great for making soft-textured chocolate chip cookies, but if you prefer canola oil or other oils use them instead. *Hellman's Real Mayonnaise* has very little sugar and a very good flavor which I think enhances many recipes. If I have listed a specific brand you might want to try it and see if you can tell a difference. Don't forget to look at my Cook's Tips at the end of each chapter, which hold important information, as well as a chuckle hopefully.

It has been a benchmark of my teaching that I thoroughly test every recipe and write them clearly. Look at the cookbook as a bountiful smorgasbord, where you can come back time and again to refill your plate with new tastes and experiences. Remember that life is a banquet—so enjoy it fully!

Fondly,
Betty Ann

Acknowledgements

I want to take this opportunity to thank some special people in my life for their much-appreciated help. No one teaches cooking or writes a cookbook alone. First on my list is my husband of more than 52 years, Ron, who survived week-long transformations of our house to accommodate the students, carried in groceries, helped set up the classroom and kept himself out of our way (it's dangerous to step into a lively group wielding knives!), taste-tested ALL my recipes, and was supportive in more ways than I could ever list. I also am enormously grateful to my culinary assistants throughout the years: from Linda Ruck, who stuck with me for 21 awesome years, to Jan Smith, David Berg, Susan Keferl, Marlene Broseman and Pam Workman. They never failed to be right there for me, stirring, chopping, timing, tasting, and, of course washing mountains of dishes, while still smiling! Linda, Marlene and Pam along with Ruth Ann Rusk, an advanced cooking student who joined us, have been an integral part of preparing this cookbook, participating in lunches where we all re-tested a number of the older recipes I had taught, to be sure they were as good as we remembered. There are truly no words to thank them sufficiently.

My wonderful sister Helene Norin, a fabulous cook, also got in on the act and tested many recipes for me, and her talented daughter Debbie Norin-Kuehn worked on the Asian section, which I appreciate so much! I thank my family, from my parents who brought me up in an ethnic culture that showed me that Food equals Love, to my three children. Alan, our son, won his wife of 20 years with "his" spaghetti carbonara in college and does a lot of the cooking in his home, Diane, a seasoned and experimental cook, has prepped and shopped with me, tested recipes, taught some cooking classes, encouraged me to write this cookbook, helped me find my voice *and* served as editor for the book, and Ayla, a very adventurous cook who shares my love of ethnic restaurants and inspired me to explore vegetarian options. I am proud that all of my children have continued the tradition of great cooking at home, and I enjoy cooking with the next generation, their children! I owe a huge debt of thanks to all my culinary colleagues and great family cooks and friends who allowed me to share their recipes, which have enriched this book hugely. Another big Thank You to all my students through the years, whose enthusiasm and interest always spurred me on!

Many thanks to colleague Andrew Schloss, author of many successful cookbooks, who coached me on preparing my proposal and gave me invaluable suggestions on the manuscript, and to the darling Shirley Corriher, award-winning cookbook author and friend, for her warm Forward. To both of them and to Raghavan Iyer and Michael Kalahny for their generous comments for the back of the book, my sincere thanks! My dear friend Sundra Spears has been supportive and encouraging from the beginning of this project—her heart is as big as the state of Texas, where she lives. I owe a huge debt of gratitude to Ruth Ann Rusk, who spent countless hours retyping many of my earlier recipes that had not been on computer. A big thank-you to Marcia Gantz for her many hours of meticulously editing and proofreading the manuscript, to Peggy Hayes for her editing suggestions, proofreading and recipe testing, to her husband Dr. David Hayes for his technical computer advice, and to my grandsons Lee and Daniel Helton, for the hours they spent teaching me new computer skills, and especially for not losing patience with me when I asked them how a flash drive works for the eighth or ninth time. Many thanks to my friend Alison Chapman, a talented personal chef and former formatter at a publishing house, for her help in formatting the cookbook.

I also want to thank Marlene Broseman and Ruth Ann Rusk, again, and dear friend Marilyn Pugliese, who generously cooked several dishes for me for the photo shoot for the book, and my grandson Daniel Helton, a chef-in-training, who helped me cook many dishes for the photo shoot. And kudos to talented friend Lisa Fox, who took all the pictures. To my amazing friend, Vinny Herwig, warm hugs for her constant friendship and support! I am so honored that Cowboy Artist Jack Wells created an original and historically authentic black and white sketch of a female chuckwagon "cookie" to accompany the recipe for "Can Do" Cowboy Beans in Chapter 3. Finally, and very importantly, I am indebted to my delightful publisher, James Clois Smith Jr., President of Sunstone Press, who believed in me and this book right away, and has been of invaluable help to me in getting this book in print—it has been a joy to work with him and his skilled staff!

1

STARTERS FOR ALL OCCASIONS

C all them appetizers, hors d'oeuvres or starters, these tasty recipes set the tone for a meal and keep your family and guests happy while you're readying the "main event." In this chapter are 20 recipes for all occasions, from simple to fancy. You'll be able to choose just the right dish to suit the menu you're planning, or consider picking three or four from the list, add a bottle of bubbly and voilà—an easy but elegant party!

Sausage and Cheese Stars (page 16) and The Colors of Italy (page 25)

SAUSAGE AND CHEESE STARS
MAKES ABOUT 2 1/2 DOZEN

This is one of my most popular appetizers—easy to make and delicious!

Crisco to grease mini muffin pans
1 cup cooked crumbled sausage
3/4 cup each grated sharp cheddar and Monterey Jack cheese
1/2 cup bottled ranch dressing
1/4 cup each sliced ripe (black) olives and chopped fresh red pepper (or bottled roasted red pepper)
1/2 package wonton wrappers (find them in produce section at the supermarket)
cooking spray

1. Preheat oven to 350°F. Grease 2 mini muffin tins with the Crisco.

2. Make the filling: In a large bowl, combine sausage, cheeses, salad dressing, olives and red pepper. Reserve.

3. Press one wonton wrapper into each cup of muffin tin. (Freeze any extra wrappers.) Spray with the cooking spray. Bake 5 minutes, or until golden. Remove from oven. (Can be made a day ahead, cooled, and reserved in airtight plastic container.) When ready to bake, fill each cup with some of the filling. Return to the 350°F. oven and bake 5 minutes more, or until cheese melts. Remove to pretty platter and serve warm.

MAHOGANY CHICKEN WINGS
SERVES 10

This marinade is an all-purpose barbeque sauce for chicken, cornish hens or large butterflied shrimp. Be sure to bring any leftover marinade to a boil before using again, to kill any bacteria from the raw food marinated in it.

4 pounds chicken wings, tips cut off (save them to make chicken stock)

Marinade:

1 cup plus 2 tablespoons hoisin sauce
3/4 cup plum sauce
1/2 cup light soy sauce
1/3 cup cider vinegar
1/4 cup each dry sherry and honey
6 green onions, minced
6 large cloves fresh garlic, minced
nonstick cooking spray

Optional garnish: one bunch green onions, to make scallion brushes (see below)

1. Cut off wing tips, then cut rest of each wing into two pieces at the joint.

2. In a large non-reactive (ceramic, plastic or glass—not aluminum) shallow casserole combine marinade ingredients. Place wings in marinade and mix well. Cover casserole and refrigerate overnight.

3. Preheat oven to 375°F. Line a large baking sheet with heavy duty foil. Spray a wire cooling rack with non-stick cooking spray and place rack in the baking sheet.

4. Drain the chicken wings. Boil the marinade and reserve it. Arrange wings on the rack and roast for 30 minutes. Remove baking sheet from the oven and carefully drain accumulated liquid, adding to reserved marinade. Baste the wings with the marinade, turn them and baste again. Return to oven and roast until the wings turn a rich mahogany color, up to another 30 minutes, basting with reserved marinade to be sure wings don't burn or dry out. Arrange on pretty platter and serve hot or at room temperature.

5. To make scallion brushes: Cut off root tip from scallions and discard, then clean scallions. With a sharp knife make lengthwise cuts at each end about 2 inches long, leaving about 1/2 inch in center uncut. Place in ice water for several hours or overnight—ends will curl. Garnish platter of finished wings with brushes if you wish.

SAVORY MUSHROOM STRUDEL
MAKES 2 LARGE STRUDELS

A wonderful recipe adapted from Betty Rosbottom's La Belle Pomme Cooking School, formerly situated at Lazarus Department Store in Columbus, Ohio, where I worked first as a volunteer and then as her culinary assistant. Betty ran the school with professionalism and panache for many years.

Filling:

2 tablespoons unsalted butter
1 1/2 pounds fresh domestic white mushrooms, cleaned and finely diced (this can be done in batches in a food processor)
3 cloves garlic, peeled and minced
1 tablespoon fresh parsley, finely chopped
3 1/2 tablespoons <u>each</u> unsalted butter and all-purpose flour
3/4 cup whole milk <u>plus</u> 3/4 cup heavy cream, warmed
1 teaspoon salt
1/2 teaspoon freshly ground black pepper

10 sheets phyllo (pronounced feelow) dough, defrosted
10 tablespoons unsalted butter, melted
<u>5 tablespoons fine unseasoned breadcrumbs, approximately</u>

1. <u>Make the filling</u>: Melt the 2 tablespoons butter in a large heavy skillet over medium-high heat and add the mushrooms. Cook until liquid has evaporated, stirring occasionally. Add garlic and parsley and sauté quickly. Reserve.

2. In a medium saucepan, melt the 3 1/2 tablespoons butter. Whisk in the flour and cook, stirring constantly with a wooden spoon 3 minutes. Add the warmed milk-cream mixture and cook, stirring constantly with a whisk and using a wooden spoon to stir any stuck sauce around edges, until mixture thickens and comes to a boil. Season with salt and pepper. Add the mushroom mixture and bring to a low boil. Cool and refrigerate until cold.

3. <u>Assemble strudels</u>: Lay a sheet of phyllo dough on a work surface and brush with melted butter. (Keep rest of phyllo dough covered with parchment or waxed paper and a damp cloth.) Sprinkle with about 1 teaspoon breadcrumbs. Add another sheet of dough, brush with more butter and sprinkle with crumbs again. Continue to stack sheets in this manner, using 5 sheets total. Lay half of the chilled mushroom filling across the width of the sheets, in about a 3 inch pile. Tuck in ends of phyllo and roll up tight, as for an egg roll. Brush the top with melted butter and use a large spatula to transfer to a rimmed buttered baking sheet. Repeat this process with the second set of phyllo sheets and filling to make a second strudel. (You can bake immediately, or cover with plastic wrap sprayed with cooking spray and refrigerate overnight.)

4. When ready to bake, preheat oven to 375°F. Bake strudels 25 minutes. Carefully remove to a wooden board using a large spatula and slice into serving pieces with a serrated or electric knife.

BAKED BRIE WITH KALAMATA OLIVES AND
ROASTED GARLIC—SERVES 8

This makes a great starter for a holiday party and it halves easily for a smaller group.

1 whole head fresh garlic
2 tablespoons extra virgin olive oil
1-pound wheel of Brie, well chilled
1/4 cup Greek Kalamata olives, pitted and quartered
2 teaspoons finely snipped fresh parsley
<u>Granny Smith apple slices, warm French bread slices</u>

1. Place whole head of garlic in a <u>heavy</u> saucepan with the olive oil and cook, stirring over medium heat for 5 minutes. Cover, reduce heat to low and cook for 10 to 15 minutes more, or until garlic is soft. Remove from pan and drain on absorbent paper. Alternately, you can put the whole head in an ovenproof casserole with the oil, cover with foil, and bake in a preheated 325°F. oven for about 30 minutes. Remove garlic from casserole, drain on absorbent paper and cool.

2. Carefully slice the thin rind off one of the flat sides of the Brie, using a sharp knife or a serrated knife. Place cheese on a baking sheet, preferably with no sides, cut side up.

3. Divide the head of garlic carefully into cloves and peel gently. With a small sharp knife slice the cloves

diagonally, being careful not to sever each slice. Gently press garlic cloves into fans. Arrange garlic fans and quartered olives on top of Brie. (At this point, you can wrap cheese in plastic wrap and chill up to 3 days.)

4. <u>When ready to serve</u>: Bake in a preheated 400°F. oven 10 to 12 minutes, or until the Brie is warm and slightly softened and runny. Sprinkle with parsley. Carefully transfer to a serving platter with a large spatula and serve garnished with the apple wedges and crusty bread slices.

SPICY POTATO CROQUETTES
MAKES 30

This recipe is from the fascinating world of Indian cuisine. Look for some of the spices and flour at an Indian grocery—it's lots of fun to explore ethnic grocery stores. Keep leftover spices in your refrigerator or freezer to keep them fresher.

3 medium Idaho (Russet) potatoes (1 1/4 pounds) peeled, boiled and mashed
1 1/2 medium onions, finely chopped
2 large eggs
2 spicy green chilis, seeded and chopped (fresh or canned, optional)
3 1/2 tablespoons chickpea flour (besan) or all-purpose flour
1/8 teaspoon <u>each</u> cumin, garlic powder, turmeric, coriander and baking soda
1/2 teaspoon sambhar spice

vegetable oil for deep frying
<u>Major Grey's Chutney or other prepared chutney</u>

1. In a medium bowl combine mashed potatoes, onion, eggs, chilis, besan flour, spices and baking soda. Mixture will be sticky.

2. Heat oil in deep fryer to 375°F. For each croquette scoop up a tablespoon of the potato mixture and with a second spoon scrape the mixture directly into the hot oil. Fry about 4 or 5 at a time, turning occasionally with a slotted spoon, for about 5 minutes, or until golden brown. As they brown, remove croquettes with a slotted spoon and drain on paper towels. Serve croquettes hot with some chutney on the side.

PANCETTA-ALMOND MEDJOOL DATES
SERVES 8

My assistant Marlene tasted this fabulous starter at Iron Chef Michael Syman's wonderful Cleveland restaurant Lolita and brought me the idea. We tweaked it a bit and here it is for you to enjoy. It is a simple but stunning appetizer.

6 slices pancetta (Italian bacon), chopped
2 tablespoons unsalted butter
32 Medjool or other pitted dates
1/2 cup sliced almonds
<u>chopped parsley leaves</u>

1. In a skillet fry the chopped pancetta until crisp. Add butter until it melts. Transfer to a small bowl and reserve.

2. Preheat oven to 400°F. Place dates on a baking sheet and bake for 6 to 8 minutes, or until they become slightly crisp. On another baking sheet place the almonds and bake until they are light brown—5 minutes or so. Watch carefully so they don't burn. Reserve.

3. <u>Assemble</u>: Put the dates on a serving platter. Pour the sautéed pancetta on top and sprinkle with almonds. Sprinkle on the chopped parsley.

GOAT CHEESE-STUFFED FINGERLING
POTATOES—SERVES 8

A truly elegant and memorable beginning for a special meal, adapted from Star Chef Hubert Keller.

12 fingerling potatoes, about 2 1/2 inches long, thicker ones preferred

Dressing:

1 teaspoon Dijon mustard
2 teaspoons sherry vinegar
2 tablespoons extra virgin olive oil

Filling:

5 ounces goat cheese, room temperature

1 teaspoon white truffle oil (or hazelnut oil or walnut oil), refrigerate after opening
1/2 teaspoon salt, 1/4 teaspoon black pepper

Garnish: snipped fresh chives

1. Wash the potatoes and slice the tips off each end, so they sit perfectly flat, then cut potatoes into 1-inch sections. You should get approximately 2 pieces from each potato.

2. Using a small melon baller or metal measuring spoon, scoop out the center of each potato section, creating a cavity for the goat cheese filling. Be careful not to go more than 3/4 of the way down the potato. Boil 2 quarts of water with 1 tablespoon of salt in a 4- quart pan. Carefully drop in the potato sections and scooped-out rounds and cook until tender, approximately 8 to 10 minutes. Save these rounds for a "cook's treat". While the potatoes cook, prepare an ice water bath—a large bowl with water and ice cubes. When potatoes are tender, use a slotted spoon to scoop them out of the boiling water, and drop them immediately into the ice water bath to stop the cooking.

3. Make the dressing: In a small bowl whisk together the Dijon mustard and vinegar. Slowly whisk in the olive oil until well blended. Set aside.

4. Remove potatoes from the ice water bath, dry them and line them up on a tray. Season lightly with salt and pepper, then drizzle with the dressing.

5. Make filling: In a bowl mix together the goat cheese, white truffle oil and the salt and pepper. Whisk until smooth.

6. Using a small measuring spoon, spoon the mixture into the potato sections, so that it completely fills each potato and comes just slightly over the top.

7. Garnish each potato with some snipped chives and serve at room temperature.

PORTOBELLO-HAVARTI TURNOVERS
MAKES 16

This is one of several of my recipes that use frozen puff pastry, a wonderful convenience product that doesn't compromise the integrity and flavor of the dish.

4 ounces (2 cups) portobello mushrooms, wiped dry with a damp paper towel, stems discarded
1 cup finely chopped onion
2 tablespoons unsalted butter
1/4 cup shredded Havarti cheese

1 sheet (from a 2-sheet package) frozen puff pastry, thawed

Egg wash: 1 egg whisked with 1 tablespoon water

1. Dice the mushrooms. In a medium skillet, sauté mushrooms with the onion in 2 tablespoons butter until onion is golden and mushrooms have exuded their liquid and it has evaporated. Remove to small bowl and cool. Add the Havarti cheese.

2. Unfold the thawed puff pastry sheet and place it on a lightly floured board. Roll pastry to a 14" x 14" square and cut into 16 squares, each 3 1/2" x 3 1/2".

3. Spoon 2 teaspoons filling onto each square. Fold each square into a triangle and seal edges with the tines of a fork. Place turnovers on a rimmed cookie sheet lined with parchment paper. Cover with plastic wrap and refrigerate 1 hour or up to overnight, or you can freeze them, and then transfer to a plastic ziplock bag and keep in freezer for up to 2 months.

4. When ready to bake turnovers: Preheat oven to 400°F. Cut a slit in the center of the top of each turnover. Brush with the egg wash, trying not to get any on the parchment paper, and bake for about 15 minutes, or until pastry is puffed and golden brown. Serve while still warm.

SMOKED SALMON BEGGAR'S PURSES
WITH CRÈME FRAÎCHE
MAKES ABOUT 20

This recipe contains the basic recipe for crêpes, which you can use in many other preparations as well.

Crêpes:

1 cup <u>each</u> cold water and cold whole milk
4 large eggs
1/2 teaspoon salt
2 cups all-purpose flour
4 tablespoons melted unsalted butter
thin strips of parchment paper
1 tablespoon vegetable oil

Filling:

2 cups chopped smoked salmon
4 tablespoons chopped chives, plus more for dip
1 cup crème fraîche

20 additional long chives, blanched in simmering water
    and drained, to wrap purses

2 ounces black lumpfish caviar (from supermarket),
    <u>gently rinsed in a fine sieve and drained</u>

1. <u>Make crêpe batter</u>: In a blender place liquids, eggs and salt. Add the flour, then the butter. Cover and blend at high speed for 1 minute. Scrape down any bits of flour with a rubber spatula, blend for 2 to 3 seconds more. Cover and refrigerate for at least 2 hours or up to overnight.

2. <u>Make crêpes</u>: Brush a 6-inch cast iron or non-stick skillet with about 1 tablespoon vegetable oil. Set over moderately high heat and heat until pan is just beginning to smoke. Immediately remove from heat and, holding the handle of the pan in your right hand, pour in 1/8 cup (can use a 2 tablespoon coffee measure) of batter into the middle of the pan with your left hand. Quickly tilt the pan in all directions to run the batter over the bottom of the pan in a thin film. This takes about 3 seconds. Return pan to heat for 60 to 80 seconds, then jerk and loosen crêpe and lift its edges with a thin spatula, if underside

is light brown, turn carefully, by either using the spatula or using your fingers. Brown lightly for about 30 seconds on second side, which will be a pale spotty brown. This is always the "nonpublic" side of the crêpe, as Julia Child used to say. Stack on a plate, separating each crêpe with a thin strip of parchment paper so crêpes won't stick together, and continue cooking crêpes until all batter is used. Can be made up to a day ahead and refrigerated, or wrapped well and frozen for 2 months. (If frozen, defrost before using.)

3. <u>Filling for crêpes</u>: Toss the smoked salmon with 4 tablespoons of chopped chives. Place 1 teaspoon of the crème fraîche in the center of the "nonpublic" side of one crêpe. Top with 1 tablespoon of the smoked salmon mixture. Carefully bundle up the crêpe, creating a little purse-shaped package. Tie it closed with a blanched chive carefully. The first few purses may be difficult, but practice makes perfect!

4. <u>To serve</u>: Mix the remaining crème fraîche with 3 to 5 tablespoons water and 3 to 4 tablespoons chopped chives, stirring until smooth. Season with salt and pepper and spoon on each plate, top with some caviar and 2 beggar's purses for each serving.

ROQUEFORT-WRAPPED GRAPES
MAKES ABOUT 5 DOZEN

Simple, fast, beautiful, and best of all, it's a make-ahead recipe! This recipe was given to me by my very creative culinary assistant David Berg.

10 ounces walnuts

8 ounces cream cheese, at room temperature
4 ounces Roquefort cheese, at room temperature
2 tablespoons heavy cream

1 1/4 pounds (about 60) red or green seedless grapes, or <u>a mixture of both, stems removed</u>

1. Heat the oven to 325°F. Spread nuts evenly on a rimmed, foil-lined cookie sheet and bake until lightly toasted and aromatic, 8 to 12 minutes. Cool.

2. Chop toasted nuts coarsely in a food processor or by hand. Transfer to a large tray or plate and spread out evenly.

3. In the bowl of an electric mixer combine the cream cheese, Roquefort and heavy cream and beat on low speed until smooth, 2 to 3 minutes. Drop the clean, dry grapes into the cheese mixture. Use a rubber spatula to stir grapes in the mixture until each grape is coated. Working a few at a time, transfer the coated grapes to the chopped nuts and roll them in the nuts until they are well coated. Transfer grapes to a rimmed baking sheet lined with parchment or waxed paper. Cover with plastic wrap and refrigerate until serving. Can be made up to 2 days ahead. Before serving cut each grape in half with a serrated knife if using large red grapes. Any leftover cheese mixture can be frozen.

NACHO POTATOES—SERVES 10

I made these for a teen cooking class, and both the kids and their parents loved them!

6 medium Idaho (Russet) potatoes, peeled and cut into
    8 wedges each
6 tablespoons extra virgin olive oil
2 teaspoons salt
1/4 teaspoon freshly ground black pepper
2 cups grated cheddar or Monterey Jack cheese
8 to 10 slices bacon, cooked crisp and crumbled
4 scallions (green onions) thinly sliced

<u>Garnish: sour cream and salsa</u>

1. Preheat oven to 375°F.

2. Put potato wedges into a large bowl. Toss with the olive oil, salt and pepper. Arrange in a single layer in a heavy ovenproof 12-inch skillet (I love a cast iron skillet for this). Cook for 8 minutes over medium-high heat on the stovetop until golden brown, then turn potatoes with tongs or a spatula and transfer the skillet carefully to the preheated oven.

3. Bake until potatoes are golden and crisp on the outside and cooked through (taste one carefully—they will be hot!), about 25 minutes.

4. Remove skillet from oven with hot pads and sprinkle potatoes with the grated cheese, the crumbled bacon and the scallion slices. Return to oven and bake until cheese melts, 3 to 4 minutes.

5. Carefully remove from oven and transfer potatoes to a platter. Serve with the sour cream and salsa on the side for guests to garnish their own servings. YUM!

SHRIMP BOMBAS—MAKES 24 PIECES

1 medium Idaho (Russet) potato (about 1/4 pound)
   peeled and quartered
2 tablespoons unsalted butter
2 ounces Muenster or smoked cheddar cheese
1 large egg yolk (you can freeze the egg white for later
   use)
2 tablespoons fresh chopped parsley leaves
1/8 teaspoon white pepper, plus salt to taste
1 to 2 tablespoons flour

1/2 cup finely minced onion
1 tablespoon unsalted butter
1/2 pound raw shrimp, peeled, deveined and coarsely
   chopped

1/4 cup flour, or more as needed
1 large egg, beaten
1/2 cup fresh breadcrumbs (made with white bread,
   crusts removed, whirled in food processor)
Crisco solid oil for deep frying

1. Cook potato in lightly salted water until tender, then
drain. Mash, then add 2 tablespoons of butter, the cheese,
egg yolk, parsley and pepper and mix thoroughly. Add 1
to 2 tablespoons flour until mixture holds together. Cover
and reserve.

2. Melt the 1 tablespoon of butter in a skillet and sauté
onions for 5 minutes. Add the chopped raw shrimp and
cook until just pink, just a few minutes. Add this mixture
to the reserved potato mixture, mixing gently. Fry a small
teaspoon of this mixture in a skillet, then taste and season
whole mixture with salt and more pepper if needed. DO
NOT taste the uncooked mixture, as it has raw eggs in it.

3. Flour hands and shape mixture into walnut-size balls.
Roll lightly in flour, dip into beaten egg and then into the
breadcrumbs. Put onto parchment paper or waxed paper-
covered cookie sheet and refrigerate at least 30 minutes
or up to 2 hours.

4. When ready to serve, heat 2 inches of Crisco oil in
a heavy pot to 375°F. and fry the bombas until golden
brown. Remove gently with a slotted spoon and drain on
absorbent paper. Arrange on a serving platter and serve
warm.

HUMMUS WITH PITA CRISPS
MAKES 4 CUPS

*You need this recipe in your cooking repertoire—easy,
make-ahead and full of flavor. If you are in a hurry you
can omit making the parsley oil, but it makes a stunning
presentation.*

4 large fresh garlic cloves, peeled
1 teaspoon salt
2 1-pound cans of chickpeas (garbanzos) drained and
   rinsed
2/3 cup well-stirred tahini (sesame seed paste—
   available at specialty food stores)
1/4 cup fresh lemon juice or to taste
1/4 cup extra virgin olive oil

Toasted pita wedges

twelve 4-inch pita loaves
1/3 cup or more extra virgin olive oil

Parsley oil:

1/2 cup fresh parsley leaves
1/4 cup extra virgin olive oil, or more as needed for
   proper consistency

2 tablespoons pine nuts, lightly toasted in a skillet
   (watch carefully as they burn easily.)

1. On a cutting board mince and mash the garlic and salt
to a paste with a large knife.

2. In the food processor purée the chickpeas with this
garlic paste, the tahini, lemon juice, 1/4 cup of olive oil
and 1/2 cup water, scraping down the sides with a rubber
spatula to make a smooth mixture. Taste and add salt if
needed. Add more water if needed to thin the hummus to
the desired consistency. Transfer to a serving bowl. Can
be made up to three days before and refrigerated. Bring
to room temperature before serving.

3. Make toasted pita crisps: Preheat oven to 400°F. Halve
the pita loaves horizontally, forming 24 rounds, and
brush the rough inside of each round lightly with some
of the oil. Cut each round into 6 triangle-shaped pieces
with kitchen scissors. Put the wedges in one layer on two

cookie sheets and bake for 8 to 10 minutes or until they are golden and crisp. Then remove from oven and let them cool. These may be made up to one week in advance and kept in an airtight container. Makes about 144 thins. Any extras make great snacks.

4. Make the parsley oil: Clean the processor bowl and purée the parsley and the 1/4 cup of olive oil until the oil is bright green and the parsley is minced. Transfer to a small glass bowl. Can be refrigerated for up to three days.

5. When ready to serve: Drizzle the parsley oil in a lattice pattern over the hummus and sprinkle with the toasted pine nuts. Serve with the pita crisps.

MUSHROOM CRESCENTS—MAKES ABOUT 60 PIECES

I got this recipe from my dear Aunt Evey. My Aunt Carol, Aunt Shirley and Aunt Betty also made them often, so I'm not sure which one of them created it. Everyone always waited for these delicious bites at family gatherings!

Dough:

9 ounces cream cheese
1/2 cup unsalted butter
1 1/2 cups flour

Filling:

2 tablespoons unsalted butter
1 medium onion, minced
1/2 pound fresh mushrooms, cleaned and chopped
3 ounces cream cheese
1/2 teaspoon salt, 1/8 teaspoon freshly ground black
    pepper
1/4 teaspoon dried thyme

Glaze: 1 egg beaten with 1 teaspoon water

1. Prepare the dough: In a large bowl combine the cream cheese, butter and flour until dough is an even consistency. Wrap in plastic wrap and chill for at least 30 minutes, or up to overnight.

2. Prepare the filling: In a large skillet melt the butter and sauté the onions until light brown. Add the mushrooms

and cook over medium heat 3 to 4 minutes. Lower the heat, add cream cheese and stir until melted. Stir in the salt, pepper and thyme and cool filling in the refrigerator.

3. Roll out the chilled dough 1/8 inch thick and cut into 2 1/2 inch circles. Fill center with 1/2 teaspoon of filling. Fold in half and press edges with the tines of a fork to seal well. Snip center top of each round with kitchen scissors to let steam escape during baking.

4. Brush pastries with glaze and freeze RAW, well wrapped, OR refrigerate until ready to use if you are planning to bake and serve them the same day.

5. When ready to bake, place on ungreased cookie sheets and bake at 325°F. to 350°F. for 30 minutes if frozen, or 20 minutes if "fresh". Watch carefully so they don't burn. Serve warm.

CRAB RANGOON
MAKES 28 WONTONS

Asian flavors using time saving prepared wonton wrappers. Remember that you can freeze any extra wrappers for another use.

Filling:

6-ounce can pasteurized lump crabmeat, drained, any
    cartilage removed (find it in the refrigerated section
    of the supermarket)
2 ounces ground pork
1/2 large egg white, lightly beaten
1/2 teaspoon each sugar and freshly ground black
    pepper
1/4 teaspoon salt
1 1/2 teaspoons each grated fresh gingerroot, dry
    sherry, and cornstarch
1 teaspoon each light soy sauce and Oriental sesame oil
2 tablespoons chopped scallions

Dipping Sauce

1/4 cup light soy sauce
2 teaspoons sugar
1/4 cup water
1/4 cup rice wine vinegar
2 teaspoons grated fresh gingerroot

1 tablespoon chopped scallions
1/2 teaspoon <u>each</u> sesame oil and chili oil

28 wrappers from a 1-pound package of prepared
   wonton wrappers
cornstarch, for dusting filled wontons
<u>Crisco solid vegetable oil, for frying wontons</u>

1. <u>Prepare the wonton filling</u>: Mix the drained crabmeat with the ground pork, egg white, sugar, pepper, salt, grated gingerroot, dry sherry, cornstarch, light soy sauce and sesame oil and let stand 15 minutes.

2. <u>Prepare the dipping sauce</u>: Place the soy sauce, sugar and 1/4 cup water in a small saucepan over moderate heat and bring to a boil. Remove from heat and stir in the remaining ingredients. Cover and set aside.

3. <u>Assemble the wontons</u>: Position a wrapper with one point toward you. Place 1 rounded teaspoon of filling just below the center of the wrapper. Lightly moisten edges of the wrapper with water. Fold wrapper in half over the filling to form a triangle. Moisten the 2 side points with water and overlap them over the filled portion, then pinch the overlapping edges firmly together to seal. Place filled wontons on a baking sheet that has been lightly dusted with cornstarch and keep covered while you fill and fold remaining wontons.

4. <u>To fry the wontons</u>: In a wok or deep fryer heat 2 to 3 inches of oil to 350°F. over moderately high heat. Add a few wontons at a time and fry until golden, about 2 to 3 minutes. Remove with slotted spoon, drain on paper towels and serve with the dipping sauce.

BEEF KNISHES—MAKES 4 1/2 DOZEN

A staple of Jewish cuisine. Time intensive, but well worth the effort…The knishes can be frozen and defrosted for a party up to three months ahead.

Dough

3/4 cup warm water (105°F. to 110°F.)
1 package active dry yeast
1/4 cup vegetable oil

1 tablespoon sugar
1/2 teaspoon salt
2 large eggs
about 3 1/4 cups flour
vegetable oil

Filling:

2 pounds ground beef
1 cup chopped onion
1 1/4 cups cooked and mashed potatoes
1 1/2 teaspoons salt
1/2 teaspoon thyme
1/8 teaspoon black pepper

<u>melted butter (or Parve margarine if you keep Kosher)
   to brush warm rolls</u>

1. <u>Make dough</u>: Place warm water in large warm bowl. Sprinkle in yeast, oil and sugar. Mix until smooth. Stir in eggs, salt and 2 cups of the flour. Beat until smooth. Add enough additional flour to form a soft dough. Turn out onto a lightly floured board and knead until smooth and elastic, about 8 to 10 minutes. Place in an oiled bowl, turning to oil top. Cover, let rise in a warm place free from draft, until doubled, about 1 hour.

2. <u>Prepare filling</u>: Brown ground beef and onion in large skillet. Transfer to large bowl with slotted spoon and discard grease. Add mashed potatoes and stir in the 1 1/2 teaspoons salt, thyme and black pepper. Cool.

3. <u>Assemble knishes</u>: Punch dough down. On lightly floured board roll dough into a rectangle 15 inches wide by 22 inches long. Spread cooled filling evenly over dough. Cut into 3 strips, 5 inches wide by 22 inches long. Roll up each strip as for a jellyroll starting from the long sides. Seal edges well by pinching, and cut with sharp knife into 1-inch pieces. Pinch ends to seal. Place on greased baking sheets. Cover and let rise for about 30 minutes in draft-free warm spot.

4. <u>To bake</u>: Preheat oven to 375°F. and bake rolls 20 to 25 minutes, or until browned. Brush with melted butter and serve warm. (Or cool completely, wrap well and freeze. To serve, thaw and reheat in 400°F. oven for about 5 minutes.)

THE COLORS OF ITALY—SERVES 8 TO 12

Although this recipe takes some time, it is showy and delicious, and oh so special. It freezes beautifully with no loss of flavor! The name of the recipe comes from the colors of the Italian flag.

1 envelope unflavored gelatin
6 tablespoons cold water
8 ounces cream cheese, room temperature
4 ounces goat cheese, crumbled
1 10-ounce jar each prepared pesto, drained well, and sun-dried tomato spread, drained well (save the oil to use in sautéing in other recipes

Garnish: fresh basil leaves

To serve: assorted crackers or party breads

1. Line a 6-inch or 7-inch bowl or 4-cup loaf pan with plastic wrap.

2. Sprinkle the gelatin over the cold water in a 2-cup microwave-safe measuring cup. Let stand for 2 minutes. Microwave on High setting for 20 seconds or until the gelatin dissolves. Cool to lukewarm.

3. Beat the cream cheese and goat cheese in a mixing bowl until blended. Stir in 2 tablespoons of the gelatin mixture.

4. Combine 2 tablespoons of the remaining gelatin mixture with the drained pesto in a separate bowl and mix well.

5. Stir the remaining 2 tablespoons of gelatin mixture into the drained sun-dried tomato spread in a separate bowl.

6. Assemble: Layer the pesto mixture, goat cheese mixture and tomato mixture in the order listed in the prepared bowl or loaf pan, evening out each layer with an offset spatula. Chill, covered with plastic wrap, 2 to 24 hours. Invert onto a serving platter and discard the plastic wrap. Garnish with fresh basil leaves and serve with assorted party crackers or party breads cut into triangles.

CHORIZO IN PUFF PASTRY MAKES 36 PUFFS

This appetizer from Spain is both easy and impressive.

1 package frozen puff pastry, defrosted
8 to 10 ounces chorizo sausage, fully cooked type, cut into 1/4-inch slices
1 large egg yolk, lightly beaten

1. Roll out one sheet of the puff pastry on a lightly floured board to a thickness of 1/8 inch. Cut into circles with a fluted or plain round cookie cutter (or glass) that is 1/4 inch larger than the chorizo slices. Center a slice of chorizo on each circle, paint the edges of the dough with the beaten egg yolk using a pastry brush, and cover with another circle of pastry. Seal the edges well with the tines of a fork. Refrigerate on ungreased cookie sheets, covered with plastic wrap, for at least 30 minutes or up to one day.

2. When ready to serve, preheat oven to 450°F. Place puffs in upper third of oven and bake for 7 to 10 minutes, or until lightly browned and puffed. Serve warm.

TANGY SHRIMP MOLD—SERVES AT LEAST 10

This is one of my Aunt Betty's recipes. She was an amazing cook and has been my inspiration and role model for many years.

1 10 3/4-ounce can tomato soup, heated
1 8-ounce package cream cheese, room temperature
1 envelope unflavored gelatin
1/4 cup cold water
1 cup Hellman's mayonnaise (do not substitute another product)
1 1/2 pounds cooked shrimp, coarsely chopped
1/2 cup each finely chopped celery and finely chopped green onions
1 tablespoon fresh lemon juice
dashes of Tabasco, garlic powder and pepper

Garnishes: black olives, green pepper rings, pimiento, etc.

crackers to serve alongside

1. In a large bowl combine tomato soup and cream cheese together and whisk until smooth.

2. Combine gelatin with water, mixing until gelatin is dissolved. Add to soup-cream cheese mixture. Stir in mayonnaise until smooth. Add shrimp, celery, green onions, lemon juice and seasonings to taste.

3. Lightly oil or spray a fish-shaped mold or other large mold with cooking spray and pour shrimp mixture into it. (I have a special mold shaped like a fish that I use, but any large mold will work) and refrigerate until set, at least 4 hours or up to overnight. Dip mold into sink filled with very warm water, invert and unmold onto a serving platter. Decorate with olives, pimiento, green pepper, etc. Serve with crackers.

CONCH SALAD WITH SALSA OF LIFE AND SAVORY CLAM PANNA COTTA SERVES 10

This spectacular appetizer is adapted from Florida Star Chef Norman Van Aken. Although the list of ingredients seems daunting, this is a completely make-ahead dish, and one of the most memorable I have ever tasted. The conch is exotic if you can get it, and the combination of flavors and the stunning presentation make it perfect for special guests! Buy some martini glasses from a dollar store and reserve them for this recipe and other savory dishes, as the flavors can permeate the glass and make an unpleasante taste to martini drinkers if you use them for drinks!

Salsa of Life:

1 1/4 pounds frozen conch (Jamaican shellfish) diced small (available at gourmet grocery stores) OR if not available, substitute same amount of fresh raw scallops or peeled, cooked shrimp, chopped
3 cloves garlic, peeled and minced
1 English cucumber (seedless), peeled, diced small, placed in a sieve with lots of salt for 10 minutes, then rinsed well
1 small red onion, diced small
1 each red and yellow bell pepper, finely diced
1 large tomato, halved, seeds removed, finely diced
1 jalapeño pepper, halved, seeds removed, finely diced
1 small white onion, peeled and finely diced
1 tablespoon lime zest, plus more for garnish
1 cup each freshly squeezed lime juice and tomato juice
1/4 cup freshly squeezed lemon juice
1/2 cup each freshly squeezed orange juice, extra virgin olive oil and sugar
1/4 cup fresh cilantro leaves, chopped, PLUS sprigs for garnish
1 teaspoon kosher salt, 1/2 teaspoon freshly ground black pepper, or to taste
Tabasco, to taste

Orange Dust to garnish rims of Martini glasses:

1 tablespoon each dried orange peel, cumin and sugar

Savory Clam Panna Cotta:

1/3 cup bottled clam juice
1 1/2 teaspoons unflavored gelatin
1 1/4 cups whipping cream
1/4 cup sugar
2 cups plain low-fat yogurt, drained in fine strainer for
    30 minutes

Accompaniment: crisp corn tortilla chips, warmed

1. Make Salsa of Life: Place all ingredients in a large
bowl and refrigerate covered for at least 2 hours or up to
overnight so that acidic ingredients can "cook" conch or
scallops.

2. Prepare glasses: Use Martini glasses (I found
inexpensive ones at Dollar Tree) for a great presentation,
or use custard cups. Mix ingredients for the Orange
Dust in a shallow bowl. Set out a shallow bowl of water,
and the Orange Dust. Dip rim of each glass in the water,
shake off excess water, then dip rim into Orange Dust. Set
aside to dry while preparing the panna cotta.

3. Make the Panna Cotta: Pour the clam juice into a large
bowl. Sprinkle gelatin over the juice, stir and let stand
10 minutes. Bring the cream and sugar to a simmer in a
heavy medium saucepan over medium-high heat, stirring
until sugar dissolves. Remove from heat and whisk into
the gelatin mixture until dissolved and smooth. Whisk
in the drained yogurt. Divide mixture evenly among the
Martini glasses or custard cups. Chill 1 hour.

4. When ready to serve, remove glasses from refrigerator,
spoon on the Salsa of Life, garnish with some lime zest
and a sprig of cilantro and serve with some warmed chips
to awed guests.

COOK'S TIP

The most basic and useful technique in cooking that
I can pass on to you is the concept of *mise en place*,
or "putting everything in its place". This classic French
plan will help you be a more relaxed and successful
cook. Begin by making a shopping list, gathering
all the ingredients you'll need for your recipe, then
prepping each food item according to the directions and
assembling all of the utensils needed. Now you're ready to
cook! You'll see how much more smoothly and efficiently
your meal comes together.

2

FIVE WITH FIVE

We all want to provide well-rounded, fresh and creative meals for our families and friends. Today's busy lifestyle challenges us to get a quality, healthy meal ready quickly. Help is on the way! Here are five of my most popular menus, each containing five recipes with only five ingredients, featuring depth of flavor and cutting-edge cuisine, to help you get a marvelous meal on the table every night. Each menu could be a complete meal, including appetizer, entrée, side dish and dessert, but feel free to mix and match. Remember that a clock icon ⏲ indicates a make-ahead recipe. Salt, pepper and water are not counted as ingredients. In some cases I have taken liberties with the number of ingredients per recipe, but the total number of ingredients for each menu is still 25.

**Quick Beef Stroganoff (page 37), Parmesan Potato Cake (page 40)
and Buttered Green Beans with Pecans (page 31)**

MENU #1:

Goat Cheese-Filled Empanadas
Brown Sugar-Grilled Pork Tenderloin
Baked Sweet Potato Fries
Buttered Green Beans with Pecans
Chocolate-Ricotta Ice Box Cake

HERBED GOAT CHEESE EMPANADAS
MAKES ABOUT 20

Fun to make with friends. This is so easy, as it uses a premade piecrust without compromising taste. Mexican oregano is somewhat stronger in flavor than Italian oregano, but you can substitute the Italian herb if you don't have the Mexican variety.

1 package (2 piecrusts) refrigerated piecrust dough
8 ounces goat cheese
2 teaspoons <u>each</u> cumin and Mexican or Italian oregano

prepared salsa of your choice

<u>Optional garnish: sprigs of cilantro</u>

1. Unroll one refrigerated piecrust on a lightly floured work surface. Using a 3-inch round biscuit or cookie cutter, cut out 9 to 10 rounds. Repeat with second piecrust.

2. In a medium bowl mix the goat cheese with the cumin and oregano. Place 1/2 teaspoon of this filling on lower half of each round. (You may have extra filling left, which is very good with tortilla chips or celery.) Lightly dot edges of the rounds with water, then fold in half and press with a fork to seal. Place on a parchment paper-lined cookie sheet.

3. Bake in preheated 375°F. oven until golden, about 20 to 25 minutes.

4. Meanwhile, put the salsa in a blender and blend until smooth, which makes it easier for dunking the empanadas. Place in a decorative bowl, or fill individual small bowls for each guest.

5. When empanadas are baked, serve with the salsa. If you want to be extra-fancy, place a sprig of cilantro on each plate. (even though that makes it 6 ingredients-ha!)

BROWN SUGAR GRILLED PORK TENDERLOIN
SERVES 8

Marinade:

1/4 cup (4 tablespoons) Worcestershire sauce
2 tablespoons brown sugar
1 tablespoon soy sauce
liberal sprinkles of garlic powder and black pepper
1/4 cup (4 tablespoons) water

2 pork tenderloins (about 2 to 2 1/2 pounds total),
    <u>silverskin and any fat removed with sharp knife</u>

1. <u>Make Marinade</u>: In a small bowl, mix the Worcestershire, brown sugar, soy sauce, garlic powder, black pepper and water. Place in a non-reactive rectangular dish or Tupperware and immerse tenderloins in this mixture. Marinate, refrigerated, for at least 30 minutes, or up to overnight, turning once or twice. Transfer marinade to a saucepan and bring to a hard boil. Taste and if too salty add water and/or brown sugar to adjust. Reserve.

2. <u>When ready to cook</u>: Light grill or broiler. Grill over medium-high heat, turning once or twice and basting with marinade, until internal temperature of meat reaches 140°F. when measured on an instant-read thermometer.

3. Remove meat from grill and tent with foil. Reboil any remaining marinade to serve as sauce, tasting to adjust seasoning. Let meat rest 5 minutes before slicing on the diagonal. Place on a platter and serve right away. Leftovers make great sandwiches for lunch.

BAKED SWEET POTATO FRIES—SERVES 8

These are all the rage in restaurants, and now you can make them at home easily. Because of the moisture content in sweet potatoes, they will not be as crisp as regular potato fries.

4 large sweet potatoes (about 1 1/2 to 2 pounds total) peeled and cut lengthwise into
3/4-inch thick slices
1/4 cup all-purpose flour
1/4 cup or more extra virgin olive oil
generous sprinkles of sweet paprika
<u>1 teaspoon or more salt, to taste</u>

1. Preheat oven to 400°F.

2. Toss cut potatoes in flour and shake off any excess, to help crisp slices. Place on a large baking sheet and toss with olive oil, paprika and salt. Place in oven and roast until browned and tender, 20 to 25 minutes, turning over once halfway through baking time.

3. Remove from baking sheet, place on a serving platter and serve hot.

BUTTERED GREEN BEANS WITH PECANS
SERVES 8

1 1/2 pounds fresh green beans, washed and ends trimmed
4 tablespoons unsalted butter, <u>DIVIDED</u>
6 tablespoons pecans, coarsely chopped
salt to taste

<u>Optional garnish: jarred sweet red pepper, room temperature</u>

1. Bring a large pot of lightly salted water to a boil. Parboil beans until crisp-tender, 5 to 8 minutes, depending on their age. Refresh in ice water, drain and reserve.

2. In a small skillet melt 1 tablespoon of the butter and toast the pecans for just a few minutes on medium heat. Watch carefully as they can burn quickly. Transfer to a small bowl and reserve.

3. Slice the red peppers into strips if using and reserve.

4. When ready to serve, place the remaining butter in a large skillet over medium-high heat. Add the green beans and stir until heated through. Taste and add salt. Place on serving platter and scatter the toasted pecans over the beans and decorate with optional red pepper strips. Serve hot.

CHOCOLATE-RICOTTA ICE BOX CAKE
SERVES 8 to 10

If you choose to use the dark rum, substitute 1/2 cup chopped and toasted almonds and 1/2 teaspoon of almond extract in the ricotta mixture instead of the orange zest, juice and orange flavoring. Both versions are delicious!

12 ounces semisweet or bittersweet chocolate, chopped
    in food processor, plus more for garnish
1 9-ounce package Famous brand chocolate wafers
8 tablespoons unsalted butter, melted
2 15-ounce containers ricotta cheese
orange zest from 1 navel orange
1 tablespoon Grand Marnier, Cointreau or orange juice
    OR 1 tablespoon dark rum (I like Myer's)

<u>Garnish</u>: chocolate shavings made from a block of
    semisweet chocolate with potato peeler, orange
    <u>segments (suprèmes) from the zested orange</u>

1. Place chopped chocolate in the top of a double boiler and place over simmering water on low heat. Cook until chocolate melts and is smooth, stirring once or twice. Let cool at room temperature and reserve.

2. Place the chocolate wafers in the food processor and process into fine crumbs. Add the melted butter and process for a few seconds more. Place in a bowl and reserve.

3. In the bowl of the cleaned food processor, place the ricotta, cooled chocolate, orange zest and Grand Marnier, Cointreau or orange juice OR rum, toasted almonds and almond extract. Process until very smooth.

4. Line an 8 1/2" x 4 1/2" loaf pan with parchment paper, leaving an overhang on all sides. Divide the ricotta-chocolate mixture into 3 even portions. Layer 1/3 of the ricotta filling in the pan and smooth it down with an offset spatula, then put 1/2 of the cookie-butter mixture on top and smooth it down evenly. Place another 1/3 of ricotta next and smooth it down, then the rest of the cookie-butter mixture, and then put the last 1/3 of the ricotta mixture on top. Cover with the overhanging parchment paper and refrigerate for at least 12 hours and up to 2 days.

5. <u>Make the orange suprèmes</u>: Remove all the white pith from the zested orange, then slice with a very sharp knife between the membranes of the orange to get perfect pieces of orange. You will need a very sharp knife to do this procedure successfully.

6. When ready to serve, uncover top of loaf pan and turn pan over onto a flat serving dish, then remove rest of parchment paper. Smooth out any "wrinkles" in top and sides of cake. Sprinkle cake with 1/4 cup of shaved semisweet chocolate. (Shave chocolate with a sturdy potato peeler onto parchment paper, then carefully transfer with a knife to top of cake.) Slice cake with a serrated knife and garnish each slice with orange suprèmes.

MENU #2:

Fast Mushroom-Sausage Strudel
Parmesan-Crusted Boneless Pork Chops
Gloucester Cheese-Garlic Mashed Potatoes
Fresh Spinach with Garlic and Chilis
Peggy's Gold Rush Bars

FAST MUSHROOM-SAUSAGE STRUDEL
MAKES 24 SLICES

1/2 pound sweet Italian sausage, casing removed
1/2 pound fresh mushrooms, cleaned and chopped
1 tablespoon Dijon mustard
1/4 cup sour cream
1 8-ounce package refrigerated Crescent rolls

1. Make the filling: In a medium nonstick skillet, sauté the sausage over moderately high heat, breaking it up to crumble it, until cooked through. Drain off any excess fat and add the mushrooms. Sauté over high heat until all the liquid has evaporated and the mushrooms begin to brown and reduce in volume. Cool the mixture and stir in the mustard and sour cream. This can be made the day before and refrigerated.

2. To assemble strudels: Remove half of the package of crescent rolls and place on a lightly floured board. Press perforations together to seal. Turn over and press perforations from the other side. Roll lightly with a floured rolling pin into approximately a 4" x 15" rectangle. Spoon one half of the cooled filling into a log down the edge of the long side of the pastry, then roll up the pastry into a log, pinching to seal the ends. Repeat with remaining crescent rolls and filling. At this point, the strudels can be covered with plastic wrap and refrigerated up to overnight, or frozen, well-wrapped. If frozen, defrost in the refrigerator before baking.

3. To bake: Preheat oven to 350°F. Bake 15 to 18 minutes or until golden brown. Remove from oven and cool slightly, then transfer to cutting board and slice into 1-inch pieces.

PARMESAN-CRUSTED PORK CHOPS
SERVES 8

This is my son-in-law Greg's recipe. Coming from Iowa, he introduced me to "Iowa chops" and this delicious way to prepare them. This is a real crowd-pleaser.

2 large eggs
1/2 cup grated good-quality Parmesan cheese
1 sleeve (1/4 pound) lightly salted saltine crackers, made into crumbs in food processor, or placed in a heavy plastic bag and crushed with a rolling pin
1/2 teaspoon salt, 1/4 teaspoon pepper
8 boneless pork chops, 1 inch thick
4 tablespoons Crisco or other vegetable oil

1. Preheat oven to 350°F.

2. Mix the two eggs with 2 tablespoons water in a medium shallow bowl.

3. Mix Parmesan cheese, saltine cracker crumbs, salt and pepper together and place on parchment or waxed paper.

4. Dip chops in egg mixture, letting excess egg drip off, then dredge in Parmesan-cracker mixture. Place on waxed-paper lined platter. (Can refrigerate for several hours at this point, or proceed with recipe right away.)

5. Melt the Crisco oil in a skillet and sauté chops about 3 minutes per side, until golden brown, then transfer to baking sheet and bake in preheated oven for 15 to 20 minutes, or until internal temperature reads 155°F. on instant-read thermometer. Don't overcook.

GLOUCESTER CHEESE-GARLIC MASHED POTATOES—SERVES 8

Be careful not to beat the potatoes in the mixer too long, or they will become rubbery.

2 pounds all-purpose or Yukon gold potatoes, peeled and cubed
12 garlic cloves, peeled and cut in half
2 tablespoons unsalted butter
3 tablespoons milk, or more as needed, heated in microwave
<u>6 ounces Double Gloucester cheese, shredded</u>

1. Place potatoes, garlic and 1/2 teaspoon salt in large saucepan, cover with cold water and bring to a boil. Reduce heat to a low boil and cook until soft, about 20 minutes. Drain water from potatoes, and place pan back on low heat until all water has evaporated.

2. Transfer potatoes and garlic to an electric mixer and beat until they are mixed but not gummy, then add butter and heated milk, mixing again for a minute or two. Add the Gloucester cheese and scrape down the sides while mixing. Season with more salt and freshly ground black pepper to taste and adjust consistency with more milk if needed.

3. Place in buttered casserole dish and bake at 350°F. for 20 to 30 minutes or until golden brown and heated through.

FRESH SPINACH WITH GARLIC AND CHILIS SERVES 8

We often forget to include vegetables in our meals. This simple but tasty dish is a great addition.

coarse salt
1 1/2 pounds baby spinach leaves, washed, stems discarded
1/4 cup extra virgin olive oil
2 to 3 cloves garlic, sliced thinly
1 fresh hot chili pepper, coarsely chopped (Use rubber gloves to protect your hands from chili juices and <u>remove seeds for less heat.)</u>

1. Pour 1/2 inch of water into a large stockpot and bring to a boil. Add the salt and spinach, cover and let cook for 1 minute. Uncover, stir with a wooden spoon and boil for another minute. Drain thoroughly in a colander, pressing out excess water with the back of a spoon carefully.

2. Using a very sharp knife, gently cut spinach into strips. Do not mince it. It will be fragile.

3. In a medium nonstick skillet heat the oil, then add the garlic and chili pepper and cook over medium heat, stirring so garlic doesn't burn. When oil begins to sizzle add cut spinach and cook for 5 minutes, turning spinach gently occasionally with a wooden spoon to combine. Taste, adjust for salt and serve hot.

PEGGY'S GOLD RUSH BARS—MAKES 16

This is my friend Peggy Hayes' treasured family recipe. I know it will become one of yours too!

Crisco to grease the pan
1 14-ounce can sweetened condensed milk
1 2/3 cups graham cracker crumbs
6 ounces semisweet chocolate chips

<u>Optional: 1 cup (4 ounces) walnuts, chopped</u>

1. Preheat oven to 350°F. Grease an 8" x 8" square pan with the Crisco.

2. In a large bowl mix the sweetened condensed milk, graham cracker crumbs and chocolate chips. Add the optional walnuts if desired. Mix well and pour into prepared pan.

3. Bake in preheated oven for 35 minutes. Let rest in pan on wire rack for 20 minutes, then cut with a sharp knife into 16 bars. These freeze very well.

MENU #3

Chili Con Queso Bites
Chicken Pompadour
Rosemary Potatoes
Fast French Bread
Sprite Bundt Cake

CHILI CON QUESO BITES
MAKES 12 LARGE or 24 SMALL BITES

cooking spray
2 large eggs
1/4 cup purchased salsa
2 tablespoons all-purpose flour
1 teaspoon chili powder
3/4 cup (6 ounces) shredded Cheddar cheese
<u>1 green onion, chopped, about 1 tablespoon</u>

1. Preheat oven to 400°F. Spray 12 3-inch muffin pan cups
or 24 mini-muffin pan cups with cooking spray. Reserve.

2. In a medium bowl mix eggs, salsa, flour and chili
powder. Stir in the cheese and green onion.

3. Spoon about 1 tablespoon of this mixture into regular
muffin cups or 1 rounded teaspoon for mini-muffin tins.
Bake 9 to 11 minutes (less for mini-muffins) or until
golden brown. Loosen with knife. Serve warm or at room
temperature. Set out a bowl of extra salsa and/or sour
cream as an accompaniment if desired when serving.

CHICKEN POMPADOUR—SERVES 8

8 boneless, skinless chicken breasts
salt and pepper
1 cup flour for dredging
3 large eggs
3 cups blanched, chopped almonds
<u>4 tablespoons each butter and oil, or more as needed</u>

1. Preheat oven to 250°F.

2. Place each breast on a piece of plastic wrap and cover
with another piece of plastic wrap. Lightly pound chicken
breasts to an even thickness with a meat pounder or
rolling pin. Season with salt and pepper.

3. Beat the eggs in a shallow bowl. Put the flour on
a dinner plate or piece of parchment paper. Put the
almonds on another dinner plate or piece of parchment
paper.

4. Dredge (dip and then shake off excess) each breast in
flour, dip it into the egg, shake off excess and then coat it
with the almonds. Press with the palm of your hand so
that the almonds stick to the chicken. Can prepare to this
point several hours ahead, cover and refrigerate.

5. When ready to cook, in a large frying pan melt the
butter. Add the oil and sauté the breasts on high heat 4 to
5 minutes on each side, until cooked through and golden
brown. Put first batch in oven while sautéing the rest,
then serve right away.

ROSEMARY POTATOES—SERVES 8

3 tablespoons butter
2 teaspoons <u>each</u> minced garlic and chopped dried
    rosemary
1 teaspoon kosher salt
1/2 teaspoon freshly ground black pepper
<u>3 pounds red new potatoes, quartered</u>

1. Place butter and garlic in a 9" x 13" glass baking
dish. Cover loosely and microwave on Medium-High
(70% power) 45 seconds or until butter melts. Add the
rosemary, salt, pepper and potatoes and toss well to coat
potatoes.

2. Cover with plastic wrap and microwave at High for 10
to 15 minutes or until potatoes are tender, testing with a
sharp knife after 10 minutes. The knife should slide out
easily. Toss again and serve.

FAST FRENCH BREAD—MAKES 2 LOAVES

From the great French chef Pierre Franey. Fast, easy and delicious!

2 1/4-ounce packages RapidRise dry yeast
2 1/4 cups warm water (90°F. when measured with an
    instant-read thermometer), <u>DIVIDED</u>
6 cups bread flour
1 tablespoon salt

<u>Optional: 1 teaspoon dried herbs</u>

1. Put the yeast into the bowl of a food processor with 1/4 cup of the warm water and pulse a bit. Add the flour and process for a few seconds. With the processor running add the salt and rest of the water, pouring through the feed tube, mixing until the dough forms a ball. Take dough out of the processor and knead it on a floured board for about 5 minutes. If you wish at this point you can add the dried herbs.

2. Shape dough into 2 equal long loaves and place on a large greased baking sheet. Cover and let rise away from any drafts until doubled, 45 minutes.

3. Preheat oven to 400°F. When ready to bake breads, cut slashes in top of breads with a safety razor (which you reserve for cooking) or very sharp knife, either lengthwise all the way down the loaf or cut 3 to 4 slashes diagonally. Place baking sheet in the oven and immediately throw a few ice cubes on the bottom of the oven, to produce steam for a crisp crust. Bake 30 minutes, then reduce oven temperature to 350°F. and bake for 10 minutes more. Test doneness by turning bread over and inserting an instant-read thermometer in center of bottom crust. It should read 190°F. Cool a bit on wire racks, then slice with a serrated knife and serve warm.

SPRITE BUNDT CAKE
MAKES ONE CAKE

A great cake with very little effort!

Crisco shortening and flour to prepare pan
3 cups sugar
3 sticks (3/4 pound) unsalted butter, room temperature
6 large eggs
3 cups flour
3/4 cup Sprite (not Diet-type)
<u>1 tablespoon pure lemon extract (flavoring)</u>

1. Preheat oven to 325°F. Grease and flour a Bundt pan and reserve.

2. In the bowl of an electric mixer cream sugar and butter until smooth, stirring down once or twice to mix thoroughly. Add one egg at a time, and beat until mixed well. Stir in the flour on low speed.

3. In small bowl combine Sprite and lemon flavoring and mix into the batter until smooth.

4. Transfer batter to greased and floured Bundt pan or angel food pan and bake for one hour or more, until a cake tester or skewer inserted near center of cake comes out clean. Cool in pan 15 minutes, then invert onto rack to cool completely. This cake freezes well!

MENU #4

Prosciutto Purses with Herbed Mascarpone
Quick Beef Stroganoff
Smashed Potato Gratin
Glazed Orange-Ginger Carrots
Italian Amaretti Cookies

PROSCIUTTO PURSES WITH HERBED MASCARPONE—MAKES 10

Mascarpone cheese from Italy is the ingredient that binds this mixture together beautifully. Any extra cheese mixture can be served on crisp crackers as a quick appetizer.

1/2 pound mascarpone cheese
1 clove garlic, peeled and crushed
2 tablespoons chopped fresh herb mix: basil, thyme, chives, OR 2 teaspoons dried herb mix
sea salt and fresh black pepper to taste
10 to 12 long chives for "ties" for purses
10 slices (about 1/2 pound) Prosciutto de Parma

Salad to serve with purses

mesclun salad mix
extra virgin olive oil
good quality balsamic vinegar

Optional accompaniment: Italian bread sticks

1. Mix the mascarpone, garlic, herbs and salt and pepper to taste together in a medium bowl. Reserve.

2. Bring a small pot of water to a boil and cook chive strips until they become pliable, but remain bright green. Drain carefully and refresh with cold water, then put into ice water, dry and place on paper towels. Refrigerate until needed.

3. Lay out slices of the prosciutto on a work surface. Put 1 tablespoon of the mascarpone mixture in the center of a prosciutto slice, then draw it up like a drawstring purse and tie with a chive ribbon. Be gentle as ribbons are fragile. Refrigerate until ready to serve. Can prepare hours ahead.

4. <u>When ready to serve</u>: Place purses on individual plates. Place some mesclun salad mixture on each plate next to each purse and dress the salad to taste with good olive oil, balsamic vinegar, salt and pepper, then put a shaving of Parmesan on top. Serve with bread sticks.

QUICK BEEF STROGANOFF—SERVES 8

Your guests will think you've been slaving for hours to prepare this dish...we'll never tell!

1 1/2 pounds filet mignon, sirloin or New York strip steak, thinly sliced
1 teaspoon salt or more to taste
about 1/4 teaspoon black pepper
4 tablespoons olive oil, <u>DIVIDED</u>
1/2 pound button mushrooms, cleaned and thinly sliced
1/2 cup <u>each</u> dry sherry and chicken or beef broth, or more broth if needed
1/2 cup sour cream

Optional: 1 onion, sliced thin, to sauté with the mushrooms

Garnish: chopped flatleaf parsley

1. Dry meat and season with salt and pepper. Heat 2 tablespoons of the oil in a large skillet over medium-high heat. Cook steak in batches, not crowding the pan, until brown on all sides, about 3 minutes, then remove to a bowl. Add the remaining oil and place over medium-high heat. Add mushrooms and optional sliced onions and cook until their juices evaporate, about 5 minutes. Add the sherry and broth and bring to a boil. Cook until liquid reduces by half, about 5 minutes more. Reduce heat to medium low, whisk in the sour cream and heat until mixture thickens.

2. Return steak with any juices that have accumulated to the skillet and adjust seasonings. Heat until warmed through. Add extra broth if you want more sauce, and serve with the potato gratin (recipe follows) or over steamed rice. Garnish with chopped parsley if desired.

SMASHED POTATO GRATIN
SERVES 8 TO 10

Leftovers are also great reheated.

4 pounds medium Idaho (Russet) or Yukon Gold
    potatoes, peeled and cut into eights
2 tablespoons softened butter to grease baking dish
7 tablespoons unsalted butter, cubed, room temperature
1 cup whole milk
freshly ground pepper to taste
1 1/2 cups (about 5 ounces) grated Asiago or Swiss
    cheese, DIVIDED

1. Preheat oven to 350°F.

2. In a large pot, cover the potatoes with salted water.
Bring to a boil over high heat and cook until tender,
about 20 minutes. Drain. Very coarsely mash the potatoes
with 6 tablespoons of the butter and the milk. Stir in 1
cup of the cheese. Season well with salt and pepper

3. Butter a 9" x 13" ovenproof baking dish. Spoon the
mashed potato mixture into the dish and sprinkle the
top with the remaining 1 tablespoon of butter and 1/2
cup grated cheese. (Can prepare hours ahead, cover and
refrigerate, in which case baking time may increase a bit.)

4. Bake the gratin for about 35 minutes, or until it is
heated through and the cheese on top is melted and
brown. If not brown enough, you can put under broiler
for a few minutes.

GLAZED ORANGE-GINGER CARROTS
SERVES 8

*So simple, yet this vegetable has a wonderful fresh flavor
that will add to your meal.*

5 cups fresh carrots, peeled and cut 1/2 inch thick with
    crinkle-cutter or plain knife, or baby carrots (no
    need to peel them)
salt
6 tablespoons ginger preserves, OR orange marmalade
    plus 1 teaspoon grated fresh ginger
4 tablespoons frozen orange juice concentrate, thawed
2 tablespoons unsalted butter

1. In a large saucepan cook the carrots, covered, in a
small amount of lightly salted boiling water for 5 minutes.
Drain and set aside in a large bowl.

2. In the same saucepan over medium heat combine the
preserves, orange juice and butter, stirring until melted.
Return carrots to saucepan and cook until just tender and
glazed, 10 to 14 minutes, stirring occasionally. Serve hot
or warm.

ITALIAN AMARETTI COOKIES
MAKES 24 TO 30

Better than from a bakery!

1 3/4 cups sliced, slivered or whole almonds, coarsely
    chopped (about 5 1/2 ounces)
1 cup confectioners' sugar
3 large egg whites
1/2 teaspoon pure almond extract

1. Preheat oven to 350°F.

2. Spread almonds in a single layer on a rimmed baking
sheet and toast until lightly browned and fragrant, 7 to 9
minutes. Remove from oven and cool.

3. Combine almonds and sugar in the bowl of a food
processor fitted with the metal blade and grind to a fine
powder. Transfer to a medium bowl.

4. In a separate bowl, beat egg whites with an electric
mixer until stiff peaks form, then fold in the almond
extract. With a clean spatula gently fold whites into the
almond mixture.

5. Line baking sheets with parchment paper. Transfer
almond mixture to a pastry bag fitted with a 1/2-inch
plain tip and pipe 2-inch rings onto the prepared sheets,
OR use a tablespoon to make mounds of batter, making
an indentation in the center of each cookie, so cookies
will bake evenly. Bake until golden brown and firm to the
touch, about 17 to 20 minutes. Remove from oven and
immediately transfer to wire rack to cool completely.

MENU #5

Focaccia with Sun-Dried Tomatoes and Herbs
Veal (or Chicken) Piccata
Parmesan Potato Cake
Sugar Snap Peas with Green Peas and Shallots
No-Fail Chocolate Mousse

FOCACCIA WITH SUN-DRIED TOMATOES AND HERBS—MAKES 1 BREAD

1 tablespoon plus 2 teaspoons olive oil, <u>DIVIDED</u>
4 cloves garlic, finely chopped
10 sun-dried tomatoes, packed in oil, drained and cut into thin strips
1 teaspoon rosemary leaves, crushed, <u>DIVIDED</u>
<u>1 10-ounce package refrigerated ready-to-bake pizza crust dough</u>

1. Preheat oven to 400°F.

2. In small saucepan heat 1 teaspoon of the olive oil, add garlic and sauté about 1 minute, until golden. Remove to a medium bowl and set aside.

3. To the garlic-oil mixture add the tomato strips, 1 tablespoon of the oil and 1/2 teaspoon rosemary, stirring to combine.

4. On a clean work surface unroll the pizza crust dough. Roll out to an even square. Spread the tomato mixture over surface and fold the dough in half crosswise, then fold in half crosswise again, shaping to make an 8-inch square. Brush dough with remaining oil and sprinkle with remaining rosemary and a dusting of freshly ground pepper if desired. Place on a small cookie sheet. Poke indentations in dough with your finger, not going all the way through to the bottom. Bake in preheated oven until dough is golden, about 13 to 15 minutes. Cut into slices and serve warm.

VEAL (OR CHICKEN) PICCATA—SERVES 8

Fast, fresh and delicious—what more could the home cook ask?

2 lemons, 1 sliced, 1 juiced
4 boneless veal scallops or 2 chicken breasts—about 1 1/2 to 2 pounds total
salt and black pepper
1 cup all-purpose flour
about 6 tablespoons vegetable oil
4 tablespoons minced (about 2 small) shallots, or 2 small garlic cloves
2 cups homemade or good quality chicken stock
4 tablespoons <u>each</u> drained, rinsed small capers and softened unsalted butter

<u>Garnish: chopped parsley leaves</u>

1. Preheat oven to 200°F.

2. Cut one of the lemons into thin slices and reserve. Juice the other lemon, strain and reserve for sauce.

3. Pound veal scallops between two pieces of plastic wrap, using a meat pounder, into even, thin cutlets, called paillards (pronounced pie-yard). Halve each for a total of 8 pieces. If using chicken breasts, first slice them in half lengthwise, then pound and halve. Sprinkle both sides with salt and freshly ground pepper. Place the flour in a shallow bowl and coat each paillard with flour, shaking to remove excess.

4. Heat a heavy-bottomed 12-inch skillet over medium-high heat until hot, about 2 minutes. Add 3 tablespoons of oil and swirl pan to coat. Place half of the paillards in the skillet in one layer. Sauté without moving them until light brown on one side, about 2 minutes, then turn and sauté on second side until light brown, about 2 to 3 more minutes. Transfer cutlets to heatproof platter and place in oven while browning the other 4 cutlets in remaining oil. Remove to oven.

5. <u>Make sauce</u>: Add the shallot or garlic to pan and sauté until fragrant, about 30 seconds for shallot or 10 seconds for garlic. Add the stock and lemon slices, increase heat to high and scrape skillet bottom with a wooden spoon to

loosen browned bits. Simmer about 4 minutes to reduce liquid slightly. Add lemon juice and capers and simmer 1 minute. Swirl in the butter until it melts, to thicken sauce. Taste and correct seasoning. Spoon over paillards and sprinkle with parsley. Serve immediately.

PARMESAN POTATO CAKE—SERVES 8

3 pounds Yukon Gold potatoes, peeled, cut into chunks
1 1/4 teaspoons salt, <u>DIVIDED</u>
1/4 cup (4 tablespoons) extra virgin olive oil, <u>DIVIDED</u>
3/4 cup grated Parmesan cheese
1/2 teaspoon freshly ground pepper

<u>Garnish: chopped parsley</u>

1. Preheat oven to 425°F.

2. In a large pot, cover potatoes in water, add 1 teaspoon of the salt and bring to a boil. Lower heat and simmer until tender, about 14 minutes. Drain and return to pot.

3. Mash potatoes, leaving them slightly chunky. Stir in remaining 1/4 teaspoon salt, 3 tablespoons of oil, the Parmesan and the pepper. Heat a 10-inch cast iron or ovenproof nonstick skillet over high heat until hot. Remove from heat, add the remaining tablespoon of oil, spoon in the potato mixture and press down evenly. Return skillet to burner on medium heat and cook for 5 minutes to set the bottom of cake. Then put in preheated oven and bake for about 30 to 35 minutes or until browned on top.

4. Cut into wedges, garnish center with chopped parsley and serve right from the skillet with a spatula, protecting your serving surface and handle from the heat of the pan with pads.

SUGAR SNAP PEAS WITH GREEN PEAS AND SHALLOTS—SERVES 8

2 tablespoons unsalted butter
2 large shallots, thinly sliced
2 cups frozen peas
1 pound sugar snap peas, strings removed
<u>1/2 teaspoon salt, 1/4 teaspoon black pepper</u>

1. Heat butter in large nonstick skilled over medium-high heat. Add shallots and sauté until golden, about 5 minutes, watching closely.

2. Add the frozen peas and the sugar snap peas, and sauté 5 minutes more or until the snap peas are crisp-tender. Sprinkle with salt and pepper and serve right away.

NO-FAIL CHOCOLATE MOUSSE
SERVES 8 TO 10

The key to success in this recipe is in the handling of the ingredients. The chocolate must still be warm to the touch when it is folded into the cream. If it is too cool it will "seize" up before it can be fully incorporated, making the mousse grainy. Likewise, the cream must be at room temperature before whipping, so that it will not harden the chocolate when it is incorporated. Whisking the chocolate all at once into the cream quickly gives the smoothest result for great texture. This recipe comes from the legendary former White House Pastry Chef Roland Mesnier.

8 ounces bittersweet or semisweet chocolate, best
    quality, finely chopped in the food processor
2 cups heavy cream, room temperature

Optional: 2 teaspoon finely chopped crystallized ginger

<u>Optional garnish</u>: 1 cup heavy cream, whipped, diced
    crystallized ginger,
<u>chocolate shavings (using a potato peeler) or mini pastel</u>
    <u>mints</u>

1. Put 2 inches of water into a medium saucepan and bring to a bare simmer. Place the chocolate in a stainless steel or glass bowl that is big enough to rest on top of the saucepan, and place it over the simmering water, making sure that the bowl doesn't touch the water. Heat, whisking occasionally, until chocolate is completely melted. Remove from the heat and let cool until chocolate is just warm to the touch, between 95°F. and 100°F. on an instant-read thermometer.

2. Bring the 2 cups of heavy cream to room temperature before whipping it with an electric mixer until it holds soft peaks. Add the whipped cream and (optional) crystallized ginger to the chocolate all at once, and whisk together. Scrape the mousse into a serving bowl or individual ramekins or goblets. Serve right away, or refrigerate, covered, for up to 1 day.

3. When ready to serve, whip the 1 cup of heavy cream to soft peaks and place a dollop on each serving of mousse, then decorate with optional garnish if desired.

COOK'S TIP

"Coming with Hot" is a phrase I often used in my cooking classes, to emphasize to my students that the kitchen can be a dangerous place if you don't give your full attention to what you're doing. Don't talk on the telephone, text, watch television or play with your children while you're cooking. Remember that you're often using sharp knives and high heat (hopefully), and you need to concentrate fully on your cooking.

3

FABULOUS FAMILY MEALS

The kitchen is the heart of the family, and sharing meals together builds priceless memories. In the frantic pace of our modern world, many people feel too rushed and stressed to find time to create these special times. One of our family's priorities all through the years was making time to eat together, and it was well worth it! The five menus that follow take into account how busy we are, but still offer many delicious options for you to enjoy together. Take the time to eat together and share the day's stories, be they triumphs or problems. Menus include: In Short Order—A Working Person's Dream, American Diner Food, Easy Does It!, A Make-Ahead Meal for Family and Friends, and Summertime Fun.

Wellesley Fudge Cupcakes (page 50)

IN SHORT ORDER—A WORKING PERSON'S DREAM

Sesame Pork and Mushrooms with Pasta
Spinach Salad with Oranges and Peanuts
Jan's Angel Biscuits
Marilyn's Chocolate Dream Cream Pie

SESAME PORK AND MUSHROOMS WITH PASTA
SERVES 8

A true fusion dish, combining the flavors of Asian and Italian food.

1 pound uncooked vermicelli or angel hair pasta
4 tablespoons butter
4 teaspoons Oriental sesame oil
2 pounds pork tenderloin or boneless pork loin chops or pork roast, sliced thin
4 green onions, thinly sliced (green part too)
3 to 4 garlic cloves, minced
2 tablespoons sesame seeds
12 ounces fresh snow peas, trimmed, or 2 6-ounce frozen packages, thawed and drained
1/2 cup grated Parmesan cheese
3 to 4 drops hot chili oil
1/2 tablespoon soy sauce

1. In large pot of boiling salted water, cook vermicelli to al dente doneness. Drain and keep warm. (Save some of the pasta water to mix in if pasta gets too dry waiting.)

2. Heat butter and oil in large skillet or wok over high heat. Add pork and stir-fry quickly until no longer pink. Add onion, garlic and sesame seeds. Add mushrooms and snow peas and cook 2 to 3 minutes until peas are crisp and bright green. Add hot chili oil and soy sauce to taste.

3. Pour pork and vegetable mixture over warm pasta. Sprinkle with the Parmesan cheese and serve.

SPINACH SALAD WITH ORANGES AND PEANUTS—SERVES 8

1 pound fresh spinach, cleaned and stemmed, torn into bite-size pieces
4 oranges, all pith (white part) removed, sectioned (or use canned Mandarin oranges)
1/2 cup salted peanuts, placed in plastic bag and crushed with a rolling pin

Optional: 6 slices bacon, fried and crumbled (or use bacon bits)

bottled Catalina dressing

1. Buy spinach in cello bag, as it is already washed and cleaned. Or if not available, wash very well (can be done day ahead and put into a plastic bag with paper toweling to keep crisp.)

2. Section oranges, or if using canned mandarin oranges, drain. Crush peanuts. Fry and crumble bacon if you are going to use it.

3. Combine all in large glass bowl. Toss with Catalina dressing.

JAN'S ANGEL BISCUITS—MAKES ABOUT 2 1/2 DOZEN

My culinary assistant Jan Smith generously shared her family's recipe with me. The first time she made these southern biscuits for her future husband (and split and buttered them for him, too) he knew she was the girl for him! A great feature of this recipe is having the dough ready in the refrigerator so you can have hot biscuits whenever you want them.

1/4 cup warm water
1 tablespoon sugar
1 package active dry yeast

5 cups all-purpose flour
2 cups buttermilk
1 cup vegetable oil
1 teaspoon baking soda
1 heaping teaspoon salt

1. In a 1-cup measuring cup combine warm water, sugar and yeast. Let sit for a few minutes to let yeast bubble up a bit. This is called proofing the yeast, to make sure it is still healthy and active.

2. In a large bowl (I like to use a Tupperware mixing bowl with a tight lid) combine flour, milk, oil, baking soda and salt thoroughly. Add the water-sugar-yeast mixture and mix thoroughly again. Cover tightly and place in refrigerator overnight or up to 3 weeks until you want to make fresh biscuits.

3. When ready to make biscuits: Grease a cookie sheet or line it with parchment paper and preheat oven to 450°F. Pinch off amount of dough you want (roughly 1/2 of the total dough amount will yield 12 to 16 biscuits, depending on size you choose) and knead on a floured surface until smooth. Dough will be very moist and "oily". Don't add too much flour as you knead, so biscuits will be light. Roll out to 3/4 to 1 inch thickness and cut biscuits with a 2 1/2-inch donut or biscuit cutter. You can reroll scraps to use up all the dough. Place 1 inch apart on the baking sheet. Bake until golden brown, about 12 to 15 minutes. Split and butter right out of the oven and serve warm!

MARILYN'S CHOCOLATE DREAM CREAM PIE SERVES 8 TO 10

This is my friend Marilyn Pugliese's wonderful recipe. You can double this recipe easily and put it into a 9" x 13" rectangular pan, then cut into squares to serve. A great, easy dessert for a crowd!

Crust:

1/2 cup almonds, slivered or sliced
3/4 cup (2 ounces or 4 whole crackers, crushed) chocolate graham crackers
1 tablespoon sugar
2 tablespoons melted butter

Filling:

1 7-ounce bar Hershey's chocolate bar with almonds
1 cup whipping cream, whipped to soft peaks
1 tablespoon confectioners' sugar
2 tablespoons Myer's dark rum

Optional garnishes: 1 cup whipping cream, whipped, sweetened with 1 tablespoon powdered sugar, OR chocolate sauce made with 2 ounces bittersweet or semisweet chocolate, melted in microwave, mixed with 1 tablespoon each heavy cream and rum

1. Make crust: In bowl of food processor place almonds and sugar and process until almonds are chopped fine. Add graham crackers and process until they are finely chopped also. Melt butter in medium glass bowl in microwave and add almond mixture, mixing well. Press mixture into bottom and halfway up sides of a 9-inch pie pan. Bake 7 minutes at 350°F. Cool.

2. Make filling: Melt the Hershey's chocolate bar, broken up, in the microwave on 50% power for 1 to 2 minutes, checking and stopping as soon as chocolate is melted. Cool slightly. Fold in the whipped cream, sugar and rum. Pour mixture into the crust and let it firm up in the refrigerator for at least 4 hours or up to overnight.

3. When ready to serve, cut pie into wedges. You can then either spoon on a dollop of the sweetened whipped cream, or drizzle with some of the warm chocolate sauce, or if you're feeling decadent use both, or serve pie plain if you prefer.

AMERICAN DINER FOOD

Boston Harbor Clam Chowder
Barbecued Baby Back Ribs
Macaroni and Cheese
Zucchini Casserole
Mile High Coconut Cream Pie

BOSTON HARBOR CLAM CHOWDER

SERVES 8 TO 10

This is the creamy style clam chowder, not the tomato-based Manhattan clam chowder.

1/4 pound unsalted butter
1 medium onion, diced
1/2 cup green pepper, diced (optional, as some people don't like green peppers)
2 carrots, peeled and diced
2 stalks of celery, diced
3/4 pound potatoes (2 to 3), peeled and diced
1/2 cup flour
3 1/2 cups clam juice, from canned clams, or bottled clam juice, warmed
2 cups chopped clams, canned is fine
1 bay leaf
1 tsp. dried thyme
1/8 to 1/4 teaspoon cayenne pepper
1/4 pound (about 4 slices) thick-sliced peppered bacon, chopped
1 1/2 cups heavy cream, warmed
<u>fresh ground black pepper and sea salt</u>

1. In a large stockpot melt the butter and sweat the onions, optional peppers, carrots and celery, covered, over low heat for 5 minutes, then uncover and add the potatoes. Stir in the flour and cook for 2 to 3 minutes. Add the warmed clam juice, whisking until thickened. Add the bay leaf. This mixture is called a roux.

2. Cook this roux until bubbly, then add the warmed cream, cayenne, thyme, salt and pepper to taste. Stir well, then lower heat, cover and cook until the potatoes are tender, about 15 minutes.

3. While this mixture is cooking, cook bacon until nicely browned. Drain, discarding the fat. Add the bacon and the chopped clams to the soup, taste for seasoning and serve, removing the bay leaf, or cool, refrigerate and rewarm later.

BARBEQUED BABY BACK RIBS—SERVES 8

This barbecue sauce is my adaptation of one from Columbus restaurateur and outstanding grillmaster Jim Budros.

3 racks of baby back ribs (about 7 to 8 pounds)
salt and freshly ground black pepper

Barbecue Sauce:

2 cups classic Coke (do not substitute diet or no-caffeine types)
2 cups ketchup
1/2 cup <u>each</u> Worchestershire Sauce and A-1 Sauce
2 teaspoons Liquid Smoke
2 tablespoons brown sugar
onion powder and garlic powder
<u>4 tablespoons unsalted butter</u>

1. Lightly salt and pepper the ribs and place on a rack in a large roasting pan. Add 2 cups of water to the bottom of the pan. Cover pan with foil and bake at 350°F. for 30 minutes, then turn and bake another 30 minutes, or until tender and no longer pink inside, checking by cutting between two ribs with knife. Can refrigerate until ready to grill.

2. <u>Prepare sauce</u>: In large saucepan mix all ingredients. Bring to a boil and simmer slowly to reduce to about 1/2 the original volume, about 30 minutes. Sauce can be made a day ahead.

3. When ready to grill ribs, preheat grill to High, then brush the less meaty side of ribs liberally with sauce and place on the grill, basted side down. Reduce heat to Medium and grill until sauce begins to bubble, watching closely so ribs don't burn (sauce can burn easily, as it has brown sugar in it), then baste other side, turn and grill until bubbly and brown. Remove to platter and cut ribs into 2 to 3 rib portions and serve with additional sauce, which you have brought to a boil. Leftovers warm up very well.

MACARONI AND CHEESE
SERVES 8 TO 10 🕐 🎩

When my daughter Diane prepared this dish for us on a recent visit to Iowa, my husband praised it and asked me to get the recipe from her. She and I chuckled, as it is one of my recipes—I just hadn't made it for a while. Now I make sure to make it for him more often.

solid Crisco to grease pan
7 ounces rigatoni pasta, cooked, drained and cooled (2 cups cooked)
8 ounces elbow macaroni, cooked, drained and cooled (2 cups cooked)
1 1/2 cups <u>each</u> small curd cottage cheese and sour cream
2 large eggs
24 ounces cheddar cheese, coarsely grated
salt and freshly ground pepper to taste
<u>1/2 cup additional cheddar cheese for topping</u>

1. Grease a 9" x 13" ovenproof casserole. Mix all ingredients except the 1/2 cup cheddar in a large bowl and transfer to casserole. (Can prepare several hours ahead and refrigerate.)

2. Preheat oven to 375°F. and bake until golden and crusty, about 40 minutes. Sprinkle with the 1/2 cup cheddar cheese and serve hot.

ZUCCHINI CASSEROLE—SERVES 8 🕐 🎩

A great old-fashioned family recipe from my Aunt Betty— even those who don't like zucchini will love this one! I don't often use prepared items like canned soup and stuffing mix but in this case, it it's not broke, don't fix it!

1 1/2 to 2 pounds small zucchini, sliced and quartered
1 onion, minced
1 tablespoon melted unsalted butter
salt and pepper to taste
1 10 3/4-ounce can cream of chicken soup
8 ounces sour cream
1/2 cup (1 stick) unsalted butter, melted
1 8-ounce package Pepperidge Farm Seasoned Stuffing Mix

<u>butter to grease casserole</u>

1. In a large pot cook the zucchini and onion in water to cover until just tender. Drain and put into a large bowl. Add the 1 tablespoon melted butter, salt, pepper, soup and sour cream and mix well.

2. In another large bowl mix the 1/2 cup melted butter with the stuffing mix. Add 1/2 of this mixture to the zucchini mixture above.

3. Butter a 2 1/2-quart ovenproof casserole. Pour the zucchini mixture in and top with the remaining 1/2 of the stuffing mixture. Bake in preheated 375°F. oven for 30 minutes. (Can prepare up to baking step a day ahead and bake when ready to eat.)

MILE HIGH COCONUT CREAM PIE
SERVES 8 TO 10 🕐 🎩 🎩 🎩

Although this pie takes some time to make, it is the best version of Coconut Cream Pie I have ever come across. It is my husband's favorite pie, and I try to make it for him for special occasions. The Crisco makes a delicious flaky crust!

Crust:

1 1/3 cups all-purpose flour
1/4 teaspoon salt
1/2 cup Crisco solid shortening, cut into small pieces, chilled
3 to 4 tablespoons ice water

Filling:

1 package unflavored gelatin (Knox)
3 cups whole milk
1 cup sugar
4 1/2 tablespoons cornstarch
1/4 teaspoon salt
3 large egg yolks, beaten lightly
3 tablespoons unsalted butter
1 1/2 teaspoons pure vanilla extract
3/4 cup coconut, for filling

Topping:

2 cups heavy cream
2 to 3 teaspoons sugar, to taste
1 teaspoon pure vanilla extract

<u>Garnish: 1/4 cup coconut, toasted in 350°F. oven for
5 minutes until golden</u>

1. <u>Make crust</u>: In medium bowl mix flour and salt. With
a pastry blender or fork mix in the Crisco until mixture
resembles small peas. Add enough ice water for dough
to hold together without being too wet. Form into a ball,
flatten into a disk and wrap in plastic wrap. Refrigerate
for one hour or up to overnight for dough to chill. Then
roll out on a lightly floured board and fit into a deep-dish
glass pie pan. Cover with plastic wrap and refrigerate for
at least 30 minutes or up to overnight for dough to relax.

2. <u>To bake crust</u>: Preheat oven to 375°F. Remove plastic
wrap and prick crust with a fork all over, then line with
a piece of heavy duty foil or parchment paper, fill with
dried beans and bake for 10 minutes. (This method is
called blind baking.) Then carefully remove foil and
beans (you can cool beans and reuse them many times)
and continue baking for about 15 to 20 minutes more, or
until golden. Cool and reserve while making filling.

3. <u>Make filling</u>: Soften the gelatin in 1/4 cup of the milk
in a small bowl. Scald (heat to just below the boiling
point) the remaining milk in a large saucepan. Add the
combined sugar, cornstarch and salt and continue heating
until boiling, whisking constantly. Whisk about 1/2 cup
of the hot mixture into the yolks, (this is called tempering
the yolks, so you don't curdle the eggs and make
scrambled eggs), then pour this mixture back into the
saucepan whisking constantly. Simmer 5 minutes more.
Stir in the gelatin mixture, butter, vanilla and 3/4 cup
coconut. Cool and then pour mixture into baked crust.
Put plastic wrap directly on the filling, to prevent a hard
crust from forming. Refrigerate for at least 3 hours.

4. When ready to serve, whip the cream until stiff, add
the sugar and vanilla and heap on top of pie. Sprinkle
with toasted coconut and serve.

EASY DOES IT!

Pan Roasted Garlic Chicken
Marlyn's Potatoes
Peasant Salad
Crunchy Corn Medley
Wellesley Fudge Cupcakes

PAN-ROASTED GARLIC CHICKEN—SERVES 8

*This simple but tasty recipe comes from fabulous chef,
cooking teacher and cookbook author Andrew Schloss,
who knows how to make food that is easy to prepare but
wonderful to eat!*

1 chicken (about 4 pounds) cut into 8 pieces, or 8
     breasts, bone-in and skin left on
kosher salt and coarsely ground black pepper to taste
2 tablespoons garlic-flavored oil, OR regular oil
20 cloves fresh garlic, peeled and root end cut off
<u>8 sprigs of rosemary, thyme or sage</u>

1. Season the chicken liberally with salt and pepper. Heat
the oil in a large, heavy skillet (preferably cast iron) over
medium-high heat. Place chicken pieces, skin-side down,
in the hot oil and cook until browned, about 5 minutes.
Turn and brown on the other side, about 3 minutes.

2. Scatter the garlic cloves around the chicken pieces and
place an herb sprig on each chicken piece. Reduce heat
to medium-low, cover and cook until chicken is cooked
through, 15 to 18 minutes. (Test by pricking meatiest
parts with a fork—juices should run clear.) Let rest for
about 5 minutes, then serve.

MARLYN'S POTATOES—SERVES 8 TO 10

Perfect for a crowd. From my cousin Marlyn Wyman, who likes to do things the easy way without sacrificing flavor!

1 30-ounce package frozen Ore-Ida hash browns-
    country style, (shredded)
1/2 cup chopped Vidalia or other sweet onions
2 cups grated sharp cheddar cheese
1 10 3/4-ounce can cream of chicken soup
1/2 cup (1 stick) melted unsalted butter
2 cups sour cream
1 teaspoon salt
1/4 teaspoon black pepper
cooking spray

Topping:

2 cups crushed cornflakes (put them in a plastic bag and
    use a rolling pin)
<u>1/4 cup melted butter</u>

1. In a large bowl mix the hash browns, onion, cheese, soup, melted butter, sour cream and salt and pepper. Pour into a 9" x 13" ovenproof casserole that has been sprayed with cooking spray. Can prepare to this point and refrigerate up to overnight.

2. Preheat oven to 350°F. Put topping on just before baking for one hour or until heated through and browned on top. Mmmmm!

PEASANT SALAD—SERVES 8 TO 10

Definitely NOT peasant food, but a fabulous salad from the now closed and sorely missed Peasant on the Lane restaurant in Columbus. A great make-ahead.

1 head iceburg lettuce, torn up
8 ounces baby spinach, stems removed, torn up
1 cup chopped celery
1 cup diced or thinly sliced red onion
1 red pepper, chopped
1 10-ounce package frozen baby peas
1 teaspoon <u>each</u> salt and black pepper
2 tablespoons sugar
8 slices bacon, cooked crispy, then crumbled

1 cup or more shredded sharp cheddar
<u>about 2 cups or more Miracle Whip dressing</u>

1. In a large punch bowl or other large bowl, place first the lettuce, then the spinach, then the chopped celery and red onion. Sprinkle on a layer of red pepper, then the frozen baby peas. Add the salt and pepper and sugar. Sprinkle on the bacon and shredded sharp cheddar.

2. "Frost" with a thick layer of Miracle Whip, then cover and refrigerate for at least 8 hours or up to 24 hours. Toss just before serving. It will be surprising if you have any leftovers, but they are still yummy the next day, although a bit "wet."

CRUNCHY CORN MEDLEY
SERVES 8 TO 10

This is a perfect dish for a crowd. Many of my friends take it to pot luck dinners, and everyone always asks for the recipe.

2 cups frozen peas, thawed
1 15 1/4-ounce can <u>each</u> whole kernel corn and white or
    shoepeg corn, drained
1 8-ounce can water chestnuts, drained and chopped
1 4-ounce jar diced pimientos, drained
8 green onions, thinly sliced
2 celery ribs, chopped
1 medium green pepper, chopped

Dressing:

1/2 cup <u>each</u> white vinegar and sugar
1/4 cup vegetable oil
1 teaspoon salt
<u>1/4 teaspoon pepper</u>

1. In a large bowl combine the peas, both cans of corn, water chestnuts, pimientos, green onions, green pepper and celery.

2. <u>Make the dressing</u>: In a small bowl combine the vinegar, sugar, oil, salt and pepper, whisking well until sugar is dissolved. Pour over the corn mixture and mix well. Cover and refrigerate for 2 hours or up to overnight. Stir just before serving and serve with a slotted spoon.

WELLESLEY FUDGE CUPCAKES
MAKES 12 ⏱ 👨‍🍳

This is a riff on the famous Wellesley Fudge Cake. These cupcakes freeze well.

For the cupcakes:

2 ounces unsweetened chocolate, chopped in the food
    processor, for faster melting
6 tablespoons hot water
6 tablespoons unsalted butter, room temperature
1 cup firmly packed light brown sugar
2 large egg yolks
1 cup all-purpose flour
1 teaspoon baking powder
1/4 teaspoon salt
4 tablespoons (1/4 cup) whole milk
1 teaspoon pure vanilla extract

Frosting:

2 ounces unsweetened chocolate, chopped fine
1 tablespoon unsalted butter
1 cup confectioners' sugar, sifted
1 tablespoon milk, plus additional to thin the frosting if
    needed
1 teaspoon pure vanilla extract

1. Preheat the oven to 375°F.

2. Make the cupcakes: In a metal bowl set over a pan of barely simmering water melt the chocolate with the water, stirring until the mixture is smooth. Remove bowl from heat. In another bowl whisk the butter with the brown sugar until the mixture is blended well. Whisk in the egg yolks and the melted chocolate mixture.

3. On a piece of waxed paper sift together the flour, baking powder and salt and add to the chocolate mixture in batches alternately with the milk, stirring gently after each addition, starting and ending with the flour mixture for better texture in your cupcakes. Stir in the vanilla. Divide the batter among 12 paper-lined standard size muffin cups and bake in the middle of the oven for 18 to 20 minutes, or until a tester comes out clean. Remove from muffin tin to a rack and let cool.

4. Make the frosting: In a metal bowl set over a pan of barely simmering water melt the chocolate with the butter, stirring, until mixture is smooth. Remove from heat and stir in the confectioners' sugar, about 1 tablespoon milk and the vanilla and blend well. It will thicken as it stands.

5. When cupcakes are cool, thin the frosting to a good spreading consistency with a bit of extra milk if needed, adding by drops. Spread cupcakes with frosting using an offset spatula. For extra fancy cupcakes, double the frosting recipe and pipe it on cupcakes with a fluted pastry tip.

A MAKE-AHEAD MEAL FOR FAMILY AND FRIENDS

Chunky Vegetable Soup
Giant Stuffed Pasta Shells
French Bread Garlic Mustard Slices
Marlyn's Black Cherry Jello Mold
Williamsburg Inn Pecan Bars

CHUNKY VEGETABLE SOUP
SERVES 8 TO 10 ⏲ 👨‍🍳

Real comfort food. Serve with slices of peasant bread and wait for raves! I adapted this recipe from a family favorite of my amazing culinary assistant Linda Ruck, who defines what a loyal friend is!

1 pound stew meat, cut into bite-size cubes, most fat removed
2 tablespoons vegetable oil
4 cups <u>each</u> beef stock (I like More Than Gourmet pucks here), and cold water
1 onion, coarsely chopped
1 15-ounce can tomatoes, with their juice, coarsely chopped
2 potatoes, peeled and cut into cubes
3 carrots, peeled, quartered and sliced
1/4 head green cabbage, about 2 cups, chopped
1/2 cup celery, coarsely chopped
2 cloves fresh garlic, chopped
1 15-ounce can green beans, drained
1 to 2 tablespoons <u>each</u> ketchup and sugar, to taste
1 to 2 teaspoons dried herbs: Italian mixed herbs, basil, oregano, thyme
1 teaspoon salt, or to taste
<u>1/2 teaspoon pepper, or to taste</u>

1. Dry the stew meat on paper towels or it won't brown. In a 5-quart stockpot heat the oil till very hot and sauté the meat on all sides for about 5 minutes. Do not crowd the pan. If you have to, brown meat in several batches. Add the beef stock and water, the onion, garlic and tomatoes and bring to a boil. Skim off any scum that rises to the top. Lower heat to a simmer and simmer for 1 1/2 hours.

2. Add the carrots, potatoes, cabbage, celery, and herbs.

Cook for one half hour longer, or until carrots and potatoes are fork-tender. Add the sugar, salt and pepper to taste. Add the green beans. This soup is even better served the next day. It freezes well too!

GIANT STUFFED PASTA SHELLS
SERVES 8 TO 10 ⏲ 👨‍🍳 👨‍🍳

A perfect family meal.

30 to 32 jumbo pasta shells for stuffing
salt for cooking pasta
2 tablespoons olive oil
1/4 cup chopped onion
1 teaspoon minced garlic
1 10-ounce package frozen chopped spinach, defrosted and squeezed dry
3/4 pound <u>each</u> ground beef and ground sausage, spicy or mild, to your taste
5 tablespoons grated Parmesan cheese
2 tablespoons whipping cream
2 large eggs, lightly beaten
1/2 teaspoon dried oregano, salt and freshly ground black pepper

Béchamel Sauce:

6 tablespoons <u>each</u> unsalted butter and flour
1 cup <u>each</u> whole milk and whipping cream, warmed
1 teaspoon salt, 1/8 teaspoon white pepper
1/4 to 1/2 teaspoon grated nutmeg

Topping:

3 cups jarred or homemade tomato pasta sauce
<u>2 or more tablespoons each Parmesan cheese and butter, cut into small pieces</u>

1. Preheat oven to 375°F.

2. Cook shells according to package directions in salted water. Drain and reserve.

3. <u>Make filling</u>: In large skillet heat olive oil, add onion and garlic and cook over moderate heat, stirring for 7 minutes or until soft but not brown. Stir in spinach

and cook, stirring constantly for 3 to 4 minutes. When moisture has boiled away and spinach sticks lightly to side of skillet transfer to large mixing bowl. In same skillet lightly brown the ground meat, breaking up any lumps. Drain meat and add to onion-spinach mixture. Add the Parmesan, whipping cream and oregano. Taste and add salt and pepper. Add eggs and with a wooden spoon mix ingredients thoroughly but gently. Reserve.

4. Make the Béchamel Sauce: Melt butter over moderate heat in a 2-quart saucepan. Stirring with a whisk add the flour and cook until bubbly. Whisk in the warmed milk and whipping cream and whisk constantly until sauce thickens enough to coat a wooden spoon. Season with salt, white pepper and nutmeg.

5. To assemble dish: Place about a tablespoon of filling in each shell. Spray a deep 9" x 13" casserole with cooking spray and pour a layer of the tomato sauce into the bottom of the pan to coat. Lay the shells side by side in one layer on the sauce. Pour the Béchamel Sauce over the shells and drizzle the rest of the tomato sauce over the top, not covering completely. Sprinkle the Parmesan over the top and dot with the butter. (Can prepare up to 2 days ahead and refrigerate.)

6. To bake: Place casserole on parchment-lined cookie sheet and bake in preheated oven 25 to 30 minutes, or until the cheese is melted and sauce is bubbly. Serve from the baking casserole.

FRENCH BREAD GARLIC MUSTARD SLICES
MAKES 24 SLICES

1/2 cup (1 stick) unsalted butter, room temperature
1/4 cup fresh chopped parsley leaves
2 tablespoons each sliced green onions and Dijon
    mustard
1 tablespoon toasted sesame seeds
1 teaspoon fresh lemon juice
1 loaf soft French bread (not a baguette), sliced into 24
    1-inch thick slices

1. Preheat oven to 375°F.

2. In a small mixing bowl stir together all ingredients except bread. Spread mixture on both sides of bread slices.

3. Arrange bread slices on foil-lined baking sheets. Toast for about 20 minutes or until golden brown, turning once. Put into breadbasket and serve right away.

MARLYN'S BLACK CHERRY JELLO SALAD
SERVES 8 TO 10

This is a very easy but delicious dish, showing "oldies" can still be "goodies"!

1 3-ounce package black cherry, raspberry or strawberry jello
1 cup boiling water
3/4 cup black cherry juice (from black cherries, below)
1 1-pound can or jar sweet black cherries, in heavy syrup, drained (reserve juice)
1 15-ounce can pineapple chunks, drained
1 8-ounce can mandarin oranges, drained
1/2 cup walnuts, coarsely chopped

1. Place jello in a large bowl and pour the 1 cup of boiling water over it, stirring to dissolve. Add the 3/4 cup of cherry juice, stirring well. Add the cherries, pineapple chunks, mandarin oranges and walnuts. Stir well and pour into large 6-cup jello mold. Refrigerate overnight, covered.

2. When ready to unmold, fill sink 1/2 full with very warm water and dip mold quickly into water, then invert onto serving plate.

WILLIAMSBURG INN PECAN BARS
MAKES 48

This recipe makes a lot of bars, so bake up a batch and freeze half, and you'll always be ready for unexpected company.

solid Crisco and flour to prepare pans
1 1/2 sticks (3/4 cup) unsalted butter
3/4 cup sugar
2 large eggs
grated rind of 1 lemon
3 cups all-purpose flour
1/2 teaspoon baking powder

Pecan Topping

1 cup each butter, light brown sugar, packed, and honey
1/4 cup whipping cream
3 cups pecans, chopped

1. Preheat oven to 375°F.

2. Grease and flour two 9" x 9" x 2" square baking pans.

3. Cream the butter and sugar in an electric mixer, add the eggs one at a time and then add the lemon rind and mix well.

4. Sift the flour and baking powder together and add them to the creamed mixture on medium speed, mixing well.

5. Press the dough onto the bottom of the prepared pans. Prick all over with a fork and bake 12 to 15 minutes or until the dough looks half done. Remove from oven and set on top of stove. Lower oven temperature to 350°F.

6. Prepare pecan topping: In a large deep heavy saucepan place the butter, sugar and honey. Bring to a boil. Cool slightly and add the cream and chopped pecans, mixing well. Spread the pecan topping evenly over the surface of the partially baked dough with an offset spatula. Return to the oven and bake for 25 to 30 minutes. Cut while still warm into 48 bars, 24 from each pan. These freeze well.

SUMMERTIME FUN

Marlene's Fresh Cream of Tomato Soup
Spicy Maytag Blueburgers with Hot Wing Sauce
Susan's Corn Pudding
"Can-Do" Cowboy Beans
Homemade Vanilla Ice Cream with warm Berry
Compote

MARLENE'S FRESH CREAM OF TOMATO SOUP
8 SERVINGS

You can make this soup up to step #3, then freeze the tomato "base" and finish soup with the white sauce at a later date. Do not freeze the completed soup, as the white sauce will curdle. Just follow the directions and you will have wonderfully fresh-tasting soup all winter long.

3 pounds fresh tomatoes, about 12, skins and seeds
    removed (see below)
1 cup water or chicken stock
1/2 cup each chopped onion and chopped celery
1/2 tablespoon sugar

3 cups whole milk, warmed
4 tablespoons each butter and flour or cornstarch
1 to 2 tablespoons brown sugar, to taste
1 teaspoon salt, or to taste
1/4 teaspoon pepper, or to taste

Garnish: 4 tablespoons fresh basil, julienned into thin
    strips with a sharp knife

1. Remove skins from fresh tomatoes by immersing them in boiling water for about 30 seconds, or until they peel off easily with the point of a knife. Quarter them and remove seeds.

2. Simmer tomatoes with water, onion, celery and sugar for 20 minutes in a 4-quart Dutch oven. Put into a blender in batches and purée until very smooth. Strain and reserve while making white sauce, OR freeze this "base" for future use.

3. Make white sauce: Warm milk in a saucepan or the microwave. In another saucepan melt butter and stir in

flour or cornstarch, stirring constantly with a wooden spoon or whisk, and cook 2 to 3 minutes until "raw" taste disappears. Add the pepper and the salt. Stir well.

4. Add this white sauce to strained tomato mixture, stirring (if you have had the tomato base in the freezer, defrost it first.) Season to taste. Garnish each serving with julienned basil before serving.

SPICY MAYTAG BLUE CHEESE BURGERS WITH
HOT WING SAUCE—SERVES 8 TO 10

On a trip to visit our daughter Diane who lives in Iowa, we had fun visiting the Maytag Blue Cheese plant in Newton, Iowa, where you can watch them as they still hand-wrap this delicious cheese.

2 pounds ground chuck (you don't want meat that's too
    lean or burgers will be dry)
1 cup crumbled Maytag or other blue cheese
1 cup finely minced onion
2 tablespoons Worcestershire sauce
2 teaspoons each freshly ground black pepper and
    prepared yellow mustard
1 teaspoon garlic powder
4 tablespoons cold water

Hot Wing Sauce:

1/2 cup (1 stick) unsalted butter, melted
4 tablespoons or more hot sauce, to your taste

8 to 10 sesame or onion buns, split, brushed with
    melted butter before grilling

Optional condiments: lettuce, sliced tomato, pickles,
    relish, etc.

1. In a large bowl, mix ground beef, blue cheese, onion, Worcestershire sauce, mustard, pepper and water, using your hands and mixing thoroughly but gently. Form into 8 to 10 patties, depending on how big you like your burgers. Do not compress them too tightly or they will be dry when cooked. Cover and refrigerate for 1/2 hour up to overnight (or you can freeze them, wrapped individually).

2. <u>Prepare the Hot Wing Sauce</u>: In a medium microwavable bowl, melt the butter and add the hot sauce to taste. Reserve at room temperature.

3. <u>When ready to grill</u>: Preheat an outdoor grill to High heat. Remove patties from refrigerator and pour enough hot wing sauce (the butter and hot sauce combined) over them to cover the top surface. Allow to sit for 10 minutes.

4. Lower heat on grill to Medium and place buns brushed with butter on the grill and close lid. Watch closely and remove as they brown. Press a small indentation into each burger with your finger, then put burgers on the grill and close lid. Cook about 5 minutes or more per side, or until no longer pink inside. The time will vary with your grill, but the internal temperature should be 150°F. when tested with an instant read thermometer for burgers to be safe to eat. For extra spicy burgers, baste with additional hot wing sauce several times while cooking.

5. Serve burgers with buns and pass optional garnishes.

SUSAN'S CORN PUDDING—SERVES 8

My culinary assistant Susan says her family has made this dish for every holiday and family get-together since she can remember, and when you taste it, you'll know why! You can fix the casserole the night before, cover and refrigerate, then bake the next day. Every year when the white corn is ripe in July or August, Susan's whole family shucks at least twelve dozen ears of corn (Bakers' dozens at that!) and strips it, measures all ingredients <u>but the milk</u> into double freezer bags, and they're ready for the next year's family gatherings.

6 tablespoons unsalted butter, softened to room
   temperature
4 tablespoons <u>each</u> sugar and flour
1 1/2 teaspoons salt
6 large eggs, lightly beaten
4 cups freshly shucked corn kernels, if possible, or
   frozen white shoepeg corn
<u>about 1 cup milk, depending on how you like your
   corn- scalloped or custardy</u>

1. Combine the butter, sugar, flour and salt in a large bowl. Add the eggs and mix well. Finally, add the corn and the milk. Pour into a buttered 9" x 12" baking dish and bake at 350°F. for 45 minutes, stirring once halfway through, until golden brown and set.

"CAN DO" COWBOY BEANS
SERVES 8 TO 10

I am privileged to count among my friends renowned cowboy artist Jack Wells. The last time he came for dinner he said that if I included a cowboy recipe in my cookbook, he'd do an original sketch for me, an offer I couldn't resist. It is a real joy for me to have his work in my book. By the way, the recipe is killer too!

l 14.5-ounce can <u>each</u> cut green beans, drained, baby
    lima beans, drained, and garbanzo beans, drained
l 14.5-ounce can hot Caliente chili beans
l 8-ounce can tomato sauce
l 10 3/4-ounce can tomato soup
l cup brown sugar
l/2 cup Open Pit Original Flavor Barbeque Sauce
<u>l pound Italian sausage, fully cooked and sliced into l/2
    inch slices</u>

1. Preheat oven to 325°F.

2. In large roasting pan or open oven-proof casserole mix the beans with the tomato sauce, soup, brown sugar and barbeque sauce. Stir in the cooked Italian sausage.

3. Bake for l l/2 to 2 hours. Makes 8 to 10 generous servings. This reheats very well.

HOMEMADE VANILLA BEAN ICE CREAM WITH WARM BERRY COMPOTE
MAKES 1 1/2 TO 2 QUARTS

This recipe does require an ice cream maker, but today they are very inexpensive, and it is so much fun to make home-made ice cream, so consider adding it to your kitchen equipment. Note the variations suggested also.

2 cups whole milk
1/2 vanilla bean, slit down the middle, OR 1 tablespoon
    real (not artificial) liquid vanilla, added <u>after</u> milk
    has been scalded and cooled)
4 large egg yolks, beaten
1 cup granulated sugar
1/4 teaspoon salt
1 quart heavy cream

Variations:

3 cups crushed peaches mixed with 1 cup sugar, 1
    teaspoon lemon juice and 1 teaspoon red wine
    vinegar <u>OR</u> 3 cups crushed hulled fresh strawberries
    <u>sweetened to taste OR any other fruit of your choice.</u>

1. In a medium saucepan combine milk and vanilla bean and scald (to a temperature of 155°F.). Cool. If using liquid vanilla, cool milk before adding it.

2. In the bowl of an electric mixer combine egg yolks, sugar and salt. Beat until mixture is light and fluffy.

3. Remove vanilla bean from cooled milk and scrape the little seeds (called marrow) into milk. Dry bean for use in vanilla sugar. Pour the milk slowly into the sugar-yolk mixture, stirring constantly. Pour this mixture into a clean saucepan and heat over moderate heat, stirring into a clean saucepan and heat over moderate heat, stirring constantly. When milk begins to warm, reduce heat and stir with a wooden spoon until a lightly thickened custard is formed which will coat the spoon and temperature of custard is 180°F. Strain at once into a large cold bowl and cool. Add the heavy cream and when mixture is very cold pour into an ice cream maker, following manufacturer's directions. If you are adding fruit, add it just as the ice cream is getting firm. This ice cream will be very soft the first day and very hard the next.

WARM BERRY COMPOTE—SERVES 8

1/2 cup water

2 cups sugar

4 teaspoons fresh lemon juice

2 cups fresh strawberries, halved or sliced

2 cups blueberries, fresh or frozen

2 cups blackberries, black raspberries or red
   raspberries, fresh or frozen

1/2 cup (1 stick) unsalted butter, cut into cubes

1 quart best quality vanilla ice cream

<u>Garnish: mint sprigs</u>

1. Made light sugar syrup by combining water and sugar in a medium saucepan, heating to a boil and stirring until sugar is dissolved. Add the lemon juice and stir.

2. Add the strawberries and blueberries and cook on medium heat 3 minutes or until heated through, shaking pan gently to coat berries with syrup. Add butter and stir gently until it melts. Stir in the raspberries very gently.

3. Spoon compote evenly into bowls and top with scoops of ice cream. Garnish with mint sprigs, if desired.

COOK'S TIP

If you don't have some of the equipment you "need" when cooking, tell your family and friends to remember you at birthdays and holidays with kitchen gifts—they'll be repaid many times over by the great food that they'll be eating! A good quality food processor, heavy duty electric mixer and a strong motor on your blender will make your cooking time so much more pleasurable and productive, and good knives and heavy bottomed pots and pans will really help you raise your cooking success level. You don't have to buy all this equipment at once—watch for sales and keep adding to your cooking arsenal. I have noticed that many home cooks have what I call "fear of high heat" and sharp knives. Actually, you need to cook on high heat to sear meats and vegetables properly, and you really are much more likely to cut yourself using a dull knife, which requires using more pressure, than with a sharp one. Hold the food you will be cutting by curling your hand into the "arthritic claw" to keep from cutting yourself. Remember that cooking is a skill, and the more you practice your technique, the better and faster you will become!

4

STELLAR DINNER PARTIES

There is nothing more satisfying to me than entertaining friends and family with a wonderful meal that encourages great conversations and camaraderie. Here are five truly spectacular menus that are designed so that you can entertain with elegance and panache. Each meal showcases seasonal ingredients and flavors. Share these dinners with the important people in your life to celebrate special moments and to create lasting memories. Menus include: An Elegant Spring Dinner Party, A Sophisticated Dinner Party for Eight, An Autumn Celebration, A Luxury Winter Dinner Party and Entertaining for the Holidays.

Chilled Cucumber Soup with Dill (page 60)

AN ELEGANT SPRING DINNER PARTY

Chilled Cucumber Soup with Dill
Marinated Butterflied Leg of Lamb
Herbed Green Rice
Mint Soufflé
L' Armagnac's Cheesecake

CHILLED CUCUMBER SOUP WITH DILL
SERVES 8 TO 10

So refreshing on a warm spring or summer day.

3 to 4 medium cucumbers (about 24 ounces total)
   peeled, seeded and sliced
1 medium onion, coarsely chopped
6 cups chicken stock (boxed or homemade), <u>DIVIDED</u>

1/2 cup flour
1 tablespoon fresh dill, chopped (no stems), plus more
   for garnish
2 cups sour cream
1 to 2 teaspoons freshly squeezed lemon juice
sea salt and white pepper to taste

<u>Garnish: 2 tablespoons fresh chives, snipped</u>

1. In a large stockpot cook the cucumber and onion in 4 cups of the chicken stock for 10 minutes. In another pot stir the flour with the two remaining cups of <u>warmed</u> chicken stock using a wooden spoon and whisk to make a smooth thickened mixture. Cook until thickened. Combine two mixtures. Cool down in an ice and water bath. Purée mixture in blender in batches, adding the dill and the sour cream. To avoid messy spills don't fill blender container too full. Blend until smooth.

2. Taste and add lemon juice and salt and pepper to taste. Chill thoroughly. Remember to taste again before serving, as chilling often changes flavors, and you may need to add more salt and pepper. To bring to an outdoor picnic pack in a vacuum thermos. Just before serving, top each bowl of soup with some chopped chives and a sprig of dill if desired.

MARINATED BUTTERFLIED LEG OF LAMB
SERVES 8

1 boned and butterflied leg of lamb (you can have
   butcher do this) about 3 to 4 pounds after deboning
4 tablespoons extra virgin olive oil
2 tablespoons soy sauce
grated peel of 1/2 of an orange, plus the juice
1/2 teaspoon or so crushed dried rosemary
<u>2 cloves garlic, mashed</u>

1. Lay the meat out, boned surface up, on your work surface, and you will notice that it forms two large lobes. For even cooking, slash the lobes in 2 or 3 places, making long cuts about 1 1/2 inch deep, or these thicker pieces will be too rare when cooked. To keep the roast in shape, you can push long skewers through the wide sides of the meat, one through the top and the other through the bottom third, if you wish.

2. Rub the unboned side of the lamb with a tablespoon of olive oil and place, oiled side down, in a non-reactive pan. Rub the rest of the oil and the soy sauce, lemon juice and peel, rosemary and garlic into the top side. Cover with plastic wrap and marinate at least 2 hours or, for better flavor, up to overnight if possible, refrigerated.

3. When ready to cook, either prepare barbeque until coals are very hot, OR heat a gas grill to High, OR preheat oven to 375°F. If grilling meat, oil barbeque rack using crumpled heavy duty foil or old newspaper. <u>To grill on a grill with coals</u>, brush meat with extra oil and turn every 10 minutes or so, for from 45 minutes to one hour, depending on size of roast and how rare you like your lamb. If using a gas grill, reduce heat to Medium before putting lamb on racks, but follow same other instructions as above. Lamb should cook to an internal temperature of about 125°F. on the grill, testing with an instant read thermometer. <u>If roasting</u> in oven, place in a roasting pan, boned side up, in the upper middle of oven. Roast for 20 to 25 minutes, or to an instant-read thermometer reading of 120°F. Do not turn the roast. Then, baste with oil and set under broiler for 3 to 5 minutes until browned lightly. Whichever method you use to cook lamb, it is very important to let it sit for 8 to 10 minutes on a carving board, loosely tented with foil, so juices can be reabsorbed back into meat. Carve by starting at either of

the small ends, and make attractively thin largish slices by beginning somewhat back from the edge, angling your knife for prettier slices.

HERBED GREEN RICE—SERVES 8

2 1/2 cups raw long grain (Uncle Ben's Converted) white rice
1 1/2 cups chopped fresh parsley, no stems
1/2 cup fresh basil, chopped
4 tablespoons chopped green onion tops
1/2 cup olive oil (approximately)
2 tablespoons unsalted butter
salt and freshly ground black pepper to taste

Optional: freshly grated Parmesan cheese

1. Put raw rice in fine strainer and rinse under cold water until water runs clear, not cloudy. Put in large heavy pot with 5 cups cold water and bring to a boil. Lower heat to a simmer and cover pot. Cook about 20 to 25 minutes, until all liquid is absorbed. Can let rest 5 minutes.

2. Place the parsley, basil, and green onion tops in bowl of food processor. With machine running, add just enough olive oil through the feed tube to make a smooth purée.

3. Toss the puréed mixture with the hot rice, along with the salt, pepper and butter. Serve immediately, or keep warm in a 225°F. oven. Sprinkle with Parmesan just before serving, if desired.

MINT SOUFFLÉ—SERVES 8

Impressive and not as difficult as you might think. Your guests will be awed. This soufflé is a wonderful accompaniment to the lamb.

3 tablespoons unsalted butter
2 tablespoons finely chopped shallots or green onions
3 tablespoons all-purpose flour
1 cup milk, warmed in microwave or on stove
3 tablespoons minced fresh mint

1 tablespoon <u>each</u> minced fresh parsley and minced fresh chives or green onion tops
1/2 teaspoon salt
1/2 teaspoon pepper
4 large egg yolks

5 large egg whites
1 tablespoon butter to butter the soufflé dish

Garnish: fresh mint sprigs

1. In heavy medium saucepan melt butter over medium heat. Add shallots and sauté until translucent, about 2 minutes Add flour and cook 2 minutes, stirring constantly with wooden spoon. Using a wire whisk, gradually whisk in warm milk. Cook until mixture boils and thickens, stirring constantly, about 2 minutes. Add herbs, salt and pepper. Remove from heat.

2. Whisk in yolks one at a time, whisking vigorously to temper them and not make scrambled eggs. Return to heat and cook over medium high heat until thick, whisking constantly, about 2 minutes. (Can be prepared one day ahead. Cover and chill.) This is your base. If you have chilled it, whisk over low heat when you take it out of the refrigerator until smooth and just heated through to barely lukewarm before continuing.

3. When ready to bake soufflé, butter a 6-cup soufflé dish. Preheat oven to 400°F.

4. Using an electric mixer, beat egg whites in medium bowl until stiff but not dry. Fold 1/4 of whites into egg yolk base to lighten. Using a clean rubber spatula, gently fold in remaining whites. Transfer soufflé mixture to prepared soufflé dish. Bake until soufflé is puffed and golden brown but center still moves slightly when dish is shaken gently, about 25 minutes. Test by inserting a metal skewer or butter knife into the center of the soufflé—it should come out almost clean. If it is not, bake another 5 to 10 minutes. Serve immediately, garnished with mint sprigs if you wish.

L' ARMAGNAC'S CHEESECAKE
MAKES 1 CAKE

In the 1970s L' Armagnac was the premier French restaurant in Columbus, Ohio. The chef shared his recipe for their ethereal cheesecake with me, and now you can make it too.

Genoise: Makes one more layer than you'll need for this cheesecake

2 tablespoons unsalted butter, melted
1 cup sifted cake flour
1/2 cup sugar, divided
1/8 teaspoon salt
4 large eggs, room temperature
1 teaspoon pure vanilla extract
Grand Marnier liqueur, to sprinkle on baked cake

Filling:

1 1/2 pounds cream cheese (NOT reduced fat type)
3/4 cup sugar
1 tablespoon each Armagnac brandy (or other brandy),
    Grand Marnier and orange juice concentrate
2 cups whipping cream
1/2 cup sugar
1 tablespoon pure vanilla
1 envelope Knox gelatin

Raspberry Coulis:

2 pints fresh raspberries OR one 12-ounce bag frozen
    berries, defrosted
1 to 2 tablespoons superfine (bar) sugar or
    confectioners' sugar
1/2 cup raspberry jam, seedless
fresh lemon juice to taste

1. Make the Genoise: Preheat oven to 350°F. Butter and flour a 10-inch cake pan. Line with a circle of parchment paper and butter and flour it as well. Reserve.

2. Pour the melted butter into a 1-quart bowl and reserve.

3. Put the sifted cake flour in a sieve and add 1 tablespoon of the sugar and the salt. Sift onto a piece of parchment paper and reserve.

4. Put eggs and remaining sugar into the bowl of a mixer. Using the whisk attachment mix ingredients to blend. Then whip mixture on high speed until airy, pale and tripled in volume, like softly whipped cream, 4 to 5 minutes, when it forms the ribbon (batter rests on the surface for about 10 seconds keeping its shape). Pour in the vanilla during last moments of whipping. Transfer this mixture to a large bowl. Sprinkle about 1/3 of the sifted flour mixture over batter and fold in with a rubber spatula, stopping as soon as flour is incorporated. Fold in rest of flour mixture in 2 more additions.

5. Gently spoon about 1 cup batter into the reserved bowl with the melted butter and fold in with a rubber spatula. Fold this mixture into the batter in the large bowl—this is the point at which the batter is at its most fragile, so fold gently. Pour batter into the prepared pan and bake immediately for about 25 minutes. Cake is done when it has puffed, is lightly brown and has just begun to show a faint line of shrinkage from the edges of the pan.

6. Remove from oven and let stand in the pan for 6 to 8 minutes. It will sink slightly and shrink more from the edges of the pan. Run a knife around the edge of the pan and reverse the cake onto a cake rack. Remove parchment paper and immediately reverse so its puffed side is on top. Allow to cool for an hour or so. Cut cooled cake into two thin layers with a serrated knife. Line a 10-inch springform pan with one of the layers and sprinkle it with Grand Marnier. Freeze the other layer for future use.

7. Make the filling: Cream together the cream cheese and 3/4 cup sugar in the bowl of an electric mixer. Add the Armagnac, Grand Marnier and orange juice concentrate. In another bowl whip the whipping cream, 1/2 cup sugar, vanilla and Knox gelatin to stiff peaks. Fold this mixture gently into the cream cheese mixture. Pour into the springform pan over the Genoise layer, and smooth top with an offset spatula. Chill in the refrigerator until set, at least 4 hours and up to overnight.

8. Make the Raspberry Coulis: In the blender or food processor place the raspberries and purée with the jam. Strain through a fine strainer to remove the seeds. Add sugar and lemon juice to taste. Place in a clean ketchup squeeze bottle and put 3 to 4 large drops of coulis on each plate with a piece of cheesecake, then pull a knife through the drops to make hearts.

A SOPHISTICATED DINNER PARTY
FOR EIGHT

Rita's Lobster Salsa Canapés
Poached Salmon with Sauce Verte
String Bean Salad with Hazelnuts and Crème Fraîche
Marcia's Frozen Lemon Mousse

RITA HOLT'S LOBSTER SALSA CANAPÉS
MAKES 24

One of the greatest thrills a cooking teacher can have is watching her students strut their stuff. Several of my advanced students decided to prepare a special meal for me, my staff, and our significant others. It was outstanding, starting with this delicious appetizer. What fun it was for me to watch them show us how to make this meal! It's a memory I hold very dear.

1 1/2 pounds live lobster, or a 16-ounce to 20-ounce
    package of frozen lobster tail
2 English cucumbers
2 tablespoons or more real mayonnaise
3 to 4 teaspoons fresh lime juice
1 teaspoon or more minced jalapeño (including seeds),
    to taste
1/4 teaspoon salt
1/3 cup finely diced peeled ripe mango
1/4 cup finely chopped celery
2 tablespoons <u>each</u> finely chopped red onion and finely
    chopped cilantro,

<u>Garnish: cilantro sprigs</u>

1. <u>Cook the lobster</u>: Bring a large pot of salted water to a rolling boil and add live lobster. Cook on high heat for 12 to 15 minutes. Cool and take meat from tail and claws, cutting into 1/4-inch pieces. Reserve. <u>Alternately</u>, defrost frozen lobster tails, oil with a bit of vegetable oil and place on a cookie sheet and roast for 10 minutes or until done, then remove from shell and cut into 1/4-inch pieces.

2. In a large bowl whisk together the mayonnaise, lime juice, jalapeño and salt. Add a pinch of pepper to taste.

3. Add the lobster, mango, celery, onion and cilantro to

this mixture and toss well. Taste and adjust seasoning. Can refrigerate, covered at this point.

4. Peel the cucumbers, or leave alternating strips of green, or run a fork down the sides of the cucumber for a fancier look. Cut into about 3/4-inch pieces and carefully scoop out the centers with a small spoon, leaving enough to keep the bottom whole.

5. Fill the cucumber rounds with approximately 1 to 2 teaspoons of the lobster salsa and garnish with cilantro sprigs.

POACHED SALMON WITH SAUCE VERTE
SERVES 8 TO 10

Elegance personified!

white wine and water to cover fish, in ratio of 2 parts
    wine to 1 part water
(I used Lindeman's Bin 65 Chardonnay, which is also
    good to drink with this dish)
1 fennel bulb, sliced, or just top fronds, or dill fronds
damp cheesecloth to wrap fish
3-pound fresh salmon fillet, skin on

<u>Garnishes</u>: black olive slice, lemon slices, sliced
    cucumbers, sliced carrots, chive

Sauce Verte:

2 tablespoons <u>each</u> finely chopped parsley, dill, chives
    and basil or watercress
1 clove garlic, crushed
1 shallot, finely chopped
touch of cayenne, sea salt and crushed white pepper to
    taste
1 cup real mayonnaise
<u>2 cups heavy whipping cream</u>

1. Bring the wine, water and fresh fennel or dill sprigs to a boil in a fish poacher or large oval roasting pan, which has a rack. Reduce heat so liquid is at a simmer. Place the salmon, which has been wrapped, skin side down, in damp cheesecloth, on the rack, cover and simmer until the salmon is opaque throughout. The rule of thumb for cooking time is 10 minutes per each inch of thickness of the fish. After about 8 minutes remove rack to a large

platter and check doneness by using two forks to break into the thickest part of the fish. If it is opaque, fish is done. Let cool to room temperature, cover with plastic wrap and refrigerate until chilled, several hours or up to overnight.

2. Carefully remove skin from the fish, using the cheesecloth to roll fish over, then transfer to a large platter. Garnish with a black olive slice for an eye, thinly sliced English cucumber, thinly sliced carrots and lemon slices to suggest the head, fins and tail, and a chive sprig for definition of the "body". Serve with Sauce Verte.

3. To make Sauce Verte: In blender, chop the herbs and add the garlic, shallot, salt, pepper, cayenne, mayonnaise and 1/2 cup of the cream. Transfer to large bowl. Whip rest of the heavy cream until slightly thickened, then fold into above mixture by hand. Taste for seasoning and refrigerate until needed.

STRING BEAN SALAD WITH HAZELNUTS AND CRÈME FRAÎCHE—SERVES 8

2 pounds young string beans , or cut regular green
  beans in half horizontally to make them thin, the
  French way
8 tablespoons crème fraîche OR 1/2 cup sour cream and
  4 tablespoons heavy cream
1 cup shelled hazelnuts (also called filberts), halved
2 tablespoons fresh chopped chervil, or parsley, or dill

Garnish: leaf lettuce

1. Try to get the freshest beans possible. Break one. It should snap. Steam beans in steamer basket over boiling water until tender. Time will vary with age and thickness of beans; keep tasting after 6 minutes or so. When done, plunge into a bowl of ice water to keep their color. When they are cold, drain and pat dry carefully with a towel and refrigerate. Can be done up to 2 hours ahead of serving.

2. Put crème fraîche or the sour cream and heavy cream in a chilled bowl. Whisk in mustard, lemon juice, salt and freshly ground pepper to taste.

3. Up to 1/2 hour before you want to serve salad, combine green beans, chopped fresh herbs and crème fraîche sauce. Taste for salt.

4. Toast hazelnuts in small skillet over high heat, stirring constantly to keep them from burning. Do not allow them to brown too much. You can toast them in a 350°F. oven for 10 minutes if you prefer, shaking the pan frequently. When done, turn out onto a pan to cool.

5. To serve salad: Arrange lettuce leaves on individual plates. Place a mound of beans on each leaf and sprinkle with hazelnuts. Serve at once.

MARCIA'S FROZEN LEMON MOUSSE SERVES 8 TO 10

Utterly delicious and totally make-ahead. If you can't find superfine sugar, it is easily made by placing regular granulated sugar into a blender and whirring until sugar is "superfine"—just be careful not to blend too long or you will make confectioners' sugar.

3 cups chilled heavy whipping cream
1 3/4 cup superfine sugar (sometimes called bar sugar)
3 tablespoons finely grated lemon zest
1/2 cup fresh lemon juice
6 to 10 drops yellow food color, optional

Garnish: mint leaves or fresh raspberries

1. Line a 9" x 4" glass rectangular loaf pan (not aluminum) with plastic wrap, leaving enough wrap hanging over sides to cover the filled pan.

2. Beat cream in large bowl of mixer with whisk attachment if you have one, until soft peaks form. Add the sugar and continue to beat until stiff. Add the lemon juice and zest. Stir in optional food coloring and pour into prepared pan. Freeze until firm, at least 2 hours or up to overnight, then unmold by quickly dipping in hot water or turning over onto a serving plate and covering with hot towels until mold releases. Peel off plastic wrap and cut into slices. Garnish with mint leaves or fresh raspberries if desired. This dessert can also be frozen in a bowl and scooped out with an ice cream scoop.

AN AUTUMN CELEBRATION

Tomato-Pumpkin Bisque
Brined Turkey Breast
Baked Duo of Rice with Butternut Squash and Leeks
Kelly's Pumpkin Bread Pudding with Brown Sugar
   Cream Sauce

TOMATO-PUMPKIN BISQUE
SERVES 8 TO 10

This wonderful soup is a favorite of everyone who tastes it. The pumpkin is not a discernible ingredient, but adds an intriguing depth of flavor.

1 tablespoon <u>each</u> vegetable oil and unsalted butter
1 large onion, chopped
1 28-ounce can diced tomatoes, undrained
2 to 3 tablespoons fresh chopped parsley
4 cups chicken stock or vegetable stock, homemade or
   canned
1 28-ounce can pumpkin (not pumpkin pie filling)
4 to 5 tablespoons pure maple syrup, to taste
1/2 cup heavy whipping cream or half and half
salt and freshly ground black pepper to taste

<u>Garnish: 2 tablespoons fresh snipped chives</u>

1. In large stockpot heat the oil and butter over medium-high heat and sauté the onion until softened, about 5 minutes.

2. Place tomatoes and parsley in food processor and pulse to make a coarse mixture with texture, not a purée. Reserve.

3. Add the chicken stock to the sautéed onions and heat through. Add the pumpkin, whisking in, and heat again. Add the reserved tomatoes and maple syrup and heat through. Whisk in the cream, season with salt and pepper and serve hot, garnished with chives.

BRINED TURKEY BREAST
SERVES 8 TO 10

A brined turkey will be moister and more flavorful than a regular roasted turkey, as the salt gets into the molecules of the meat and plumps them up. Just remember to discard the salty drippings and you may never make turkey the conventional way again.

6 to 7 pound turkey breast, with bones and ribs,
   defrosted if frozen, gravy packet discarded
3 tablespoons <u>each</u> kosher salt and sugar
1 large sprig fresh sage
4 tablespoons butter to put on turkey as it roasts
4 tablespoons <u>each</u> unsalted butter and Wondra flour,
   for gravy
<u>homemade chicken or turkey broth, or More Than
   Gourmet brand</u>

1. Place the salt and sugar in a large 2-gallon plastic bag and place in a large deep bowl. Add 4 cups of cold water to begin. Wash turkey breast and place in the bag. Add additional cold water to cover the breast, seal the bag and place in its bowl in the refrigerator for 10 to 24 hours.

2. When ready to roast the breast, remove from bag and discard the water. Rinse well. Place on a rack in a roasting pan and roast at 325°F. approximately 25 minutes per pound, or until meat thermometer inserted into the thickest part of the breast reaches a minimum internal temperature of 170°F. Juices should run clear when breast is pricked with a fork. During this time you can place 4 tablespoons unsalted butter on top of breast, but DO NOT BASTE WITH DRIPPINGS FROM THE PAN, as they are very, very salty. Remove from oven and tent loosely with foil. Let rest 15 minutes before slicing.

3. <u>To make gravy:</u> DO NOT USE THE DRIPPINGS FROM THE ROASTING PAN . Remember that they are very very salty. Instead, melt the 4 tablespoons butter in a medium saucepan, stir in the Wondra flour (very good for gravy, as it doesn't lump) and stir until bubbly. Can add pepper and dried sage to taste, but do not add salt. At this point you can add 4 cups good quality chicken or turkey broth, heated, whisking constantly until mixture comes to a boil. Taste for seasoning. I add garlic powder, more sage or poultry seasoning and pepper. You can

also carefully add a tablespoon or so of the roasting pan drippings carefully tasting to be sure you don't make the gravy too salty. You can also add some cream to smooth out the taste of the gravy. Keep hot to serve with sliced turkey breast.

BAKED DUO OF WILD AND WHITE RICE WITH BUTTERNUT SQUASH AND LEEKS
SERVES 8

3/4 cup <u>each</u> wild and white rice, rinsed well separately until water in sieve is clear, drained
1 teaspoon salt, <u>DIVIDED</u>
3 cups (1 1/2 pounds) peeled butternut squash, peeled and cut into 1/2 inch cubes
1 1/2 cups finely chopped leeks (white part only)
1 teaspoon fresh thyme or 1/4 teaspoon dried
3 tablespoons extra virgin olive oil
6 tablespoons (3/4 stick) unsalted butter, divided
<u>1 tablespoon chopped fresh Italian parsley</u>

1. <u>Cook both rices:</u> Put white rice in pot with 1 1/2 cups cold water and 1/2 teaspoon salt. Put wild rice in another pot with 3 cups water and the other 1/2 teaspoon salt. Bring both mixtures to a boil, then lower heat to a simmer and cover. The white rice will be cooked in about 25 minutes, and the wild rice will take about 45 minutes. Check wild rice to see if some of the kernels have popped open and rice is tender but slightly chewy. White rice will absorb all its water. Drain the wild rice when it is done and discard the water. Reserve both rices. Can make one day ahead and refrigerate.

2. <u>Prepare butternut squash:</u> Preheat oven to 350°F. Oil a rimmed baking sheet. Toss the squash cubes with 3 tablespoons of the oil in the baking sheet and arrange in a single layer. Sprinkle with salt and pepper. Roast just until tender but firm enough to hold their shape, stirring occasionally, about 15 minutes. Transfer squash to a bowl. Can make one day ahead and refrigerate.

3. In a large skillet melt 4 tablespoons of the butter. Add the leeks and 3/4 cup water. Simmer until leeks are heated through and water is absorbed, about 7 minutes. Add the two rices and roasted squash and simmer until heated through, about 4 minutes. Stir in the remaining 2 tablespoons of butter and the parsley and thyme. Season with salt and pepper to taste and transfer to a serving rimmed platter. Serve warm.

KELLY'S PUMPKIN BREAD PUDDING WITH BROWN SUGAR CREAM SAUCE
SERVES 8 TO 10

This is my daughter-in-law Kelly's marvelous recipe. It is always in demand in the fall, and when you make it you'll see why.

2 cups Half and Half
1 15-ounce can pumpkin (NOT pumpkin pie filling)
1 cup plus 2 tablespoons packed brown sugar
2 large eggs
1 1/2 teaspoons <u>each</u> pumpkin pie spice, ground cinnamon and pure vanilla extract
10 cups 1/2-inch cubed day-old white bread or egg bread
1/2 cup golden or dark raisins

Sauce:

1 1/4 cups packed brown sugar
1/2 cup (1 stick) unsalted butter
1/2 cup heavy whipping cream

<u>Optional:</u> 1 tablespoon whiskey or dark rum
<u>vanilla bean ice cream</u>

1. Preheat oven to 350°F. Spray a deep 9" x 13" baking dish with cooking spray.

2. In a large bowl whisk together the Half and Half, pumpkin, sugar, eggs, spices and vanilla extract to blend well.

3. Fold in the bread cubes and stir in the raisins. Transfer mixture to baking dish.

4. LET STAND FOR 15 MINUTES. This is critical to the success of the dish.

5. Bake approximately 40 minutes, or until a toothpick inserted in the center comes out clean.

6. <u>Make the Sauce</u>: In a heavy medium-size saucepan whisk brown sugar and butter until butter melts. Whisk in the heavy cream and stir until sugar dissolves and sauce is smooth, about 3 minutes. Remove from heat and add whiskey or rum if desired.

7. Let bread pudding cool about 30 minutes, then serve with the sauce. Serve with a scoop of good quality vanilla bean ice cream if desired. Reheats well.

A LUXURY WINTER DINNER PARTY

Shrimp and Avocado on Red Pepper Purée
Veal Medallions with Morels
Winter Vegetable Gratin
Poached Pears Topped with Chocolate Glaze on a
    bed of Crème Anglaise, garnished with Raspberry
    Coulis

SHRIMP AND AVOCADO ON RED PEPPER PURÉE
SERVES 8

Court Bouillon:

2 cups water
2 stalks celery
2 cloves garlic
2 bay leaves
5 to 6 whole cloves
juice of 1 lemon
1 1/2 cups dry white wine

24 raw shrimp, shelled (save shells to make a lovely
    shrimp bisque)

6 sweet red peppers
4 ounces walnut or hazelnut oil
2 tablespoons shallots, coarsely chopped
1 teaspoon dried French tarragon OR 1 tablespoon
    fresh
salt, pepper and Tabasco to taste

3 ripe California avocados

<u>Garnish: lemon slices and chopped parsley</u>

1. <u>Make court bouillon</u>: In a 4 to 5-quart Dutch oven put 2 cups water, 2 stalks celery, 2 cloves garlic, 2 bay leaves, the cloves, juice of one lemon and 1 1/2 cups dry white wine. Bring to a boil and simmer 15 to 20 minutes. Clean, peel and devein shrimp. Put shrimp in court bouillon and cook just until no longer opaque. Do not boil. Drain and cool. (You can reuse the court bouillon to make a shrimp bisque: Add shrimp shells, bring to a boil, then strain and add heavy cream and seasoning.)

2. <u>Make Red Pepper Sauce</u>: Roast red peppers by holding over gas flame or broil in oven or place on outdoor grill until skins blacken. Put in plastic or paper bag, seal and set aside 15 minutes. Slip off skins. Add walnut or hazelnut oil, shallots, and tarragon. Season with salt and Tabasco to taste, seasoning it highly. Process in food processor until very smooth. Chill slightly.

3. <u>To serve</u>: Spoon a layer of sauce on appetizer plate. Arrange 4 slices avocado and 3 shrimp on sauce. Garnish with a slice of lemon and parsley if desired.

VEAL MEDALLIONS WITH MORELS
SERVES 8

A heavenly dish that is sure to please even the most discriminating guest. Do not overcook the veal, as it takes very little sautéing and can go from meltingly tender to hard and chewy very quickly. Serve a soft red wine such as a Merlot or gentle Pinot Noir with this dish.

2 pounds veal medallions, cut from the veal loin, cut into 8 4-ounce portions
sea salt and freshly ground black pepper
1/2 cup all-purpose flour
2 tablespoons <u>each</u> unsalted butter and vegetable oil
1 to 2 ounces dried morels, or other dried wild mushrooms, reconstituted in 2 cups boiling water
3 tablespoons chopped shallots
2 tablespoons unsalted butter
2 tablespoons good-quality Cognac
1/4 cup or more <u>each</u> heavy cream and veal demiglace (More Than Gourmet pucks are excellent)

<u>Garnish: 2 tablespoons fresh parsley leaves, chopped</u>

1. Trim any fat from the 8 medallions and lay each between two sheets of plastic wrap. Pound gently with a plumber's rubber hammer (kept only for culinary use) or rolling pin until meat spreads out almost double, about 1/4 inch thick. Cut each medallion in half , making 16 2-ounce slices, and refrigerate meat.

2. When ready to cook, sprinkle each medallion lightly with salt and pepper and dust lightly with flour. In a large skillet, melt butter, add oil and sauté over medium high heat about 2 minutes, or until golden brown on each side.

Remove to a heat-proof casserole and reserve in a very low oven while making the sauce.

3. <u>To make the sauce</u>: Strain the reconstituted morels, using a coffee filter to catch any dirt, reserving the soaking liquid, then cut each morel in half and dry them with a paper towel. Melt 2 tablespoons of butter in another skillet and sauté them along with the shallots on high heat for 2 minutes. Pour in the cognac and *if you wish* carefully ignite with a fireplace match, averting your face so as not to singe your eyebrows. Wait until the flames subside. This step will burn off the excess alcohol in the sauce, but if you don't want to do this, just bring the sauce to a boil for a few minutes, which will help dissipate the alcohol. Add the demiglace, the reserved mushroom soaking liquid and the heavy cream, bringing this mixture to a boil. Taste and adjust seasoning with salt and pepper.

4. <u>To serve</u>: Place several medallions on each plate, pour some sauce and morels over the meat and sprinkle with chopped parsley. Serve extra sauce in a separate gravy boat.

WINTER VEGETABLE GRATIN—SERVES 8

An easy and delicious side that rounds out this menu beautifully.

4 Idaho (Russet) potatoes, peeled
4 <u>each</u> carrots, peeled, leeks, white part only, and small zucchini
2 tablespoons butter
2 cloves garlic, minced
1 teaspoon thyme
salt, freshly ground pepper, freshly grated nutmeg to taste
<u>one quart Half and Half</u>

1. Preheat oven to 350°F. Scald Half and Half to 155°F., add minced garlic and set aside. Cut peeled potatoes into very thin slices and reserve under a damp towel. Do not rinse potatoes, as you want the starch to thicken the sauce. In a saucepan bring the Half and Half to a simmer and add potatoes. Stir constantly, not letting it come to a boil. When the mixture begins to thicken, remove from the heat and season with salt, pepper and nutmeg.

2. Cut the 4 peeled carrots into 1/4-inch slices. Boil 2 to 3 minutes in salted, sugared water. Drain and add to cream-potato mixture.

3. Cut the 4 leeks lengthwise. Clean under running water to remove all grit. Cut into pieces 1/2 inch thick. Lightly sauté leeks in 1 to 2 tablespoons butter with thyme until softened. Add to cream mixture.

4. Wash the 4 zucchini and cut into 1/2-inch slices and then quarter slices. Add to cream mixture. Turn into 9" x 13" buttered gratin dish and bake until browned and crusted on top, 45 minutes to 1 hour. Can "hold" up to 30 minutes before serving.

POACHED PEARS WITH A CHOCOLATE GLAZE ON A BED OF CRÈME ANGLAISE GARNISHED WITH RASPBERRY COULIS (PRONOUNCED KOOLEE)

Although there are several steps in preparing this dessert, most of them can be made ahead. This is truly an impressive ending to this wonderful meal. You will be learning the techniques of poaching pears and making a Crème Anglaise. A coulis is a purée and is elegant and easy to make in the blender. My adorable granddaughter Courtney made this dessert for her parents' anniversary when she was 12, saying it reminded her of her grandmother's style of cooking. Gotta love that girl!

8 large pears, Bosc or Comice

Poaching syrup:

1 1/2 cups granulated sugar
1 cinnamon stick, broken in two
6 whole cloves
1/2 of a vanilla bean
zest of 1 lemon, cut into julienne strips
1 quart water

Crème Anglaise

4 tablespoons sugar
pinch salt
8 large egg yolks

2 cups milk
1 to 2 teaspoons pure vanilla, to taste

Raspberry Coulis (Purée):

1 12-ounce package frozen raspberries with no sugar or juice added
1 teaspoon lemon juice
superfine sugar to taste

Glaze:

8 ounces semisweet chocolate chips
<u>2 to 3 tablespoons Crisco solid shortening</u>

1. <u>To poach pears</u>: Prepare the poaching syrup, combining in a non-aluminum pot and simmer for 10 minutes. Peel pears, leaving on stem. Do not core. Poach pears in simmering, not boiling, liquid for from 15 minutes to 1 hour, depending on the degree of ripeness of pears. Test pears to see if they are tender by piercing with a paring knife, which should easily slide out of pear when properly done.

2. Remove from poaching syrup and let cool, covered with plastic wrap. This can be done the day before serving. The morning or afternoon you plan to serve pears, core them carefully, using a small paring knife and a melon baller or baby spoon to carefully scoop out core. Cover and refrigerate until just before serving.

3. <u>Prepare Crème Anglaise</u>: Have a fine strainer ready near the stove, suspended over a small glass bowl. In a small heavy saucepan on low heat stir together the sugar, salt and yolks until well blended, using a wooden spoon.

4. In another small saucepan (or small glass measuring cup if using a microwave oven on High power) heat the milk to the boiling point. Carefully stir a few tablespoons of the hot milk into the yolk mixture; then gradually add the remaining milk, stirring constantly, being careful not to curdle the yolks or you'll have scrambled eggs. Heat the mixture to just before the boiling point, 170°F. when measured with an instant-read thermometer. Steam will begin to appear and the mixture will be slightly thicker that heavy cream. It will leave a well-defined track when a finger is run across the back of the spoon. Remove immediately from heat and pour through the strainer, scraping up the thickened cream that settles on the

bottom of the pan with a rubber spatula. Cool crème anglaise in an ice-water bath, or refrigerator. Stir in the vanilla when cool. Can be made 2 to 3 days ahead. Sauce thickens slightly overnight in refrigerator.

5. <u>Make raspberry coulis:</u> Thaw raspberries completely. Purée with their juice in processor or blender. Strain through a fine strainer, to remove all the seeds. In a saucepan, boil the sugar, juice and berries until the purée is of desired consistency, meaning that it will drop slowly from a spoon. Cool and put into squeeze bottle and reserve, to decorate crème anglaise before presentation.

6. <u>Make Chocolate Glaze to drizzle on tops of pears:</u> Melt chips and Crisco together in double boiler over simmering water. Cool slightly.

7. <u>To Assemble and Serve:</u> Place 3 tablespoons crème anglaise on a dessert plate, make two small circles of raspberry purée around rim. Using small paring knife, make design by pulling knife through circles. Center pear on Crème Anglaise and drizzle with chocolate glaze.

ENTERTAINING FOR THE HOLIDAYS

Whole Tenderloin of Beef with Horseradish Sauce
Gourmet Make-Ahead Mashed Potatoes
Red and Golden Beet, Blood Orange, Endive and
    Walnut Salad with Orange-Scented Vinaigrette
Gâteau Royale

WHOLE TENDERLOIN OF BEEF WITH HORSERADISH SAUCE
SERVES 8 TO 10

You can serve this beef warm, room temperature, or cold. I like to prepare the beef about 2 hours before company arrives, and then serve at room temperature. To serve cold, make it the morning of the party and refrigerate it.

1 4 to 5-pound filet of beef tenderloin, trimmed of any
    fat
1 large onion, chopped
2 <u>each</u> carrots, chopped, and stalks of celery, chopped
1/2 pound bacon, blanched in a pot of boiling water for
    5 minutes
salt and freshly ground pepper
3 tablespoons olive oil
1 puck More Than Gourmet beef or veal concentrate,
    reconstituted in 2 cups boiling water, or 2 cups
    boxed beef stock
1 tablespoon Dijon mustard
1 clove garlic, crushed
breadcrumbs

Horseradish Sauce:

1/2 cup grated radishes (grate on fine grater, then drain)
3 tablespoons prepared horseradish
2 tablespoons sour cream
1 tablespoon Dijon mustard
1 teaspoon sugar
1/2 cup chilled heavy whipping cream, whipped to
    medium peaks
<u>salt and pepper to taste</u>

1. In a large heavy skillet melt olive oil on high heat. Add dried filet and brown rapidly on all sides, about 5

to 10 minutes. Season meat with salt and pepper. Place on a rack in a large roasting pan. Mix chopped onion, carrot and celery, which is called a mirepoix, and place on top of the meat. Lay slices of blanched bacon all over top of beef. Put into preheated 450°F. oven for 30 minutes, then reduce heat to 375°F. and roast to internal temperature of 130°F. for medium rare. Remove from oven, scrape off vegetables and bacon and reserve. Spread 1 tablespoon Dijon mustard and 1 crushed garlic clove on filet. Sprinkle with breadcrumbs and drizzle with 2 tablespoons melted butter. Then return to 450°F. oven for about 15 minutes or until it reaches 140°F. Remove from oven, cover loosely with a foil tent and let rest 10 minutes. Cut into 1/2- inch slices and place on platter.

2. Make Sauce for meat: When meat is roasted, in a saucepan add reserved vegetables and bacon to the reconstituted More Than Gourmet stock or boxed stock. Bring to a boil on top of the stove, then strain through a fine strainer, discarding vegetables and bacon. Serve sauce warm on the side along with the following horseradish sauce.

3. Make Horseradish Sauce: Mix first five ingredients in medium bowl. Fold in whipped cream. Season with salt and pepper. Can be prepared up to 3 hours ahead. Refrigerate until serving.

GOURMET MAKE-AHEAD MASHED POTATOES
SERVES 8

3 pounds Idaho potatoes (Russet), peeled and cubed

1/4 to 1/2 cup heavy cream, as needed
1 8-ounce package cream cheese, room temperature
2 tablespoons unsalted butter
approximately 1/2 teaspoon salt, 1/4 teaspoon white
    pepper, to taste
optional: a few shakes of Tabasco
4 tablespoons green onion, minced

1. Cook cubed potatoes in cold, salted water until a knife inserted in a potato comes out easily, about 20 minutes. Drain the potatoes as soon as they are done. Mash well with potato masher.

2. In a medium saucepan heat the cream, cream cheese and butter, or heat in microwave. Place mashed potatoes in bowl of electric mixer and add warmed mixture, whipping carefully, until fluffy but not gummy. Add salt, pepper and Tabasco to taste. Stir in green onions and mound in buttered casserole. Can prepare ahead, put in cooking-sprayed ovenproof casserole, refrigerate, and reheat in oven or microwave gently.

RED AND GOLDEN BEET, BLOOD ORANGE, ENDIVE AND WALNUT SALAD WITH ORANGE-SCENTED VINAIGRETTE
SERVES 8

From the innovative California chef Alice Waters, who was the first to champion the use of fresh organic produce. If you can't find golden beets, use all red ones.

1 1/2 pounds <u>each</u> medium-sized red and golden beets

1 cup shelled walnuts

Orange-Scented Vinaigrette:

4 tablespoons <u>each</u> red wine vinegar and fresh orange juice
zest of 1 orange
salt and freshly ground black pepper
1/2 cup extra virgin olive oil

4 blood oranges (or use navel oranges if blood oranges are not available)
<u>1/2 pound Belgian endive</u>

1. Preheat oven to 400°F.

2. <u>Cook beets</u>: Trim and wash beets, leaving 1 inch of stem and tails on. Put in a baking pan with a splash of water. Tightly cover with foil and bake 45 minutes to 1 hour, or until they can be easily pierced with a sharp knife. Uncover and allow to cool. Peel off skin and cut off tops and bottom tails. Keep red and yellow beets separate, or red will color the yellow ones. Slice into rounds and dress in two separate bowls, one for each color, with vinaigrette (below). While oven is on, toast walnuts on a baking sheet for about 5 minutes.

3. <u>Make vinaigrette</u>: In a medium bowl mix together the vinegar, orange juice and zest. Season with salt and pepper, then whisk in the olive oil. Use about 3/4 of this mixture to dress both red and yellow beets.

4. <u>Prepare oranges and endive</u>: With a sharp paring knife trim off top and bottom of each orange. Remove rest of peel, including all the white pith, which is bitter. Slice oranges into 1/4-inch rounds. Separate endive leaves, cutting off bottom stems.

5. <u>To assemble salad</u>: Arrange beets on individual plates with the orange slices and endive leaves. Drizzle over any vinaigrette remaining and garnish with the toasted walnuts.

GÂTEAU ROYALE
SERVES 10 TO 12

Sumptuous and impressive.

Cake:

5 ounces bittersweet chocolate, best quality (Valrhona is a quality brand) chopped in processor
4 tablespoons unsalted butter, cut into pieces
3 large eggs, <u>separated</u>
3/4 cup sugar, separated into 1/2 cup and 1/4 cup
3/4 cup (3 ounces) <u>sifted</u> cake flour (measure after sifting)
1/8 teaspoon cream of tartar
1/4 cup raspberry or apricot preserves (strained), room temperature
4 ounces almond paste

Glaze:

6 ounces bittersweet chocolate, best quality (Valrhona or Lindt), chopped
1/2 cup (1 stick) unsalted butter, cut into pieces
<u>1 tablespoon light corn syrup</u>

1. Preheat oven to 350°F. Line the bottom of a 9" x 2" round cake pan with a circle of parchment paper. Do not butter it.

2. <u>Make the cake</u>: In a microwavable large measuring cup melt chocolate, butter and 3 tablespoons water at 50% power for about 1 minute. Stir until smooth.

3. Beat the egg yolks and 1/2 cup sugar together until pale and thick in electric mixer. Transfer to large bowl. Stir in the warm chocolate mixture. Stir in the flour. Set aside.

4. Beat the egg whites with cream of tartar in a clean dry mixing bowl until soft peaks form. Gradually sprinkle in the remaining 1/4 cup sugar, beating at high speed until

stiff but not dry. Fold 1/4 of the whites into the chocolate batter to lighten it. Then fold in the remaining whites gently. Turn the batter into prepared pan. Bake about 25 minutes, or until a toothpick inserted into the center comes out just dry. Do not overbake.

5. Cool cake 10 minutes on rack, then run small knife around edge and invert onto a cardboard cake circle. Peel off parchment. Remove cake circle carefully and cool cake completely on rack. Top of cake may be crusty—don't worry, as this will be the bottom when you assemble the cake. Place cake back on cake circle, crusty side down. (May be made, wrapped well and kept at room temperature up to 2 days, or frozen up to 3 months. Let come to room temperature before glazing or serving.)

6. Roll almond paste between 2 sheets of plastic wrap until 1/8 inch thick and at least 8 inches in diameter. Cut into a neat 8-inch round, saving scraps for another use. (Can do 1 day ahead and refrigerate. Bring to room temperature before using.)

7. <u>To assemble cake</u>: With serrated knife split cake horizontally into 2 thin layers. Carefully set upper layer aside, using another cake circle lined with plastic wrap if needed to transfer. (If either layer breaks, just piece them together, no one will ever know!) Warm the preserves for easier spreading. Spread bottom layer evenly with half of the preserves. Place top layer on bottom layer. Spread with remaining preserves. Center the almond paste round on top of the cake.

8. <u>Make glaze and glaze the cake</u>: Place chocolate, butter and corn syrup in large microwaveable measuring cup and microwave at 50% power for 1 1/2 minutes, or till just melted. Stir gently with spoon until completely smooth; do not whisk or beat. When glaze is at about 90°F. using instant-read thermometer and the consistency of heavy cream pour <u>all of the glaze</u> in puddle in the center of the cake. Working quickly, use just 2 or 3 spatula strokes to spread glaze over the top of the cake so that it runs over all sides of cake, rotating cake gently. Use spatula to scoop up any excess glaze from work surface to touch up any bare spots on sides. The best looking glazes are poured, not spread. If needed, jiggle cake gently to settle any uneven glaze. Attempting to respread or resmooth glaze will cause streaks and marks. Once glazed, do not refrigerate cake. Can keep at room temperature 1 to 2 days.

COOK'S TIP

Cooking is a very sensual art. By that I mean that you need to use all of your senses in your preparation and presentation. Use your sense of *smell* by noting the freshness of the ingredients before cooking and being aware of the aromas as the recipe nears completion. *Taste* as you are cooking to make mid-course corrections in herb and spice quantities. *Feel* your food, especially helpful in testing when the meat or fish is done, by noting how it springs back and feels to the touch. Finally, make the dish *look* appealing, since we eat with our eyes first! Set a lovely table with colorful flowers and use those gorgeous dishes that Aunt Hattie left you— you'll get more pleasure out of using them than letting them gather dust in a cupboard!

5

FUN PARTY AND BUFFET MENUS

Cooking and entertaining should be all about fun, both for the cook and those lucky enough to have someone cooking for them. These menus are filled with easy and delectable offerings for all types of gatherings. Get into the kitchen and cook up a party! Menus include Superbowl Buffet, Academy Awards Party, Tailgate Food, Tapas for a Crowd—the Little Dishes of Spain, and A Festive New Year's Eve Buffet.

Texas Chili Con Carne (page 82)

SUPERBOWL BUFFET

Tortilla Roll-Ups
Kelly's Fantastic Potato Soup
Marcia's Gridiron Gumbo
Buckeye Cheesecake

TORTILLA ROLL-UPS—MAKES 48

Timeless and always popular, as well as being a make-ahead that's very easy to make!

2 8-ounce packages cream cheese, room temperature
1 1-ounce package Hidden Valley Ranch Milk Recipe
    Original Ranch Dressing Mix
2 green onions, minced
2/3 cup each diced sweet red pepper and sliced black
    ripe olives, coarsely chopped
1/2 cup diced celery
6 10-inch flour tortillas
parsley

1. In a large bowl, mix cream cheese with dressing mix, minced onions, sweet red pepper, olives and celery.

2. Spread each tortilla with 1/2 cup filling. Roll up tightly. Wrap each rolled tortilla in plastic wrap and chill for from 2 hours to overnight on a baking sheet or in a brownie pan to support the rolls.

3. When ready to serve, slice into 1-inch slices on the diagonal with a sharp or serrated knife. Save ends for "cook's treats" and arrange on large platter with chopped fresh parsley leaves around the edge of the platter.

KELLY'S FANTASTIC POTATO SOUP
SERVES 8

My daughter-in-law Kelly always scores a touchdown when she serves this soup!

6 tablespoons unsalted butter
1 large onion, peeled and coarsely chopped
8 green onions, coarsely chopped
2 cloves garlic, peeled and minced
8 Idaho potatoes, about 4 pounds total, peeled and
    coarsely chopped
6 cups chicken broth (homemade or boxed, low-salt,
    organic)
1 1/4 cups heavy whipping cream
2 cups whole milk
1 1/2 teaspoons salt or to taste
black pepper and freshly grated nutmeg to taste

Garnish: unseasoned store-bought croutons and fresh
    chives, snipped

1. Melt the butter in a large stockpot and add the onions, green onions and garlic and sauté 2 to 3 minutes. Add the potatoes and chicken broth. Bring to a boil, lower the heat to simmer and cook uncovered for about 20 minutes or until the potatoes are tender.

2. Purée the soup in a blender or food processor in batches. Do not overfill the blender or food processor or it will overflow and make a mess.

3. Return soup to the stockpot and add the cream, milk, salt, pepper and nutmeg. Taste and correct seasonings. You can prepare the soup up to this point and refrigerate it overnight.

4. When ready to serve, reheat and garnish each filled bowl with croutons and chives.

MARCIA'S GRIDIRON GUMBO
SERVES 8

Once when Marcia made this dish for her husband's family who were to be visiting that evening, she had to run to the store to pick up some additions for the dinner. Curt arrived home hungry and mentioned to Marcia that he had "tasted" some of the gumbo. She never thought of checking how much he had eaten, until the company arrived and she found to her horror that he had eaten almost all of it! They ordered pizza for their meal. Honestly, folks, it's THAT good!

1 whole chicken breast, about 2 pounds, not skinned or boned, split in half lengthwise

1 pound Italian sausages, sweet or hot, or a mixture of both

1 28-ounce can tomatoes, not drained

2 large cloves garlic, minced

1/4 teaspoon dried thyme

1 12-ounce jar or less Picante sauce, medium or hot, to your taste

2 cups chicken broth (can use the liquid from poaching the chicken breasts, below)

1/2 pound baked ham, sliced 1/2 inch thick, cut into cubes

2 tablespoons sugar, or more to taste

Tabasco sauce to taste

2 tablespoons unsalted butter

3 tablespoons flour

1 small onion, chopped

2 ribs celery, chopped

1 large green pepper, seeds and ribs removed, chopped

1 cup warm chicken stock

1 pound raw shrimp, deveined and shelled

1 1/2 cups raw rice cooked in 3 cups water (Uncle Ben's Converted Rice, rinsed in a fine sieve under cold water till water runs clear before cooking)

1. In a large pot bring 3 cups water to a simmer, add the chicken and poach (cook gently, simmering below the boiling point), covered, for 25 minutes or until the juices run clear when breast is pierced with a fork. Remove from broth with a slotted spoon and cool slightly. Discard the skin and bones and cube the chicken meat. Strain broth created by cooking the chicken to use in the recipe. You should have 2 to 3 cups left.

2. Cook the Italian sausage in a frying pan with 1 cup water, starting on high heat and reducing to medium when water comes to a boil. Cover. When water evaporates and sausages are browned, cut into one to be sure it is no longer pink in the center. Remove from pan, slice into 1/2-inch rounds and set aside.

3. Purée tomatoes with their juice in blender or processor. Put into a large stockpot with the garlic, thyme, picante sauce, the 2 to 3 cups chicken broth and sugar. Add the chicken, sausages and ham and bring to a boil. Lower heat to simmer, cover and cook 1 hour.

4. Meanwhile, make the roux: In a large skillet (I like cast iron) sauté the onions, celery and green peppers (these three vegetables are called "The Holy Trinity" in Cajun cooking) in the 2 tablespoons butter over medium-high until tender. Whisk in the 3 tablespoons flour, stirring constantly, then add the 1 cup of warm stock and bring to a boil, stirring. This roux will thicken the gumbo towards the end of cooking. Carefully (it will be very hot) transfer roux to a bowl and reserve.

5. When almost ready to serve, whisk the roux into the pot to thicken sauce, bringing it to a boil. Cook 10 minutes, stirring occasionally. (You can stop here and refrigerate overnight, then return to heat before serving.) Just before serving, add the raw shrimp and cook 5 minutes more. Taste and adjust seasoning. Serve in bowls over scoops of the cooked rice.

BUCKEYE CHEESECAKE
MAKES ONE CAKE

No way could I leave out this one—GO BUCKS! The classic combination of chocolate and peanut butter is irresistible.

1 9-ounce package Famous Chocolate Wafer cookies

5 tablespoons unsalted butter, melted

2 1/4 pounds (36 ounces or 4 1/2 8-ounce packages) cream cheese, softened to room temperature

1 1/2 cups sugar

6 large eggs

2 teaspoons vanilla extract

10 ounces semisweet chocolate, melted

1 cup smooth peanut butter (not natural or no-salt types)

2 Reese's peanut butter cups, chopped, for garnish

Garnish: 1 cup heavy cream, whipped with 1 teaspoon confectioners' sugar

1. Preheat the oven to 350°F.

2. In a food processor or blender grind the cookies into fine crumbs. Add the melted butter and process until well mixed. Press crumb mixture into the bottom and 1/2 up the sides of a 10-inch springform pan. Wrap outside of pan with heavy duty foil and place on a cookie sheet, to prevent leaks onto your oven floor.

3. In a large bowl, beat cream cheese and sugar with electric mixer on medium speed until light, fluffy and smooth, 2 to 3 minutes. Beat in eggs one at a time, beating well after each addition. Beat in vanilla. Beat about 2 minutes, until smooth.

4. Transfer 1/3 of batter to another bowl and set aside. Beat the melted chocolate into the remaining batter. Turn chocolate mixture into prepared crust in the springform pan.

5. With mixer at medium speed, beat peanut into remaining 1/3 of batter until thoroughly mixed. Carefully spoon peanut butter mixture on top of chocolate cheese mixture in pan. With the long handle of a wooden spoon, swirl the two flavors together.

6. Bake in preheated oven for about 1 hour, or until cheesecake is set around edges and puffed but still jiggles in the center. Let cake cool 2 hours, then refrigerate, covered with a cardboard round, until well chilled, 6 hours or overnight. (The cardboard cover will not collect moisture beads, which could fall on the top of the cake and make it soggy.)

7. Run a knife around edge of pan to loosen cake and remove the springform side of pan. Put onto platter.

8. Garnish the cheesecake: Pipe whipped cream rosettes around top of cake, or spoon on mounds with a small spoon. Sprinkle whipped cream with chopped peanut butter cups. Serves 12.

AN ACADEMY AWARDS PARTY

Twelve Oaks Apricot-Rum BBQ Ribs
Tim's Curry in a Hurry
Aladdin's Herbed Sesame Bread Sticks
Attack of the Killer Tomatoes Salad
Better Than Brad Pitt Chocolate Cake

TWELVE OAKS APRICOT RUM BBQ RIBS
SERVES 8

Scarlett O'Hara would have eaten her fill of these…Be sure to check that the ribs are completely cooked in the oven, by cutting between two ribs which should no longer be pink, before brushing on the glaze.

4 to 5 pounds baby back ribs
generous sprinkles of garlic powder, onion powder and black pepper

Glaze:

1 15-ounce jar apricot preserves, large pieces of apricot cut into small pieces
4 tablespoons unsalted butter
3 tablespoons dark rum (preferably Myer's)
3/4 teaspoon dry mustard
1/8 to 1/4 teaspoon cayenne pepper, to taste
1/2 teaspoon ground ginger

1. Season ribs with garlic powder, onion powder and black pepper. In a large metal baking pan fitted with a rack, arrange ribs in one layer if possible, or use two pans. Add 2 cups water and cover pan with aluminum foil. Bake in preheated 375°F. oven for about 60 minutes, or until ribs are no longer pink when cut between two ribs, turning ribs once during cooking.

2. Meanwhile, make the glaze: In a small saucepan combine all glaze ingredients and cook and stir over medium-high heat until butter is melted and glaze has boiled.

3. When ribs are done, place them in a single layer either on a gas grill on Medium heat setting, on a charcoal grill 4 to 6 inches from coals, or in a broiler pan placed on the

lowest rack possible under a preheated broiler. Whichever method you choose, brush the ribs generously with the glaze. Cook about 20 minutes, basting and turning frequently so they don't burn. Cut into individual ribs or sections of 2 to 3 ribs and serve with any remaining glaze, which has been reheated to boiling.

TIM'S CURRY IN A HURRY
SERVES 8

When my daughter Ayla was about 11 years old, she entered a rice contest with this recipe and won honorable mention! It truly is a prizewinner. Check to be sure your curry powder is fresh, that is, it doesn't have a musty odor—remember that you only get out of a recipe the quality of ingredients you are willing to put into it.

3 1/2 to 4 pounds chicken breasts, with bones and skin
1/3 cup butter
3 tablespoons <u>each </u>chopped onion, chopped celery and
    chopped Granny Smith apples
12 whole peppercorns
1 bay leaf
1/3 cup flour
1 1/2 teaspoons <u>fresh</u> curry powder (check that it's not
    musty smelling)
1/4 teaspoon sugar
1/8 teaspoon nutmeg
2 1/2 cups milk, warmed
2 teaspoons fresh lemon juice
1/2 teaspoon Worcestershire sauce
1/2 teaspoon salt, or to taste
1/2 cup heavy cream
2 tablespoons Sherry

<u>Condiments</u>: choose as many as you like…chopped
    egg whites, chopped egg yolks, crisply fried and
    crumbled bacon, toasted coconut, diced apple, Major
    Grey's chutney, sliced bananas, chopped peanuts,
    raisins, diced red onions

<u>2 cups uncooked converted rice (Uncle Ben's), rinsed,</u>
    <u>cooked in 4 cups water, as per package</u>

1. <u>In a 5-quart Dutch oven or stockpot</u>, poach chicken breasts in salted water to cover for about 30 minutes, or until no longer pink inside. Remove from broth and cool,

reserving broth. When cool remove skin, debone and dice meat. (Can be done a day ahead.)

2. <u>Make the sauce</u>: In a heavy 2-quart pan, heat butter. Add onion, celery, apple, peppercorns and bay leaf. Cook on medium heat, stirring until lightly browned. Blend in the flour, curry powder, sugar and nutmeg and heat until mixture bubbles, stirring constantly. Using a whisk, gradually stir in warmed milk and bring to a boil, stirring constantly. Cook until thickened, about 1/2 minute. Remove from heat and whisk in lemon juice, Worcestershire, salt and heavy cream. Remove bay leaf.

3. Place sauce in blender or food processor and blend until smooth. Return sauce to pan and reheat, whisking in some of the reserved chicken stock, any fat layer removed, as needed to thin to desired consistency, thick enough to coat a wooden spoon. When heated, add Sherry and diced chicken, cooking another 3 to 4 minutes or until heated through. Place in large bowl and serve surrounded by cooked rice and bowls of your choice of condiments. Let guests serve themselves, mounding some rice in the center of their dishes, spooning on the chicken and then adding their favorite condiments.

ALADDIN'S HERBED SESAME BREAD STICKS
MAKES ABOUT 3 DOZEN
6-INCH STICKS

1 teaspoon active dry yeast
1/4 cup warm water
2/3 cup whole wheat flour
2 or more cups white flour
3/4 teaspoon salt
2/3 cup skim milk
2 tablespoons olive oil
2 teaspoons dried oregano, basil, or thyme
1 large egg white
2 teaspoons water
<u>7 tablespoons sesame seeds</u>

1. Place yeast and warm water in bowl of food processor and let proof until bubbly, about 5 minutes.

2. Add both flours and salt. (If you don't want to use whole wheat flour, you can use all white.) Add milk, olive

oil and herbs and process until the dough is smooth and elastic, adding more flour if necessary. Remove from processor and knead a bit if needed. Place dough in ungreased bowl, cover with a towel and let rise 1 hour.

3. Preheat oven to 400°F.

4. On a lightly floured surface, roll the dough into a 1/4-inch thick rectangle, making one side of the rectangle 6 inches for the length of the breadsticks. Cut dough into 1/2-inch strips, or if you prefer thicker breadsticks, cut into 1-inch strips, in which case you will get about 18 breadsticks. Roll each strip in your palms to make a round breadstick shape and place on ungreased baking sheet. Place sticks in a line, about 1/2 inch apart.

5. Beat the egg white and water together and brush on breadsticks. Place sesame seeds on a plate and roll each breadstick in the seeds and replace them on the baking sheet. Bake for 10 to 20 minutes, or until golden brown. Cool on a rack. Can make up to 4 hours ahead.

ATTACK OF THE KILLER TOMATOES SALAD
SERVES 8

Dressing:

4 tablespoons red wine vinegar
1 clove garlic, crushed
1/2 teaspoon salt
3/4 teaspoon freshly ground pepper
1 teaspoon Italian herbs
2/3 cup extra virgin olive oil

8 ripe plum tomatoes, sliced medium-thin
6 scallions, washed, root ends discarded, sliced thin
1 small jar ripe black pitted olives, thinly sliced

1. Make the dressing: In a medium bowl place the red wine vinegar. Add garlic, salt, pepper and Italian herbs. Slowly whisk in the olive oil.

2. Place tomatoes, scallions and olives in a large rectangular ceramic serving dish. Pour dressing over them and marinate for 30 minutes to marry flavors.

BETTER THAN BRAD PITT CHOCOLATE CAKE
SERVES 10

When I first started making this cake, it was called Better Than Robert Redford Cake. The leading man may have changed, but the cake is still a star!

3/4 cup plus 2 tablespoons cake flour
1 teaspoon baking powder
1/2 teaspoon each baking soda and salt
2 ounces (2 squares) unsweetened baking chocolate, broken in pieces
1 1/4 cups sugar
1 tablespoon cocoa
1/3 cup boiling water
2 large eggs
1 1/2 sticks unsalted butter, room temperature, cut into 6 pieces
1/2 cup sour cream
1 tablespoon dark rum (I use Myer's, which has the best flavor for cooking)

Chocolate Rum Glaze

3 ounces sweet chocolate, chopped fine in processor
2 tablespoons water
2 tablespoons unsalted butter
4 tablespoons sifted confectioners' sugar
pinch of salt
1 teaspoon dark rum

1. Cut a round of parchment paper to fit the bottom of an 8-inch or 9-inch springform pan. Do not substitute an 8-inch or 9-inch regular cake pan, as batter will spill over the top. Place round in the bottom of the pan and butter the paper and up the sides of the pan.

2. Make the cake: In the food processor fitted with the metal blade place flour, baking powder, baking soda and salt. Process 5 seconds to blend. Transfer to small bowl and reserve. Wipe out processor before proceeding.

3. Put the chocolate, 1/4 cup of the sugar and the cocoa in the processor and process for 1 minute, or until chocolate is finely chopped. With the machine running pour the hot water through the feed tube. Process until the chocolate is melted. Add the eggs and process 1 minute. Add the remaining sugar and process 1 minute, stopping

once to scrape down the bowl with rubber spatula. Add the butter in pieces and process 1 more minute. Add the sour cream and rum and process 5 seconds. Add the reserved dry ingredients and turn the machine on and off 3 to 4 times, just until the flour disappears. Do not overprocess.

4. Preheat oven to 325°F. and set a rack in the middle of the oven. Transfer the batter to the prepared pan and spread it evenly with the spatula. Bake 50 to 55 minutes, or until the cake begins to withdraw slightly from the sides of the pan. Let cake cool in the pan on a cake rack.

5. <u>Meanwhile Prepare the Glaze</u>: Put all ingredients except rum in top of a double boiler and cook slowly till chocolate is melted. Add the rum and refrigerate until glaze <u>just begins</u> to thicken.

6. When the cake is cool, remove from the pan and spread the glaze over the top and sides with an offset spatula.

GAME-ON—TAILGATE FOODS

Diane's Layered Dip
Texas Chili Con Carne—A Bowl of Red
Easy Refried Black Beans
Biscochitos

DIANE'S LAYERED DIP—SERVES 8

My daughter Diane's dip is so delicious it will disappear quickly, so you might decide to double it for a crowd!

1 10 1/2-ounce can Frito Lay bean dip
1/3 cup sour cream
1/4 cup Miracle Whip dressing
1/2 package Taco Seasoning Mix
1 bunch green onions, thinly sliced
1 to 2 fresh tomatoes, diced
7 ounces extra sharp cheddar cheese
<u>tortilla chips</u>

1. Spread the bean dip in an even layer on the bottom of a pie plate.

2. Mix the sour cream, Miracle Whip and Taco Seasoning together and spread this over the bean dip.

3. Sprinkle with the sliced green onions, then sprinkle on the diced tomatoes. Top with the shredded cheddar cheese. Cover and refrigerate until served. This dish is best served the day you prepare it, especially if the tomatoes are very juicy. We have never had any leftovers, so there's no problem there!

TEXAS CHILI CON CARNE—A BOWL OF RED
SERVES 8 🕐 👨‍🍳 👨‍🍳 👨‍🍳

This is the "real deal" of chilis—hearty, spicy, and NO BEANS. The heat of various chilis is measured by the Scoville Scale. Wilbur Scoville was an American pharmacist who in 1912 devised a measurement to analyze the strength of the capsaicin (heat element) found in each variety of pepper. There is a larger amount of heat in the seeds and membranes of peppers, so if you want your food less spicy remove them before cooking. Heat numbers range from 0 for bell peppers to over 2,000,000 for the Trinidad Moruga Scorpion pepper, which is very dangerous to eat unless you have been raised on them, as in some remote areas of India. Ancho, Pasilla, Guajillo and New Mexican and California chilis are in the 3,500-8,000 range, relatively mild. The Japones, Chili de Arbol and bird chilis or Thai chilis are much hotter, at 50,000 to 100,000 range. Individual peppers from the same bush can vary in heat also, so a good suggestion when cooking with chilis is to taste your sauce after putting in half of the suggested amount of chilis, and adding more to adjust the heat you want in the dish. I have found that the amount of heat people enjoy varies greatly. Find the dried chilis at a Mexican grocery store or online—they will last for years if you keep them refrigerated in an airtight container, and they are very inexpensive.

2 dried Ancho, Pasilla or Guajillo chili pods
3 dried New Mexico or California chili pods
4 to 6 dried Japones, Chili de Arbol or Thai Bird Chilis
5 cups boiling water
1/4 cup (4 tablespoons) solid (more traditional) or
   liquid Crisco shortening
3 pound boneless chuck roast
2 to 3 cups beef broth
3 fresh garlic cloves, chopped
1 teaspoon <u>each</u> Mexican oregano and cumin
1 to 2 teaspoons salt, or to taste
2 to 3 tablespoons Masa Harina or cornmeal, for
   thickening as needed

warmed flour tortillas
1 cup shredded cheddar cheese
<u>sour cream</u>

1. Use plastic gloves when handling the chilis, as their oil can stay on your hands and burn them as well as your eyes if you touch them. Tear the dried Japones or Bird chilis in half and shake them to extract the seeds, and discard them, as they have the most heat. Place the three dried chili types in a large bowl and cover with boiling water. Let them soak for one hour.

2. While chilis soak, place the Crisco in a large heavy-bottomed pot or Dutch oven. Brown the meat in batches on high heat, turning once. When browned, add 2 cups of the beef broth, the garlic, oregano, cumin and salt and bring to a boil. Lower heat, cover and cook for 1 1/2 to 2 hours, or until meat is tender.

3. <u>Make chili water</u>: When chilis have soaked an hour, strain them, reserving them and the chili water separately. Add half of the chili water to the cooked meat in the Dutch oven.

4. <u>Make chili paste</u>: Using plastic gloves, hold each chili pod under running water to extract seeds. Discard stems and seeds. Don't put them in your disposal, as their volatile oil will send up fumes that can cause you to cough. Place chili pods in a blender with 1/2 cup of the chili water and purée. Strain this purée to get rid of any skins. Reserve purée.

5. When meat is tender, remove to cutting board and shred with 2 forks, discarding any large chunks of fat. Return to pot and add the chili purée. Cook another 15 minutes or so, adding more chili water or broth if mixture is too dry. If mixture is too liquid, add a tablespoon or so of Masa Harina or cornmeal. Taste for seasoning and add more salt if needed, then serve with the warmed tortillas, shredded cheddar cheese, refried beans, (recipe follows) or rice. Serve a dish of sour cream to cut the heat for guests who need relief. The perfect beverage with this dish is Mexican beer, such as Dos Equis or Corona, with wedges of lime.

FAST REFRIED BLACK BEANS—SERVES 8

A super easy accompaniment to the chili.

2 1-pound cans black beans
2 tablespoons vegetable oil
3 cloves garlic, minced
1 medium onion, finely chopped
1/2 teaspoon <u>each</u> Mexican oregano, cumin and salt
<u>1 cup grated cheddar cheese</u>

1. Drain liquid from beans and reserve liquid.

2. Heat the oil in a large skillet and sauté the onions and garlic until the onion is translucent. Stir in the beans and seasonings. Mash the beans using a potato masher. Heat over medium heat, adding some of the bean liquid and stirring until desired consistency. Serve with the grated cheese on the side.

BISCOCHITOS
MAKES 4 DOZEN COOKIES

The New Mexico state legislature passed a bill in 1989 making these the official state cookie. You can substitute vanilla for the anise seed and butter for the lard, as I suggest, but to make it a truly classic recipe, try it with these ingredients. Either way, these cookies are outstanding.

1 cup unsalted butter (2 sticks) (the traditional recipe
     calls for lard), room temperature
1/2 cup sugar
1 large egg
3 cups all purpose flour
1 to 2 teaspoons anise seed, pounded or ground
     (traditional, but not to everyone's taste, so if you
     don't care for the taste substitute pure vanilla)
1 1/2 teaspoons baking powder
1/2 teaspoon salt
1/4 cup orange juice

Topping:

2 teaspoons ground cinnamon (Mexicans call it canela)
<u>1/4 cup sugar</u>

1. In the bowl of the electric mixer beat the butter until creamy. Add the 1/2 cup sugar and beat until fluffy. Beat in the egg. Combine the flour, ground anise seed, baking powder and salt, and gradually add to the butter mixture, alternating with the orange juice (mixed with the vanilla if that is your choice).

2. Divide the dough in half and flatten each portion into a disk. Wrap each in plastic wrap and refrigerate at least one hour or up to overnight.

3. When ready to bake cookies, preheat the oven to 350°F. Roll out one disk to 1/4 inch thickness on a lightly floured board. Cut out cookies, using Southwestern cookie cutters for fun, or any other cutters you choose. Place cookies slightly apart on ungreased baking sheets. Sprinkle lightly with the cinnamon-sugar mixture and bake 10 to 12 minutes, or until edges are lightly browned. Let cool on racks. Can reroll scraps once to make more cookies. Roll out second disk until you have all cookies cut out and baked. Store in airtight containers. These cookies freeze well.

TAPAS FOR A CROWD—THE LITTLE DISHES OF SPAIN

Tapas are called the "Little Dishes of Spain", and they originated to cover the glasses of wine served at taverns to keep the flies out of the drink! Since then they have evolved into delicious little bites of heaven.

Shrimp in Garlic Sauce
Fried Salted Almonds
Spanish Potato Omelet
White Bean Salad
Spicy Sweet Red Pimientos with Garlic Croutons
Sangria

SHRIMP IN GARLIC SAUCE—SERVES 8

1 pound raw shrimp, preferably small, shelled and
      deveined
Coarse salt
1 cup olive oil
6 large cloves garlic, peeled and chopped coarsely
2 dried red chili peppers, stem and seeds removed,
      broken into 4 pieces
1 teaspoon good quality sweet paprika
2 tablespoons minced parsley
French bread (to mop up juices)

1. Dry the shrimp well and sprinkle both sides with salt. Let sit at room temperature 10 minutes.

2. Heat the oil in 2 large skillets. Add the garlic and chili peppers and when the garlic starts to turn golden (not brown, as it will be bitter) quickly add the shrimp. Cook over medium-high heat, stirring for 2 minutes or until the shrimp are just done. Sprinkle in the paprika. Transfer to a serving dish and provide lots of good bread for soaking up the juices.

FRIED SALTED ALMONDS—SERVES 8

8 ounces whole raw almonds
coarse salt
Crisco oil for deep frying

1. Blanch almonds: Pour boiling water over almonds that have been placed in a bowl. Let sit 5 minutes, drain them, and you can easily slip off their skins. Allow them to dry on paper towels for several hours at room temperature before frying them. Can be done several days ahead.

2. In a deep fryer or deep heavy pot heat oil at least 2 inches deep to a temperature of 400°F. Carefully immerse almonds in a frying basket and fry until lightly golden, about 2 minutes, stirring with long spoon.

3. Drain well and sprinkle with coarse salt. Serve freshly fried.

SPANISH POTATO OMELET—SERVES 8

1 cup olive oil
4 large potatoes (about 1 1/2 pounds) peeled and cut
      into 1/8-inch slices
1 large onion, thinly sliced
coarse salt and pepper to taste
4 large eggs

1. Heat the oil in a 12-inch nonstick skillet and add the potato slices slowly so they do not stick together. Alternate layers of potato slices with layers of onion slices and salt the layers lightly. Cook slowly over medium heat (the potatoes will really "boil" in the oil rather than fry), lifting and turning the potatoes occasionally, until they are tender but not brown. The potatoes should remain separated, not in a "cake." Drain the potatoes in a colander, reserving the oil, which will have a wonderful flavor for many other uses. You will need only 3 tablespoons of oil for this recipe, but save the rest!

2. Wipe out the skillet. It must be completely clean to prevent any sticking of the omelet.

3. In a large bowl beat the eggs with a fork until they are slightly foamy. Add 1/4 teaspoon salt and 1/4 teaspoon

pepper. Add the potatoes to the eggs, pressing the potatoes down with a pancake turner so that they are completely covered by the egg. Let mixture sit for 10 minutes.

4. Have a plate the size of the top of the skillet ready. Heat two tablespoons of the reserved oil in the skillet until it reaches the smoking point (it must be very hot or the omelet will stick) and add the potato-egg mixture, spreading it out rapidly with a pancake turner. Lower the heat to medium-high and shake the pan often to prevent sticking. When the eggs begin to brown on the bottom, place the plate over the skillet and flip the omelet onto the plate carefully, using hot pads. Do this job over the sink or a counter lined with newspaper, to catch any oil drippings.

5. Add about 1 tablespoon more oil to the pan, then slide the omelet back into the skillet carefully, to brown the other side. Lower the heat to medium and flip the omelet one more time, using the plate method described above. Cook briefly, as the omelet should be juicy inside. Transfer to a large plate and cool slightly, then cut into thin wedges or into 1 1/2 inch squares that can be picked up with toothpicks. Serve at room temperature.

WHITE BEAN SALAD—SERVES 8

2 1-pound cans cooked white beans, or chickpeas, drained
1 medium tomato, cubed
1 large hard-boiled egg, sliced, each slice cut in half
8 pitted cured black olives, each cut into 4 pieces
2 tablespoons minced fresh parsley

4 tablespoons extra virgin olive oil
2 tablespoons white wine vinegar
1/4 teaspoon salt
<u>2 cloves garlic, mashed to a paste or put through a garlic press</u>

1. In a glass bowl gently combine the beans, tomato, egg, olives and parsley.

2. In a separate bowl whisk the oil, vinegar, salt and garlic. Fold into the bean mixture and marinate in the refrigerator for several hours.

SPICY PIMIENTOS WITH GARLIC CROUTONS
SERVES 8

4 medium fresh sweet red peppers
3 tablespoons chicken broth or water
2 tablespoons olive oil
4 cloves garlic, peeled and crushed
1/4 teaspoon cayenne pepper
salt to taste

For garlic croutons:

6 tablespoons olive oil
4 cloves garlic, mashed or put through a garlic press
<u>1 loaf coarse Italian bread, cut 1 inch thick</u>

1. <u>Prepare the peppers</u>: Place whole peppers in an ungreased roasting pan in a preheated 375°F. oven for 17 minutes. Turn the peppers over and continue roasting for another 17 minutes. Remove from the oven, cover the pan tightly with foil and let cool.

2. Remove peppers from pan and deglaze pan with chicken broth, stirring and bringing liquid to a boil. Reserve this liquid.

3. Peel the peppers, remove core and seeds and cut each pepper into strips. In a skillet heat the 2 tablespoons oil until warm but not sizzling hot. Add sliced peppers, garlic, cayenne and salt, and sauté slowly over medium heat for 3 minutes. Add the reserved pan juices, cover, and cook slowly 5 minutes more. (May be prepared ahead and refrigerated.) Serve at room temperature with garlic croutons (below).

4. <u>To Prepare Croutons</u>: Combine the oil and garlic. Toast the bread slices lightly at 350°F. on a cookie sheet, then rub with garlic mixture. Toast other side of bread, brushing with oil-garlic mixture again. If made ahead, toast again briefly to crisp and serve warm.

5. To serve, put several pepper strips on each crouton. Or serve bowl of peppers separately and let guests assemble them themselves.

SANGRIA—A SPANISH WINE PUNCH
SERVES 8

Add the sparkling water to this traditional drink right before serving and serve icy cold. Or you might choose to serve beer with the Tapas.

1 bottle red wine, dry and full-bodied, chilled
juice of 1 lemon
1 <u>each</u> thinly sliced lemon, thinly sliced orange, thinly
   sliced lime
sparkling water to taste, chilled
sugar to taste

<u>Optional: 4 to 8 tablespoons Cognac</u>

1. Combine wine, lemon juice and sliced fruit. Prepare several hours ahead, so the wine can become more infused with the fruit flavors. Add sugar to taste and refrigerate. Add sparkling water (and Cognac if desired) right before serving.

2. Put into large glass pitcher with plenty of ice cubes and serve.

A FESTIVE NEW YEAR'S EVE BUFFET

Caviar Cheesecake
Swedish Meatballs
Boursin Potato Gratin
Grasshopper Sundaes

CAVIAR CHEESECAKE
SERVES 12 TO 16

Although this sounds very expensive, it uses jarred caviar from the canned tuna fish aisle at your supermarket, NOT the Russian kind that is so rare and pricey. The trick is to put the caviar gently into a fine strainer and run a slow stream of cold water over it, to rinse off the salty brine. Handle it carefully so you don't crush the little "eggs," and it will be a spectacular offering.

2 tablespoons unsalted butter, room temperature
5 tablespoons freshly grated Parmesan cheese,
   <u>DIVIDED</u>
2 tablespoons fine dry breadcrumbs

3 tablespoons unsalted butter
1 cup finely chopped onion

28 ounces cream cheese, room temperature
4 large eggs
1/2 cup <u>each</u> whipping cream and freshly grated
   Gruyère cheese (about 2 ounces)
1/2 teaspoon <u>each</u> salt and freshly ground black pepper
1/2 cup sour cream
2 ounces black caviar, rinsed and drained (I like the
   Romanoff brand)
2 ounces red caviar, rinsed and drained

<u>Garnish: thin slices of lemon, cut in half</u>

1. Preheat oven to 300°F. Butter a 9-inch springform pan with 2 1/2-inch sides with the 2 tablespoons butter. In a small bowl mix 2 tablespoons Parmesan with the breadcrumbs. Sprinkle into pan, turning to coat bottom and sides. Wrap heavy duty foil around *bottom* and 2 inches up *outside* of pan, and put on a cookie sheet, to prevent leakage onto your oven floor. Set aside.

2. Melt the 3 tablespoons butter in a heavy medium skillet over medium heat. Add onion and sauté until tender, about 5 minutes. Cool slightly.

3. In an electric mixer, beat cream cheese, eggs and heavy cream until well blended. Fold in sautéed onions, Gruyère and remaining 3 tablespoons Parmesan cheese. Season with salt and pepper. Pour this batter into prepared pan.

4. Place cheesecake in large baking pan. Add enough boiling water to larger pan to come 2 inches up the sides of cheesecake pan. This is called a Bain Marie, or water bath, and diffuses the heat, to bake the cheesecake uniformly. Bake until firm to touch, about 1 hour and 40 minutes. Remove cheesecake from water bath and discard water carefully. Turn off oven and return cheesecake to oven for one hour.

5. Transfer cheesecake to rack and cool 1 to 2 hours. Remove from springform pan. Serve the cheesecake at room temperature or slightly warm.

6. When ready to serve, drain each jar of caviar in two fine strainers by running a slow stream of cold water over caviar, which will remove the salty brine. Lay strainers on paper toweling to drain any excess water. Spread sour cream over top of cake evenly, then with a knife, mark top into 8 even pie wedges. (Make a cardboard guide for ease of dividing and filling.) Carefully fill alternate wedges with red and black caviar. Place on pretty platter and garnish with lemon slices.

SWEDISH MEATBALLS
SERVES 8 TO 10

Perfect buffet choice, as it doesn't hurt the dish at all to sit in a slow cooker on low heat for hours.

1/2 cup fresh breadcrumbs (whirl torn pieces of white
    bread, crusts removed, in processor)
1/3 cup heavy cream or Half and Half
3 tablespoons unsalted butter
1 medium onion, peeled and minced
salt and black pepper to taste
1/2 pound each ground beef, ground pork and ground
    veal, or all beef if you prefer

1 large egg
pinch of ground cloves or allspice

Sauce:

4 tablespoons (1/2 stick) unsalted butter
4 tablespoons Wondra flour (this grainy flour prevents
    lumps in sauces)
1 cup each chicken or beef stock and Half and Half,
    warmed
salt and pepper to taste

1. In a large bowl soak the breadcrumbs in the 1/3 cup of cream or Half and Half. Put 1 tablespoon of the butter in a large skillet over medium high heat and add the onion and a bit of salt and pepper and cook, stirring occasionally until onion softens, about 5 minutes.

2. Add the onions, meat and spices to the breadcrumbs. Do not overmix or overhandle, or your meatballs won't be tender. With wet hands or wet spoons (or a very small ice cream scoop) form mixture into small meatballs, about 1 tablespoon each. This makes about 40 meatballs, depending on size you make them. At this point fry one meatball at medium-high to taste to see if you need to add salt and pepper. Do not taste the raw meat mixture!

3. Put 2 more tablespoons of the butter in the skillet. When the butter melts, begin adding meatballs, a few at a time, cooking in batches if needed. Brown evenly on all sides and turn off heat. Drain any fat. (I use a turkey baster for this job.)

4. Make the sauce: In a Dutch oven, melt the 4 tablespoons butter and whisk in the Wondra flour until bubbly, stirring constantly. Whisk in the warm stock and Half and Half and cook until thickened. Taste and adjust seasoning, then pour over the meatballs. Can make ahead and refrigerate, then reheat before serving.

BOURSIN POTATO GRATIN—SERVES 8 TO 10

This flavorful dish is best served the day it is made.

2 cups heavy (whipping) cream
1 5-ounce package Boursin cheese with herbs and garlic
2 tablespoons minced shallots
2 medium cloves garlic, crushed in a garlic press
2 teaspoons extra virgin olive oil
2 1/2 pounds Yukon Gold or redskin potatoes, peeled and sliced 1/3 inch thick (about 8 cups)
salt and freshly ground black pepper
2 tablespoons minced fresh chives
<u>1/2 cup (2 ounces) shredded Parmesan cheese</u>

1. Place a rack in the center of the oven and preheat the oven to 400°F.

2. Place the cream, Boursin, shallots and garlic in a medium saucepan over low heat. Cook, stirring, until the Boursin melts and the mixture thickens, 4 to 5 minutes.

3. Meanwhile, brush a 9" x 13" glass or ceramic baking dish with the olive oil. Arrange half of the potato slices in the baking dish, overlapping them as needed. Season with salt and pepper to taste and sprinkle 1 tablespoon of the chives on top.

4. Pour half the Boursin mixture over the potatoes. Arrange the remaining potato slices on top, season them with salt and pepper and scatter the remaining tablespoon of chives over them. Pour the remaining Boursin mixture over the potatoes. Scatter the Parmesan cheese over the top.

5. Bake the gratin, uncovered, until it is deeply browned and the potatoes are tender, 45 to 50 minutes. Can serve at once or let rest 15 to 20 minutes before serving.

GRASSHOPPER SUNDAES—SERVES 8

Retro and fabulous! So easy to put together while your guests are gearing up for dessert.

6 brownies, store-bought or your favorite recipe (see below)
1 quart mint chocolate chip ice cream
about 1 tablespoon green crème de menthe per martini glass
1 cup heavy cream, whipped

<u>Optional garnish: chocolate shavings</u>

1. Purchase some inexpensive martini glasses from The Dollar Store or similar discount store. Crumble into 1/2-inch pieces or cube 6 brownies and divide them among the glasses. Place a large scoop of ice cream on top of the brownies in each glass.

2. Pour 1 tablespoon of the crème de menthe over the ice cream, and top with the whipped cream and chocolate shavings.

<u>If you want to make your own brownies, the recipe which follows is very simple.</u>

WORLD'S EASIEST BROWNIES
MAKES 24

Unlike many brownie recipes, this one calls for unsweetened cocoa powder, not unsweetened chocolate.

1/2 pound (2 sticks) unsalted butter
1 cup unsweetened cocoa powder
2 cups sugar
1 teaspoon salt
4 large eggs
1 1/2 cups all-purpose flour
1/4 teaspoon baking powder
1 teaspoon vanilla extract

Optional: 1 cup chopped pecans or walnuts

1. Preheat oven to 350°F.

2. In a medium heavy bottomed saucepan melt the butter over medium heat. Add cocoa powder, sugar and salt. Stir until sugar dissolves. Remove pan from heat and cool slightly.

3. Beat in eggs one at a time. Add flour, baking powder, vanilla extract and optional nuts. Batter will be thick. Pour mixture into a 9" x 13" ungreased pan and bake for 30 minutes. Allow to cool on a rack before slicing into 24 squares, then remove from pan. You will only need 6 of these brownies for the sundaes, so enjoy the rest another time. These freeze well.

COOK'S TIP

Although cooking can be a serious business that requires your attention for success, it should also be a joyous activity for you. I had so much fun putting together the Academy Awards menu! Presenting your friends and family with outstanding dishes is always a kick. Don't forget to enjoy the process of cooking!

6

REGIONAL AMERICAN ADVENTURES

America—What a country! From the Atlantic to the Pacific and every state in between, we have a treasure chest of culinary riches. In this chapter we'll savor tastes of New Orleans, Middle America, California, the Carolinas and the Southwest. Menus include: New Orleans Cooking—A Mardi Gras Party, A Harvest Bounty from the Heartland, California Wine Country Dinner, Carolina Low Country Feast and A Southwestern Meal.

Asparagus-Red Pepper Salad (page 98)

NEW ORLEANS MENU
A Mardi Gras Party

The Big Easy is known for its fabulous food. During Mardi Gras (translation: Fat Tuesday) the locals throw caution to the wind (as well as beads) and enjoy rich foods, since it is traditionally the last decadent meal before Lent. So get your party on and Let The Good Times Roll!

Shrimp Rémoulade
Muffuletta Sandwiches
Red Beans and Rice
Commander's Palace Bread Pudding with
Whiskey Sauce

SHRIMP RÉMOULADE—SERVES 8

2 lemons, one halved for cooking shrimp, other wedged
    for presentation
1 onion, halved
salt and pepper
24 (15 to 20 count size) large green (raw) shells-on
    shrimp

Rémoulade Sauce:

1 1/4 cups prepared Creole mustard
1/4 cup each minced flat leaf parsley, shallots, celery,
    dill pickle, green onion
1 tablespoon each minced garlic, horseradish and
    mayonnaise
1/4 cup each white vinegar and salad oil
1/4 cup water or less, to thin to desired consistency

Optional: sugar, paprika and more horseradish and
    mayonnaise to taste

Garnishes: shredded iceberg lettuce, tomato wedges,
lemon wedges, avocado slices, chopped parsley

1. Bring 1 quart of water to a boil. Add 1 halved lemon and onion half, salt, pepper and shrimp. Cook just until shrimp turn pink, curl and are no longer translucent, 1 to 2 minutes. Do not overcook or they will be tough. Immediately remove from water and put into an ice water bath to cool. Peel, devein and refrigerate.

2. Make rémoulade sauce: In a medium bowl mix all ingredients together in order given. Taste and if needed, add up to 1/4 cup water to make a smooth consistency. Chill.

3. To serve: Place 3 shrimp per serving on a bed of shredded lettuce. Spoon on some sauce and garnish with tomato wedges, lemon wedges, avocado and parsley if desired.

MUFFULETTA SANDWICHES
SERVES 8

Great to take on a picnic, just be sure to bring plenty of napkins to catch the drippings. Traditionally it's not an authentic muffuletta sandwich unless the oil from the olive salad drips down your arm!

1 long loaf Italian bread

Olive salad:

1 cup each pitted and chopped black olives and broken
    pitted green olives
1/2 cup chopped pimientos or roasted red peppers
1/3 cup olive oil
3 tablespoons red wine vinegar
2 cloves garlic, mashed
1 teaspoon dried oregano
3 tablespoons fresh parsley, chopped
1/2 teaspoon freshly ground black pepper

Cold Cuts:

1/4 pound each thinly sliced: Genoa or other Italian
    salami, Mortadella (Italian bologna), baked ham,
    Swiss cheese, Provolone cheese

1. Cut bread in half horizontally. Scoop out half of the soft insides of the bread and reserve for other use. (For example, toast and throw into food processor for homemade breadcrumbs.)

2. Make Olive Salad: Combine all ingredients in a medium bowl. You can make this ahead and refrigerate it for up to 3 weeks.

3. <u>To assemble muffaletta</u>: Place half of the olive salad in each side of the hollowed-out halves of bread. Begin layering the cold cuts in the bottom half of the bread, alternating meats and cheeses, salami first, then half the Provolone, all the ham, Swiss and Mortadella, and finishing with the rest of the Provolone. Carefully replace top of bread. If any olive salad spills out, spoon it back in.

4. Wrap entire uncut loaf in plastic wrap tightly. Place in large plastic bags and put on a tray, then lay two 5-pound bags of sugar or flour on top, to weight sandwich down. Refrigerate for one hour or up to overnight. You can take the muffuletta to a picnic this way and cut it there, or cut into individual sandwiches and wrap each separately. Makes 8 sandwiches.

RED BEANS AND RICE—SERVES 8

1 pound dry red kidney beans
1/2 cup chopped white onion
1/4 cup chopped shallots
2 tablespoons unsalted butter
1/2-inch thick sliced smoked ham, about 8 ounces, cut into 1/2-inch dice
1 teaspoon <u>each</u> minced garlic, salt, dried thyme and oregano
1/2 teaspoon <u>each</u> black and white pepper
1/4 teaspoon red pepper (cayenne)
1 bay leaf
4 to 6 cups water
2 cups uncooked Uncle Ben's converted rice
<u>4 cups water</u>

1. Soak kidney beans in water to cover overnight. Drain next day and reserve.

2. In a Dutch oven or saucepan sauté onion, shallots and garlic in butter until tender. Add ham and continue cooking until lightly browned. Add drained kidney beans and remaining ingredients except water. Now add 4 cups of water and bring mixture to a boil. Lower heat to medium and simmer for 1 hour, adding more water as skillet becomes dry, stirring occasionally. Cook for another hour, or until beans begin to break up and soften, adding water as needed and stirring so beans won't burn. Remove bay leaf and serve over rice.

3. <u>To make rice</u>: Place rice and 4 cups of water in a medium saucepan, bring to a boil, then lower heat to low and cover. Cook for about 20 to 25 minutes or until rice is tender and liquid is absorbed.

COMMANDER'S PALACE BREAD PUDDING WITH WHISKEY SAUCE—SERVES 8

1/2 cup (1 stick) unsalted butter, softened
1 cup granulated sugar
5 large eggs, beaten
1 pint (2 cups) heavy cream
1 tablespoon vanilla extract
pinch of cinnamon
1/4 cup raisins
12 slices of fresh or stale good-quality French bread, cut 1 inch thick

Whiskey Sauce

1/2 teaspoon cornstarch
1 cup heavy cream
1 cup sugar
pinch of cinnamon
1 tablespoon unsalted butter
<u>1 tablespoon good-quality bourbon or other whiskey</u>

1. Preheat oven to 350°F. In a large bowl, beat the butter and sugar together with an electric mixer until creamy. Add the eggs, cream, vanilla and cinnamon and beat until thoroughly combined. Stir in the raisins. Pour this mixture into a 9-inch square baking pan.

2. Place the bread slices in the pan and let stand for 5 minutes to soak up some of the mixture. Turn the bread over and let stand for 10 minutes longer. Then push the slices down so that most of each slice is submerged. Don't break up the slices.

3. Set the pan into a larger pan and pour in enough boiling water to reach within 1/2 inch of the top of the inner pan. (This is called a Bain Marie or water bath and helps the custard bake evenly.) Cover the whole pan with aluminum foil and bake for 35 minutes.

4. While pudding is baking, <u>Make the Whiskey Sauce</u>: In a small bowl dissolve the cornstarch in 1/4 cup of water. In a medium saucepan, combine the cream, sugar, cinnamon and butter. Bring to a boil over high heat, stirring, and cook and stir frequently to dissolve the sugar, about 3 minutes. Whisk in the cornstarch mixture and cook until the sauce thickens slightly, about 3 minutes. Remove from the heat and stir in the bourbon.

5. Uncover the pan and bake for 10 minutes longer, or until the top of the bread is brown and the pudding is still soft. If not brown enough, turn on the broiler and, watching carefully, brown for a few seconds, until golden and bubbly.

6. Spoon the pudding into shallow bowls and pass the Whiskey Sauce separately. Serve slightly warm.

A HARVEST BOUNTY FROM THE HEARTLAND

Tomato, Basil and Cheese Tart
Orange Glazed Loin of Pork
Kansas City Corn Bread
Michigan Apple, Dried Cherry and Walnut Strudel

TOMATO, BASIL AND CHEESE TART
SERVES 8

You'll need a 9-inch tart pan with a removable bottom for this recipe. Consider making individual tarts for special company—a bit more work but a lovely opener to this meal.

Crust:

1 1/4 cups all-purpose flour
3/4 stick (6 tablespoons) cold unsalted butter, cut into cubes
2 tablespoons cold solid vegetable shortening
1/4 teaspoon salt
3 to 4 tablespoons ice water

Filling:

4 large firm-ripe tomatoes (about 2 pounds) sliced into 1/3-inch slices
1 teaspoon salt, <u>DIVIDED</u>
1 cup fresh basil leaves, firmly packed, plus basil sprigs for garnish
1/2 cup plus 2 tablespoons whole-milk ricotta cheese
2 large eggs, lightly beaten
1/4 pound (4 ounces) whole milk mozzarella, coarsely grated
1/2 cup freshly grated Parmesan cheese
1/2 teaspoon freshly ground black pepper
<u>liquid vegetable oil to brush tomatoes</u>

1. <u>Make the crust</u>: In a large bowl blend the flour, butter, shortening and salt with a pastry blender or two forks until mixture resembles small peas. Add 3 to 4 tablespoons ice water, enough to form a dough, tossing mixture just until water is incorporated. Knead dough

lightly with heel of hand on a flat work surface for a few seconds to distribute the fats evenly, then form into a ball. Flatten slightly, dust with flour, wrap in plastic wrap and chill 1 hour or up to overnight.

2. When dough is chilled, roll into a 1/8-inch thick round on a floured surface and fit into a 9-inch tart pan with a removable bottom. Prick shell lightly with a fork and chill again for 30 minutes to prevent shrinkage in baking. (If you decide to make the individual tarts, use 8 small tart pans with removable bottoms.)

3. When ready to bake, preheat oven to 425°F. Remove shell from refrigerator, line with foil, fill with raw rice, dried beans or pie weights and bake 15 minutes. Remove the foil and weights carefully, then bake shell for 3 to 5 minutes more, or until pale golden color. Let cool in its pan on a rack.

4. Make the filling: Sprinkle the tomato slices on both sides lightly with 1/2 the salt and let them drain on paper towels. In a food processor purée the basil leaves with the ricotta. Add the eggs and blend to combine. Add remaining 1/2 teaspoon salt, the mozzarella, Parmesan and pepper. Pulse until just combined. Pat tomato slices dry with paper towels and line bottom of the partially-baked shell with the end slices, then spoon the cheese mixture over the tomato layer, smoothing the mixture. Arrange remaining tomato slices in one layer, overlapping them slightly. Brush tomatoes with vegetable oil, then bake in a preheated 350°F. oven for 40 to 50 minutes, or until cheese mixture is set. If making individual tarts adjust time accordingly, using the test of when the cheese sets to remove from oven. Transfer to a rack and let stand for 10 minutes, then place pan on an overturned bowl or large glass. Gravity should remove the outer rim easily, but you might need to loosen edges with a sharp knife. Place tart on a pretty plate and garnish with basil sprigs if desired. Serve hot or at room temperature.

ORANGE GLAZED LOIN OF PORK
SERVES 8 TO 10

3 pounds rolled loin of pork
3 cloves of garlic, cut into slivers
1/2 teaspoon each dried rosemary, salt and pepper
1 6-ounce can frozen orange juice concentrate, thawed
3/4 cup orange marmalade
4 navel or Valencia oranges, peeled, white pith removed, segmented
1/4 cup vegetable oil
1 tablespoon sugar, or to taste
2 tablespoons brandy
up to 1 cup additional orange juice

1. Make several deep cuts all over the roast and insert the garlic slivers into each cut. Rub roast with the rosemary, salt and pepper. Place roast on a rack in a shallow roasting pan and roast in a preheated 325°F. oven, allowing 30 minutes per pound to cook. Total roasting time is about 2 hours, when roast reaches 165°F. measured with an instant-read thermometer.

2. Prepare basting sauce: Mix the orange juice concentrate, orange marmalade, vegetable oil and sugar to taste in a medium bowl. Baste roast every half hour with this basting sauce. Add water if pan is becoming dry. The surface of the roast should be nicely glazed and there should be a nice amount of juice in the pan.

3. When roast reaches 165°F. remove it to a cutting board and cover loosely with foil. Let rest 15 minutes while preparing sauce.

4. Prepare sauce: Skim any visible fat from the roasting pan and discard. Pour drippings into a saucepan. Combine with the prepared orange segments, brandy and orange juice to taste. Correct seasonings and bring to a simmer on top of the stove.

5. Slice roast and arrange on serving platter. Surround with orange segments and spoon some sauce over slices. Serve additional sauce in a gravy boat.

KANSAS CITY CORN BREAD
MAKES 1 BREAD

An easy, quick bread to have in your bag of tricks anytime you want to round out a meal.

12 ounces bacon
1 cup <u>each</u> stone-ground yellow cornmeal and whole
    wheat flour
1/3 cup sugar
2 1/2 teaspoons baking powder
1/4 teaspoon salt
1 cup buttermilk
6 tablespoons (3/4 stick) unsalted butter, melted
1/2 cup sour cream
1 large egg, lightly beaten
<u>1/4 teaspoon salt</u>

1. Preheat the oven to 400°F.

2. Sauté the bacon in a heavy skillet until crisp. Drain on paper towels, reserving bacon fat. Crumble bacon and reserve. Lightly brush an 8-inch square cake pan with the bacon drippings.

3. In a large bowl combine the cornmeal with the whole wheat flour, sugar, baking powder and salt. Stir in the buttermilk, melted butter, sour cream and egg. Mix in the crumbled bacon.

4. Put oiled pan in the hot oven for 5 minutes. When smoking hot, carefully remove pan from oven and quickly pour batter into the pan. Return to oven and bake until golden, about 20 minutes. Serve warm, cut into 8 to 12 squares.

MICHIGAN APPLE, DRIED CHERRY AND
WALNUT STRUDEL—MAKES 2

1/2 cup (1 stick) unsalted butter
1 cup brown sugar
1 teaspoon ground cinnamon
6 Granny Smith apples, peeled, cored and diced
1/4-ounce package Michigan dried cherries
2 tablespoons Amaretto or Applejack Brandy or other
    brandy, or apple juice
1/2 teaspoon vanilla extract
1/2 cup (4 ounces) coarsely chopped walnuts, toasted in
    a 350°F. oven 8 to 10 minutes, until fragrant
1/2 cup breadcrumbs
1/2 cup (1 stick) unsalted butter, melted
10 sheets phyllo pastry, defrosted

<u>Garnish: confectioners' (powdered) sugar</u>

1. <u>Make apple filling</u>: In a 12-inch skillet put 1 stick butter, brown sugar, cinnamon, apples and cherries. Stir in brandy. Cook over medium heat 5 minutes, stirring occasionally. Add vanilla extract and toasted walnuts and cool mixture. (Can be made a day ahead and refrigerated.)

2. On large work surface, place 1 sheet of phyllo. Keep rest of sheets covered with a sheet of parchment paper and a slightly damp towel. Brush sheet with melted butter and sprinkle with 1 tablespoon bread crumbs. Add another sheet, brush with butter and sprinkle with breadcrumbs. Continue to build until you have 5 sheets stacked. Do not put breadcrumbs on top sheet. Put one half of the cooled apple filling on top of the short side of the phyllo, fold in as for an egg roll, brush exposed edges with butter, and roll up tightly. Place on lightly buttered cookie sheet with sides. Repeat above procedure with other 5 sheets of phyllo and rest of apple mixture to make a second strudel.

3. Bake in a preheated 400°F. oven for 15 to 20 minutes, or until pastry is golden and crisp. Carefully remove, using large spatulas, onto a rack to cool. Gently cut into serving pieces with a serrated knife and serve warm, sprinkled with powdered sugar.

CALIFORNIA WINE COUNTRY DINNER

Bruschetta with Kalamata Olive-Goat Cheese Purée
Blackened Salmon on Designer Greens
Asparagus-Red Pepper Salad
Chez Panisse Almond Tart

BRUSCHETTA WITH KALAMATA OLIVE-GOAT CHEESE PURÉE—SERVES 8

The quintessential California appetizer that reflects the casual chic of the state!

6 ounces chèvre (goat cheese)
1/4 cup Kalamata (Greek) olives, pitted and coarsely diced
1 pound crusty French or Italian long loaf, cut into 20 diagonal slices
extra virgin olive oil, for brushing slices of bread
3 Roma tomatoes, finely diced

Garnish: sprigs of fresh rosemary, extra olive slices

1. Place chèvre and the 1/4 cup of the diced olives in the bowl of a food processor and process until well mixed into a purée. Transfer to a bowl and reserve.

2. Brush bread slices with olive oil and grill or broil lightly on each side.

3. Spread a scant tablespoon of the purée on each slice and sprinkle with some diced Roma tomatoes. Add a small sprig of rosemary and a few slices of olive on each slice and serve.

BLACKENED SALMON ON GREENS WITH CITRUS VINAIGRETTE—SERVES 8

A classic California dish which I first experienced at a lovely outdoor restaurant in Beverly Hills with my sister Helene.

Citrus vinaigrette:

1/4 cup orange juice concentrate
2 tablespoons sherry wine vinegar or champagne vinegar
salt and freshly ground pepper to taste
1/4 cup extra virgin olive oil

2 pounds fresh salmon fillets, skin removed, cut into eight 4-ounce servings.
olive oil or salad oil

Seasoning mix:

1 tablespoon sweet paprika
1 teaspoon each onion powder, garlic powder and cayenne pepper
1/2 teaspoon each dried oregano and thyme
3/4 teaspoon each white and black pepper and salt

about 8 cups designer lettuces
3 seedless oranges, peeled and cut into 24 thin slices
1 red onion, peeled and cut into thin rings

1. Heat 2 large (10 to 12-inch) cast iron skillets on outdoor gas grill grid with the lid closed until skillets are very hot, 10 minutes or more. You can't heat them too much for this recipe!

2. Make citrus vinaigrette: Mix ingredients in order given, whisking in the olive oil last. Reserve.

3. Make seasoning mix in a small bowl. Brush salmon filets with olive oil and sprinkle with the seasoning mix. Place salmon in single layer in the two very hot skillets and carefully drizzle each filet with 1/2 teaspoon more olive oil, being careful of flame flare-ups. Close lid of grill and cook salmon 3 minutes. Turn over carefully with wide spatula and drizzle other side with another 1/2 teaspoon olive oil, then close lid again. Cook 3 to 5 minutes more, testing to be sure center is no longer raw.

4. Toss 1/2 of the dressing with greens and arrange on large flat platter. Arrange orange and onion slices around edges. Place cooked salmon on dressed greens on platter and serve right away. Serve any extra dressing separately.

ASPARAGUS-RED PEPPER SALAD
SERVES 8

This colorful dish shouts fresh and fabulous.

1 small red pepper
2 pounds fresh asparagus, ends snapped and stalks
    peeled

Dressing:

zest (outer color portion of skin) of 1 orange
2 tablespoons <u>each</u> orange juice, soy sauce, sesame oil
    and rice wine vinegar
1 1/2 tablespoons sugar
4 tablespoons peanut oil

<u>1 tablespoon sesame seeds, toasted in dry skillet until
    golden</u>

1. Roast or grill red pepper until skin is blackened, then put into a paper or plastic bag and close, so pepper steams and skin loosens, about 5 minutes. Remove from bag and remove skin, then cut pepper into thin strips. Reserve.

2. Cook asparagus in a skillet large enough to hold spears lying flat, in 1 inch of salted water, covered, until crisp-tender, about 4 minutes. Drain under cold running water to stop cooking, dry and reserve while making dressing.

3. <u>To make dressing</u>: In a medium bowl, whisk together the zest, orange juice, soy sauce, sesame oil, vinegar and sugar. Whisk in the peanut oil slowly. This dressing can be prepared ahead of time and refrigerated.

4. Arrange the asparagus spears on a serving platter with tips pointing out in a circular pattern if you wish. Lay the pepper strips over the asparagus. Drizzle the dressing over the platter and refrigerate at least 1 hour or up to 4 hours. Sprinkle the sesame seeds over top and serve.

CHEZ PANISSE ALMOND TART
SERVES 10

A specialty of Chef Alice Water's ground breaking Berkeley restaurant.

Tart dough:

1 cup all-purpose flour
1 tablespoon sugar
1/4 teaspoon <u>each</u> salt and grated lemon zest
1/2 cup (1 stick) unsalted butter, cut into cubes, chilled
1/2 teaspoon pure vanilla extract
1 tablespoon water, if needed

Filling:

3/4 cup <u>each</u> heavy cream and sugar
1/8 teaspoon almond extract
1 teaspoon Grand Marnier liqueur
1 cup sliced almonds, toasted in 350°F. oven 7 minutes

Topping:

<u>1 cup heavy cream, whipped with 1 tablespoon sugar</u>

1. <u>Make tart dough</u>: In a food processor combine the flour, sugar, salt, lemon zest and butter. Add the vanilla and process until the dough forms a ball that leaves the side of the bowl and whirls around blade. If too dry and dough does not form a ball, add the water and process a few seconds more. Pat dough into a small disk, wrap in plastic wrap and chill at least 30 minutes or up to overnight.

2. Preheat oven to 425°F. Roll out dough on floured surface and fit it into a 9-inch tart pan with a removable bottom, folding over excess dough to make a double edge to strengthen shell. Prick all over with a fork, then press a piece of heavy-duty foil that has been sprayed heavily with cooking spray firmly over dough. Place on rimmed cookie sheet and bake 8 minutes, then remove foil carefully and bake for about 4 more minutes, until shell appears baked but not browned. Remove from oven and reduce oven temperature to 400°F.

3. <u>Make filling</u>: Warm the cream and sugar in a small saucepan, stirring until sugar has melted and mixture is

translucent. Add almond extract and liqueur, then stir in the almonds. Pour into the tart shell, spreading evenly.

4. Bake for about 25 minutes, turning tart once or twice if not browning evenly. Mixture will bubble throughout baking. Cover edges with foil if browning too quickly. Filling should be a deep golden brown when done. Remove from oven and let rest 5 minutes, then remove outer tart pan ring by placing pan on a small overturned bowl and letting ring drop, so you do not burn yourself. Cool completely on wire rack. Serve with sweetened whipped cream.

CAROLINA LOW COUNTRY FEAST

What treasures the South holds for foodies!

The Best Crabcakes
Pecan-Crusted Chicken Breasts with Peach Salsa
Shirley's Awesome Biscuits
Orange Chiffon Cake

THE BEST CRABCAKES
SERVES 8 TO 10

Novelist Pat Conroy calls these "Matrimonial Crabcakes", as he won his wife by preparing them for her on their first shared meal together. She was so impressed she married him. Be sure to read the recipe and do your mise en place before starting to cook the crabcakes for best results.

2 pounds lump crabmeat
1 1/2 lemons, <u>DIVIDED</u>
salt and black pepper
2 large egg whites
flour
10 tablespoons unsalted butter, <u>DIVIDED</u>

3 tablespoons capers, rinsed and drained

8 to 10 handfuls baby arugula, butter lettuce or spring
   mix
champagne vinegar to taste
extra virgin olive oil
<u>salt and freshly ground black pepper to taste</u>

1. Put crabmeat in a bowl and pick over to remove any shells or cartilage. Squeeze juice of 1 lemon over the crab. Salt and pepper lightly.

2. In a small dish, beat egg whites until foamy with a whisk. Pour over crab and mix in gently. Using as little flour as possible (2 to 4 tablespoons) form mixture into 8 to 10 crabcakes using your hands. Handle gently. Because these crabcakes have so little filler, they are very fragile.

3. Melt 4 tablespoons of the butter in a large heavy skillet on medium high heat, until sizzling and just beginning to brown. Carefully add the crabcakes. Brown on one side

until crispy, then turn carefully and brown the other side. Remove to a plate and keep warm while making sauce.

4. <u>Make the sauce</u>: Add the remaining 6 tablespoons butter to the hot skillet, stirring to dislodge any crab bits still stuck to skillet. When butter begins to brown, squeeze in the juice of the remaining 1/2 lemon and turn off the heat. Throw in the capers and toss sauce.

5. Put the lettuce in a large bowl and dress with about 3 tablespoons of the vinegar and 2 tablespoon of the olive oil, tossing gently, adding salt and pepper to taste. Mound on plates, top with one crabcake, then pour sauce over top of each plate and serve right away.

PECAN-CRUSTED CHICKEN BREASTS WITH PEACH SALSA—SERVES 8

You can use this versatile salsa to top fish fillets as well.

Peach Salsa:

2 tablespoons <u>each</u> honey and red wine vinegar
2 teaspoons Dijon mustard
1 teaspoon Tabasco or other red hot sauce (or to taste)
1/2 teaspoon <u>each</u> ground ginger and salt
6 medium peaches or 1-pound bag of frozen peaches, defrosted, cut into 1/4-inch dice
1 cup <u>each</u> minced sweet red pepper and red onion

8 skinless, boneless chicken breast halves (about 4 to 6 ounces each)
1 1/2 cups pecan halves
4 tablespoons flour
1/2 teaspoon salt
4 large eggs, lightly beaten with 1/4 cup cold water
2 cups fresh dried breadcrumbs, about 8 slices, slightly stale white bread, whirled in food processor into fine crumbs
<u>4 tablespoons or more olive oil</u>

1. <u>Make Peach Salsa</u>: In a large bowl stir together the honey, vinegar, mustard, Tabasco, ginger and salt. Add the peaches, sweet red pepper and onion and stir to combine. Can make up to a day ahead and refrigerate.

2. Place each chicken breast half between two layers of plastic wrap and pound with a meat pounder to 1/2 inch thickness. Reserve.

3. In food processor combine the pecans, flour and salt and process until finely ground. Transfer to a large piece of waxed or parchment paper. Beat eggs with the cold water in a shallow bowl. Pour breadcrumbs onto another piece of waxed paper.

4. Dip chicken into the pecan mixture first, pressing it into the chicken. Dip next into egg mixture, then in breadcrumbs, pressing crumbs into chicken. Transfer to platter lined with waxed or parchment paper and refrigerate 30 minutes to one hour.

5. Preheat oven to 350°F. Lightly rub a baking sheet with

oil. In a large skillet, heat 1 to 2 tablespoons of the oil over medium-high heat. Sauté chicken about 2 minutes per side until golden brown. Transfer to prepared baking sheet and repeat with remaining oil and chicken. Bake chicken 8 to 10 minutes or until cooked through. Serve right away with Peach Salsa.

SHIRLEY'S AWESOME BISCUITS—MAKES 8

Shirley Corriher lives in the South, and you can bet these are the most mouth-watering biscuits ever! A noted food chemist and cooking teacher, Shirley's cookbooks Cookwise and Bakewise have taught me to really understand food chemistry! Be sure to follow the unusual directions for shaping the biscuits, which makes them super moist.

nonstick cooking spray
1 1/2 cups Southern self-rising flour (I like White Lily)
1/4 teaspoon <u>each</u> baking soda and salt
1 tablespoon sugar
3 tablespoons shortening (solid Crisco)
3/4 cup buttermilk
1/2 cup heavy (whipping) cream
about 1 cup all-purpose flour (for shaping)
cooking spray
<u>2 tablespoons butter, melted</u>

1. Preheat oven to 475°F. Spray an 8-inch round cake pan with cooking spray.

2. In medium bowl combine the self-rising flour, baking soda, salt and sugar. With a pastry blender or your fingers work the shortening into flour mixture until shortening is size of small peas. Stir in the buttermilk and cream and let stand 2 minutes. This dough is so wet that you cannot shape it in the usual way.

3. Pour the all-purpose flour onto a plate. Spray a medium-size (2-inch) ice cream scoop with cooking spray and scoop biscuits onto the all-purpose flour, then shape and place in the cake pan. Continue to make and fill the pan with the 8 biscuits. Brush the tops of the biscuits with the melted butter and bake about 20 minutes until lightly browned. Cool 1 to 2 minutes in the pan, then turn out onto a plate carefully, reverse right-side up onto a second plate, and serve hot. Pass the butter and butter 'em while they're hot!

ORANGE CHIFFON CAKE WITH ORANGE BUTTER CREAM
MAKES 1 CAKE

An old-fashioned recipe that is well worth revisiting. If you can't find superfine sugar at the grocery store, you can easily make it by whirling regular granulated sugar in the blender, but don't let the blender run too long or you'll make confectioners' sugar! Be sure to follow the directions in Step #3 to get a lovely light cake.

2 1/4 cups sifted cake flour
1 1/2 cups superfine sugar, <u>DIVIDED</u>
2 teaspoons baking powder
1/2 teaspoon salt
1/2 cup vegetable oil
7 large eggs, room temperature, <u>separated</u> plus 3
    additional egg whites
2 tablespoons grated orange zest
3/4 cup strained orange juice, preferably freshly
    squeezed
1 teaspoon vanilla
1 1/4 teaspoon cream of tartar

Orange Butter Cream Frosting:

1/2 cup (1 stick) soft unsalted butter
1/8 teaspoon salt
1 tablespoon <u>each</u> grated orange zest and orange juice
1 teaspoon pure vanilla extract
about 3 cups sifted confectioners' sugar
<u>about 2 tablespoons whole milk or light cream</u>

1. Preheat oven to 325°F. Set out an ungreased 10-inch two-piece tube pan. Wrap the outside bottom and up the sides of the pan with foil, to prevent any batter from leaking out.

2. In mixing bowl of an electric mixer combine the flour, all but 2 tablespoons of the sugar, baking powder and salt and beat 1 minute. Add the oil, egg yolks, orange zest and juice and vanilla and beat 1 minute or till smooth.

3. In another large mixing bowl beat the egg whites until frothy, add the cream of tartar and beat until soft peaks form. Beat in the remaining 2 tablespoons sugar and beat until stiff peaks form. Gently fold 1/3 of the whites into batter with a clean rubber spatula until just blended.

Fold in the rest of the whites gently. Don't use a spatula that has any fat or grease on it, or it will deflate the egg whites. As the expression goes, "Ask me how I know!" Once you deflate the whites, there's no way to get air back into them, and your cake won't be high and light. Pour batter into the tube pan and bake for 55 to 65 minutes, or until cake tester inserted in center comes out clean and cake springs back when lightly pressed in center. Invert pan, placing tube opening over the neck of a wine bottle, coke bottle or small vase, propping it up if necessary, to suspend it above the counter to let it cool properly, and cool cake completely in pan, about 1 1/2 hours. Loosen sides and center post with a long metal spatula or thin knife and remove both parts of the pan carefully. I like to place the cake on a cardboard cake round for ease of frosting the cake later, then set it on a serving plate.

4. <u>Make the Frosting</u>: In bowl of an electric mixer thoroughly mix butter, salt, vanilla and 1 cup of the confectioners' sugar until light and fluffy. Add rest of sugar, zest, juice and milk and continue to beat until smooth and of spreading consistency. Frost top and sides of cooled cake.

SOUTHWESTERN ADVENTURES

Many of the ingredients for this menu are easily available at most grocery stores today. If you can't find some of the ingredients there, look for a Mexican grocery store in your city.

Black Bean Soup
Bean and Rice Enchiladas
Carne Adovada
Churros

BLACK BEAN SOUP—SERVES 8

1 pound dried black beans
4 cloves garlic, minced
1 large onion, chopped
2 carrots, chopped
2 tablespoons olive oil
1 to 2 teaspoons <u>each</u> cumin and dried oregano, to your
   taste
1 teaspoon salt
1/4 teaspoon hot red pepper flakes
1-pound can tomatoes, chopped, with their juice
6 cups water, or chicken or beef stock
2 cups cooked white or brown rice
<u>2 to 3 tablespoons white vinegar</u>

1. Cover dried black beans with cold water and soak overnight, or cover with boiling water and let soak for 3 hours.

2. Drain beans, discarding soaking water. Place beans in large stockpot. Add water or stock to cover and simmer until tender, about 1 to 1 1/2 hours.

3. Meanwhile, in medium skillet, sauté onions, carrots, and garlic in olive oil until tender but not brown. Add tomatoes and cumin, oregano, salt and hot pepper flakes.

4. When beans are tender, add sautéed vegetable mixture and taste for seasoning. If soup is too thick for your tastes, add additional stock or water. Add 2 to 3 tablespoons white vinegar to taste.

5. Place 1/4 cup cooked rice in each soup bowl and ladle soup over rice.

BEAN AND RICE ENCHILADAS
MAKES 11 TO 12 10-INCH ENCHILADAS
OR 20 8-INCH ONES ☺ 👨‍🍳 👨‍🍳

My husband is a confirmed meat-eater, yet he loves these tasty and filling enchiladas.

3/4 cup raw rice, white or brown (I prefer Uncle Ben's converted)
2 tablespoons extra virgin olive oil
2 medium onions, finely chopped
4 garlic cloves, finely chopped
2 jalapeño peppers, ribs and seeds removed for less heat, chopped
1/2 teaspoon ground cumin, or more to taste
coarse salt and ground black pepper
3 tablespoons tomato paste
3 15-ounce cans pinto beans or black beans, drained and rinsed
10 ounces corn kernels, frozen or canned, drained
6 scallions (green onions) thinly sliced
11 to 12 10-inch burrito-size flour tortillas (or 20 8-inch ones)
2 cups (8 ounces) shredded Cheddar or Monterey Jack cheese

Optional garnishes: salsa and sour cream

1. Cook rice: Rinse rice in fine strainer under cold water until water runs clear. Place in saucepan with 1 1/2 cups cold water and bring to a boil. Reduce heat, cover and cook for about 20 to 25 minutes or until all liquid is absorbed. Reserve.

2. In a large saucepan heat oil over medium-high heat and add the onions, garlic, jalapeno and cumin. Season with salt and pepper. Cook, stirring occasionally, until golden, 10 to 12 minutes. Add tomato paste and cook, stirring, 1 minute.

3. Add the beans and 1 1/2 cups water, reduce heat to medium and simmer, stirring occasionally, until thickened, about 10 minutes. Add the corn to heat through, 2 to 3 minutes. Remove from heat and stir in the rice and scallions.

4. Heat the tortillas according to package instructions (I use the microwave). Lay them out on a flat surface and fill each with 1 cup of the bean mixture, and 1/4 cup of the cheese, on one side of the tortilla. Fold at end of filling and hold in sides. Starting from the filled end, holding sides as you work, tightly roll into a compact bundle.

5. Place on a baking sheet or in a ceramic casserole, seam side down. Continue with other tortillas. If you want to serve them immediately, heat for a few minutes in a 350°F. oven for 5 minutes, or in microwave oven for about 3 minutes on High.) If you prefer to freeze them for later consumption, wrap each burrito individually in plastic and freeze for up to 3 months. To reheat from frozen, place as many as you want to reheat on a microwave-safe plate and microwave on High for 3 minutes, then transfer to a baking sheet and bake at 450°F. until crispy, about 10 minutes. Serve with optional salsa and sour cream. Great to have extras in your freezer for an emergency meal!

CARNE ADOVADA WITH HOMEMADE TORTILLAS—SERVES 8 🕐 👨‍🍳 👨‍🍳 👨‍🍳

The slow cooking in this recipe really brings out wonderful flavors of the chili peppers without being too spicy. The term adovada means cured or pickled meat, which in this case translates to the use of the chili spice mixture. This recipe includes instructions on how to make your own tortillas; however, feel free to use store bought corn tortillas.

Meat :

1/3 cup vegetable oil
3 1/2 pounds pork loin, fat layer removed, cut into 3/4 inch cubes
2 cups diced white onion
2 tablespoons minced garlic
3 cups chicken broth, <u>DIVIDED</u>

Chili Mixture:

1 teaspoon <u>each</u> ground Ceylon cinnamon (Mexicans call it canela), cumin and coriander
2 teaspoons dried Mexican oregano
1/4 teaspoon crushed red chili pods, no seeds (unless you like a lot of heat!)
1 tablespoon <u>each</u> ground red chili, mild or medium, and honey
2 tablespoons sherry vinegar or red wine vinegar
½ to 1 teaspoon salt, or to taste

Corn Tortillas: Makes 16

3 cups Quaker Masa Harina
<u>2 cups water</u>

1. Preheat the oven to 350°F.

2. <u>Brown pork</u>: In a 4-quart ovenproof stockpot heat the oil on high and brown the pork in batches. Don't crowd the pan or you won't get a nice sear on the pork. Remove to a bowl and reserve. Lower heat to medium, add the onions to the stockpot and sauté until golden. Add garlic and sauté 1 minute. Deglaze the skillet with 1 cup of the chicken stock, loosening the browned bits by rubbing the pan with the back of a spoon.

3. <u>Make the chili mixture</u>: Place the canela, cumin, coriander, oregano, crushed red pepper, honey, vinegar and 1/2 teaspoon salt in the workbowl of a food processor and run the machine until mixture is thoroughly combined. Add the onions, garlic and broth from the stockpot, then add 1 more cup of broth to processor and run the machine until mixture is thoroughly combined. Reserve.

4. Return the browned pork with any accumulated juice, the chili mixture and the last remaining cup of broth to the ovenproof casserole, stir to combine well, and bake for 1 1/2 hours or until the pork is tender. Serve hot with freshly made tortillas. Rewarms and freezes well.

5. <u>To make tortillas</u>: Combine Masa Harina and water. Dough should be pliable and moist, but not sticky or wet. Can add 1 to 2 teaspoons water if needed. Shape to form 12 balls. Keep balls covered to prevent drying. Roll each out between two sheets of waxed or parchment paper or pat out by hand to form a 6-inch circle. Carefully peel off paper. (A really handy gadget in making tortillas is a tortilla press, which is made of heavy metal and flattens the dough out to just the right thickness.) Cook on hot lightly greased griddle or in heavy skillet over medium heat until lightly browned, about 1 minute per side, brushing top with oil before turning. Tortillas should be pliable and soft. As each is done, wrap in foil to keep warm. Remember that practice makes perfect! Can make one hour ahead, wrapped, then rewarm in microwave.

CHURROS-MAKES 30 OR MORE

Grab a group of friends and make these treats together. Than eat them while they're still warm…Yum!

Cinnamon-Sugar mixture:

1 tablespoon ground cinnamon (Mexicans call
    cinnamon canela)
3/4 cup sugar

Batter:

1 cup whole milk
6 tablespoons unsalted butter
1 teaspoon sea salt
1 cup all purpose flour
3 large eggs, lightly beaten
<u>5 to 6 cups vegetable oil (I like Crisco solid) for deep
    frying</u>

1. Make cinnamon-sugar mixture by stirring the two ingredients together in a shallow bowl. Reserve.

2. <u>Make batter</u>: In a medium saucepan bring milk, butter and salt to a boil over medium heat. Whisk in the flour all at once and cook, stirring, until mixture forms a ball and pulls away from sides of the pan, about 30 seconds. Remove from heat and let cool 3 minutes. Whisk in the eggs and stir until batter is smooth.

3. Spoon mixture into a pastry bag fitted with a large open-star tip, or use a sealable plastic bag, filling the bag and cutting a small slanted slit at one corner.

4. Heat 4 to 5 inches of oil in a large Dutch oven or deep fryer until it registers 330°F. on a deep-fry thermometer. Holding pastry bag 3 to 4 inches above the oil, squeeze out batter, snipping off 3 to 4 inch lengths with kitchen shears or a knife. Fry 6 to 8 churros at a time, turning once, until deep golden brown all over, about 4 to 5 minutes. Transfer to a paper towel-lined plate to drain.

5. Roll churros in the cinnamon-sugar mixture. Serve immediately. Great with hot chocolate made with some cinnamon, as they do in the Southwest.

COOK'S TIP

There are really very few mistakes you can make while cooking that can't be fixed with a mid-course correction. If the cake falls, cut it into small squares and serve as bite-size yummy treats, if the white sauce curdles, throw it into the blender to smooth it out, or if the soup is too spicy add some peeled cut up potatoes and cook until potatoes are tender, to tame the heat. Cooking is supposed to be fun, so don't stress yourself out—you're usually alone in the kitchen, so your guests will never know about the train wreck you dodged.

7

ITALIAN FARE

Everyone loves Italian food, and these six menus show the rich variety to be found in Italian cuisine. In this chapter you'll find Southern Italian red-sauced pasta, sophisticated Northern Italian recipes and fun-to-make American style pizzas. Get out a bottle of chianti, a red checkered tablecloth, put some Frank Sinatra on the stereo, and celebrate Italian style! Menus include: A Zesty Italian Home Meal, Under the Tuscan Sun, Northern Italian Cuisine, Italian Immigrant Cooking, A Trattoria Menu and Pasta and Pizza Party.

Lidia's Stuffed Mushrooms (page 108) and Grilled Sausages with Tricolor Peppers (page 120)

A ZESTY ITALIAN HOME MEAL

Lidia's Stuffed Mushrooms
Pasta Carbonara
Grissini—Italian Bread Sticks
Vanilla Panna Cotta With Velvety Chocolate Sauce

LIDIA'S STUFFED MUSHROOMS
MAKES 12

This recipe is adapted from PBS personality and restaurateur Lidia Bastianich, one of our finest chefs today. Her recipes are authentic as well as delicious.

12 white or cremini mushrooms, with caps about 1 1/2 inch in diameter
1 tablespoon extra-virgin olive oil, plus more for tops of mushrooms
1/4 cup <u>each</u> finely chopped scallions and red bell peppers
1/4 cup <u>each</u> coarse breadcrumbs and grated Parmiggiano Reggiano cheese
2 tablespoons finely chopped fresh Italian (flat-leaf) parsley
2 tablespoons softened unsalted butter
1/4 teaspoon <u>each</u> salt and freshly ground black pepper
1/4 cup chicken stock or vegetable stock

<u>Optional: 2 tablespoons dry white wine</u>

1. Preheat oven to 425°F.

2. Remove the stems from the mushrooms and chop stems finely. Reserve.

3. Heat one tablespoon olive oil in a medium skillet over medium-high heat and add the scallions. Cook until wilted, about 1 minute. Stir in the red peppers and chopped mushroom stems and cook, stirring until tender, about 3 minutes. Remove and cool.

4. In a medium bowl toss the breadcrumbs, grated cheese, 1 tablespoon of parsley and sautéed vegetables until thoroughly blended. Season to taste with salt and pepper. Stuff cavity of each mushroom with filling, pressing it in with a teaspoon until even with the sides of the mushrooms.

5. Grease a 12" x 18" shallow baking pan with 1 tablespoon of the butter. Arrange the mushrooms side by side in the pan, and using the remaining 1 tablespoon of butter, dot the top of each mushroom. Add the stock and wine, if using, and 1 tablespoon of the parsley to the pan. Drizzle tops of mushrooms with oil. (At this point you can cover and refrigerate the pan for several hours.) When ready to bake, put pan in preheated oven until mushrooms are cooked through and breadcrumbs are golden brown, about 20 minutes.

6. Transfer to a warm platter. Pour pan juices into a small saucepan and bring to a boil on top of the stove. Boil until lightly thickened, 1 to 2 minutes, then spoon juices over the mushrooms and serve immediately.

PASTA CARBONARA—SERVES 8

Rich but worth every calorie. Definitely an entertaining standout!

1 pound very thin spaghetti

5 large eggs
1 cup freshly grated Parmesan cheese
2 cups Half and Half
3 cloves garlic, crushed
1/2 teaspoon <u>each</u> dried oregano, sweet basil, and fresh parsley
1/2 teaspoon <u>each</u> salt and freshly ground black pepper

1 pound sweet or hot Italian sausage, or half of each, crumbled, browned and drained
1/2 pound bacon, fried crisp and crumbled

4 tablespoons unsalted butter
<u>additional Parmesan cheese to serve at the table</u>

1. Bring a large pot of salted water to a rolling boil and cook the spaghetti until it is at the al dente (slightly chewy to the tooth) stage. Drain and reserve. Reserve in a large rectangular shallow serving pan. Save 1/2 cup of the pasta cooking liquid to soften any clumps that occur after pasta rests a bit.

2. In a large bowl combine the eggs, cheese, Half and Half and spices. Melt the butter in a large heavy saucepan on medium high and as soon as it starts to turn a light brown pour the egg mixture in, stirring constantly. AS SOON AS it just begins to thicken, pour this over the spaghetti in the serving pan, along with the sausage and bacon. It is important to have the spaghetti cooked and drained when the eggs just begin to thicken, as they should not be allowed to overcook, but should be moist. Serve IMMEDIATELY with extra Parmesan cheese.

BROCCOLI WITH OLIVE OIL AND GARLIC
SERVES 8

4 heads broccoli (about 1 1/2 to 2 pounds)
salt
3 tablespoons extra-virgin olive oil
4 cloves garlic, peeled
1/4 teaspoon crushed hot red pepper, or to taste
1/4 cup or more chicken stock or reserved broccoli cooking water, as needed

1. Cut tough ends off broccoli stalks. Peel stalks with a vegetable peeler or paring knife up to the florets. Cut each head of broccoli lengthwise into three or more spears, depending on thickness of the stalk. (Cut stalks should be no more than 1/2 inch thick at their widest point.)

2. Blanch the broccoli spears in a large pot of boiling salted water for 3 minutes, then drain in a colander, reserving 1/2 cup of the cooking liquid if not using chicken stock.

3. In a wide skillet heat the olive oil over medium heat. Whack the garlic cloves with the flat side of a knife and toss into the oil. Cook, shaking pan, until lightly brown, about 2 minutes. Add broccoli and season lightly with salt and the crushed red pepper. Turn broccoli in oil until coated. Pour in stock or water, cover skillet tightly and cook until tender, about 8 minutes, adding a few tablespoons of stock if liquid evaporates. Taste and correct seasoning, then serve immediately.

GRISSINI—HOMEMADE ITALIAN BREAD STICKS—MAKES 16

These are fun to make and so much better than store-bought.

1 cup lukewarm milk (105°F.)
1 package active dry yeast
1 tablespoon sugar
4 tablespoons unsalted butter, room temperature
1 teaspoon salt
1 egg white
about 2 1/2 cups all-purpose flour, less 2 tablespoons to start

Egg wash:

2 large egg yolks mixed with 2 tablespoons water
coarse salt, poppy seeds and/or sesame seeds

1. Fill bowl of an electric mixer with very hot water for about 5 minutes, then drain and dry. Put milk in the warmed bowl. Slowly mix in the yeast and sugar. Cover and let proof 5 minutes. Mixture will bubble up to prove it is active.

2. Add the softened butter, salt and egg white. Mix well. Using the dough hook if you have one, on low speed gradually add the flour, beating thoroughly between each addition of flour. Then beat dough 5 minutes. Add enough additional flour to make the dough just barely firm enough to handle (it should not be too stiff.) Turn out onto a lightly floured work surface and knead for about 5 minutes, or until smooth.

3. Preheat oven to 425°F.

4. Shape dough into 16 bread sticks, 1 1/2" x 7", by rolling into strips between lightly floured hands. On 2 parchment lined baking sheets sprinkled with a light coat of flour, arrange the breadsticks about 1 inch apart. Brush with egg wash and sprinkle with coarse salt, poppy seeds or sesame seeds. Cover and let rise 15 minutes.

5. Bake for 10 minutes, then lower oven temperature to 350°F. and bake another 5 to 10 minutes, or until sticks are golden brown. Remove to wire rack to cool. Can make a day ahead and store in airtight container.

VANILLA PANNA COTTA WITH VELVETY CHOCOLATE SAUCE
MAKES 8

A classic Italian dessert with a wonderful mouth-feel. You can use the chocolate sauce over ice cream or fresh berries as well.

3 tablespoons water
1 tablespoon powdered gelatin (Knox)

4 cups heavy cream
1/2 vanilla bean, split lengthwise
1/2 cup sugar

Velvety Chocolate Sauce:

1 ounce unsweetened chocolate, chopped in processor
5 ounces semisweet chocolate, chopped in processor
1/4 cup <u>each</u> light corn syrup and hot water
1/2 cup heavy cream or more

fresh raspberries, blueberries, blackberries or
    <u>strawberries</u>

1. <u>Make panna cottas</u>: In a small bowl combine the water and gelatin and let soak about
5 minutes.

2. Meanwhile, in a medium saucepan, heat the cream, vanilla bean and sugar to a simmer over medium heat, stirring occasionally to dissolve sugar. As soon as it simmers, turn off the heat and add the gelatin mixture, stirring to dissolve gelatin. If gelatin doesn't completely dissolve in 3 minutes, return mixture to the heat and warm gently until dissolved. Pour the mixture into 8 ramekins or custard cups and chill, uncovered, 2 hours, or overnight, in which case cover them.

3. <u>Make the Chocolate Sauce</u>: In the top of a double boiler, combine the two chocolates over simmering water, stirring constantly until melted, then whisk in the corn syrup and water without removing double boiler from the heat. Whisk until smooth and shiny. Remove from heat and stir in heavy cream until mixture is to your desired consistency and taste. Can make up to 24 hours in advance, refrigerate and rewarm carefully in microwave when ready to use.

4. When ready to serve, place chocolate sauce into a squirt bottle and decorate the plate in a Jackson Pollack style (splash on creatively). Run a knife around the edge of each ramekin and unmold onto plate. If panna cotta sticks, dip ramekin in very hot water for 10 seconds, then turn out onto plate. Squirt on more chocolate, then garnish with berries and serve.

UNDER THE TUSCAN SUN

Polenta Triangles With Red Pepper Purée
Tuscan Pot Roast
Wild Mushroom Lasagna
Chocolate Hazelnut Semifreddo

POLENTA TRIANGLES WITH RED PEPPER PURÉE—SERVES 8 ⏲ 🍳 🍳

A very special presentation.

Polenta:

1/2 cup onions, finely chopped
2 tablespoons extra virgin olive oil
3 cups chicken stock (homemade or boxed, low sodium)
2 cups water
1 1/3 cups yellow cornmeal
2 tablespoons freshly grated Parmesan cheese
1/2 teaspoon salt, or to taste

Red Pepper Purée:

5 to 6 fresh red peppers
1 tablespoon fresh lemon juice
1/2 teaspoon salt
1/8 teaspoon cayenne pepper
2 tablespoons chopped fresh basil or Italian parsley
  leaves
2 tablespoons olive oil

Garnish: fresh basil or parsley sprigs

1. Make polenta: In a 5-quart saucepan combine onion and olive oil and cook until the onion is tender but not brown, about 5 minutes. Stir in the chicken stock. In a separate bowl combine the water and cornmeal. Stir this into the stock and cook, stirring, until the mixture is thick and boils, about 10 minutes. Add Parmesan cheese and salt.

2. Line two 8" x 8" or 9" x 9" square baking pans with heavy-duty foil and spray with olive oil cooking spray. Pour the polenta evenly into the pans and spread into a smooth layer with an offset spatula. Refrigerate until cold and firm, about 2 hours or up to overnight. Turn polenta out of the pan onto a work surface and peel off foil. Cut into 16 triangles, total.

3. Preheat oven to 425°F. Spray a baking sheet with olive oil cooking spray generously and arrange the triangles on the sheet without touching. Bake until browned on bottom, about 30 minutes, then turn them and bake another 15 minutes until browned and crisp. If you want them extra-crisp and brown, turn on the broiler the last few minutes.

4. Make the pepper purée: While the polenta is baking, cut each pepper in half and discard ribs and seeds. Place on a baking sheet and broil until skin is completely blackened, or you can put them on your outdoor grill on High heat. Place blackened peppers in a paper or plastic bag for 15 minutes to steam, then remove from bag and peel off skins. Reserve 1 pepper, cut into strips, for garnish. Cut rest of peppers into cubes and place in food processor with the lemon juice and cayenne and process until smooth. Reserve.

5. When ready to serve: Place 3 to 4 tablespoons of the red pepper purée on individual plates, then arrange two triangles on top, and garnish with a pepper strip. Sprinkle with chopped basil or parsley and drizzle with olive oil. Serve warm or at room temperature.

TUSCAN POT ROAST—SERVES 8

This dish is best served as soon as it has rested, although it does make divine sandwiches later on.

1 tablespoon chopped fresh rosemary leaves
2 strips lemon zest, minced
2 cloves garlic, peeled and coarsely chopped
coarse salt and freshly ground black pepper
2 pound beef rump roast, in one piece
1/4 cup extra virgin olive oil
1 teaspoon Dijon mustard
1 cup dry red wine
2 to 3 cups beef stock—one puck of More Than
    Gourmet glace de viande, reconstituted in 3 cups
    <u>boiling water, or boxed stock</u>

1. On a cutting board mince together the rosemary, lemon zest and garlic. Season with salt and pepper. Using a long sharp knife, make 3 to 4 holes right through the meat. Push the seasoning mixture into the meat with the handle of a wooden spoon.

2. Put oil in a heavy Dutch oven and heat on high heat. Brown the meat on all sides, about 10 minutes.

3. In a medium bowl, stir the mustard into the wine and stock and add to the Dutch oven. Season with salt. Lower heat to medium and continue to cook, covered, turning the meat often, so that each side of the meat is immersed in the bubbling liquid. Cooking time will be determined by the size of the roast, about 22 to 25 minutes per pound, and when the internal temperature of the meat when taken with an instant-read thermometer is 145°F. for rare, 150°F. for medium to 155°F. for well done. Remove meat to carving board and cover with foil to rest for 15 minutes.

4. Adjust seasoning for the sauce in the Dutch oven, reducing to thicken if needed.

5. Slice meat very thin and serve with the gravy spooned over it.

WILD MUSHROOM LASAGNA
SERVES 8 TO 10

An outstanding take on a traditional lasagna, and it can be made ahead!

Béchamel Sauce:

6 tablespoons <u>each</u> unsalted butter and flour
3 cups whole milk, <u>warmed</u>
salt and pepper to taste

3 tablespoons extra virgin olive oil
1 pound Portobello mushrooms, with optional
    1/2-ounce package dried porcini mushrooms,
reconstituted in boiling water, drained, then coarsely
    chopped
3 cloves garlic, crushed
1 teaspoon dried thyme or 1 tablespoon fresh thyme
    leaves

3 tablespoons unsalted butter
1 cup fresh breadcrumbs (whirl white bread, crusts
    removed, in processor until fine)

3 sheets, about 1 pound, fresh pasta, available at Italian
    groceries OR l pound of dried lasagna noodles

1 1/2 cups freshly grated Parmiggiano Reggiano cheese,
    <u>divided into three 1/2 cup measures</u>

1. <u>Make the Béchamel sauce</u>: In a large saucepan, melt the butter. Whisk in the flour and continue to cook on medium until bubbly. Whisk in the warm milk and salt and pepper to make a medium white sauce, cooking until it comes to a boil and thickens. Adjust salt and pepper. Reserve.

2. In a large skillet heat the olive oil and sauté the chopped Portobello mushrooms. Add the porcini mushrooms if you are using them. Stir in the garlic and thyme, taste and adjust seasonings. Reserve.

3. Butter a 9" x 13" ovenproof casserole and reserve. In a large skillet melt the 3 tablespoons butter. Add the breadcrumbs and stir to coat. Remove to bowl and reserve.

4. Bring a large pot of heavily salted water to a rolling boil and place the sheets of fresh or dried pasta in pot and cook until just done, al dente (literally meaning with a little bite to the tooth), then remove from water with a large Chinese strainer and drain well. Run cold water over pasta and reserve.

5. <u>Assemble the Lasagna</u>: Place a layer of the Béchamel sauce on the bottom of the buttered casserole. Add a layer of cooked pasta, then a layer of the Béchamel, then a layer of the sautéed mushrooms, and 1/2 cup of the grated cheese. Next, place another layer of cooked pasta down, and spoon on another layer of Béchamel, then mushrooms, then another 1/2 cup of the cheese. Lay down the last layer of pasta over the cheese, add Béchamel, the last mushrooms, and last 1/2 cup of cheese, then the reserved buttered breadcrumbs. You can prepare the casserole to this point and refrigerate it, covered, or bake right away in a preheated 350°F. oven for about 30 minutes. If refrigerated, bake longer, until heated all the way through. Either way, take out of oven and let rest 10 minutes, for easier cutting. Cut into squares to serve.

CHOCOLATE HAZELNUT SEMIFREDDO
SERVES 10 TO 12

The term semifreddo means half-frozen, but you can translate it as fabulous!

cooking spray
4 large eggs
1/4 cup granulated sugar
3/4 cup Nutella (chocolate-hazelnut spread), warmed slightly (in microwave for 5 seconds at high power, or on Low on stovetop) <u>DIVIDED</u> into 1/2 cup and 1/4 cup
1 cup heavy whipping cream, whipped to medium peaks and reserved in refrigerator
1/2 cup hazelnuts, toasted, skins removed and coarsely chopped

Garnish: chocolate curls made with a block of chocolate <u>and a potato peeler, and mint leaves</u>

1. Spray a 9" x 5" glass or metal loaf pan with non-stick cooking spray. Line the pan with plastic wrap, letting the wrap extend beyond the short sides of the pan.

2. Place the eggs and sugar in the bowl of an electric mixer and whisk to blend. Place the mixing bowl over a pot of just simmering water, not letting the bottom of the bowl touch the water. Whisk constantly, beating until the eggs are just warm, about 2 minutes.

3. Place the bowl in the mixer stand, and using the whisk attachment, whip eggs on high speed until pale and tripled in volume, about 7 minutes. Add the 1/2 cup of Nutella and mix on low speed until blended. Gently by hand fold in the whipped cream and chopped hazelnuts. Scrape the mixture into the prepared pan.

4. Spoon the remaining 1/4 cup of Nutella lengthwise down the center of the pan, letting it sink into the semifreddo. Cover the top of the pan with plastic wrap and freeze for at least 4 hours, or overnight, until firm.

5. <u>To serve</u>: Unmold semifreddo from loaf pan by turning upside down onto a platter and pulling on the plastic wrap. It should drop right out. Let sit at room temperature for 15 minutes or so, then use a long sharp knife to cut 3/4 inch slices of the semifreddo and place on dessert plates. Garnish with chocolate curls and mint sprigs, if desired.

NORTHERN ITALIAN CUISINE

Chicken Liver and Sage Spiedini
Pici with Simple Red Sauce
Salad with Prosciutto and Parmiggiano
Reggiano in a Balsamic Vinaigrette
Fruit Crostata

CHICKEN LIVER AND SAGE SPIEDINI
(PRONOUNCED SPYDEENEE)
SERVES 8

Don't dismiss this recipe because of "fear of liver". It is outstanding and worth pushing your culinary boundaries for a new taste sensation!

1 pound chicken livers, washed and cut in half, about 24 to 30 pieces
acidulated water (cold water with juice from one lemon, halved)

6 to 8 slices bacon, cut into about 24 pieces
3 tablespoons unsalted butter
24 medium mushroom caps, cleaned

6 tablespoons unsalted butter (to sauté livers)

3 tablespoons unsalted butter
about 12 slices Italian-style bread, 1/4-inch thick, ends cut off, cut into 1 inch squares, toasted
24 fresh sage leaves, OR if not available, 1 teaspoon dry sage (sprinkle over livers before sautéing)
wooden skewers, soaked in cold water for 10 minutes
salt and freshly ground black pepper
breadcrumbs

Optional: 8 slices buttered toast to serve under skewers

1. Soak livers in acidulated water (water with fresh lemon juice squeezed into it) for 1 hour.

2. Cut bacon into 2-inch pieces and sauté until almost crisp. Drain and make a hole in each piece with a skewer while still hot, or bacon will split when assembling skewers. Reserve bacon drippings in the sauté pan.

3. In a medium saucepan cook the mushroom caps in 3 tablespoons of the butter and a bit of salt and pepper for 5 minutes over medium heat. Drain, reserving pan juices.

4. Melt 6 tablespoons butter in a large frying pan. Drain the livers, pat dry and sauté them over high heat for 5 minutes. Remove livers, add the mushroom liquid and remaining 3 tablespoons butter and bacon drippings to the pan and tilt and scrape with a wooden spoon to deglaze, then remove pan from heat. Quickly dip the squares of bread into this sauce.

5. Assemble skewers (spiedini): Alternately thread pieces of liver, sage leaves, bacon, mushrooms and toasted bread cubes on 8 to 10 skewers. Dust lightly with breadcrumbs, salt and pepper. Place in a shallow baking dish and pour the remaining pan juices, if any, and the remaining butter, melted, on top, and place under a broiler flame until well browned. Place one skewer on 8 individual plates, on a slice of buttered toast if desired, spoon over any pan juices and serve at once.

PICI WITH SIMPLE RED SAUCE
SERVES 8 TO 10

Get your friends together and have a party making this hand-rolled pasta. This pasta recipe represents peasant cooking, "la cucina povera", as it doesn't use eggs (which were expensive) in the mixture. I have fond memories of making this dish with a travel group in a Tuscan kitchen a few years ago.

Pici (Pronounced peachy) Pasta-Makes 1 1/2 pounds:

3 1/4 cups plus 2 tablespoons (500 grams) Italian Type 00 flour OR unbleached all-purpose flour (Find the Type 00 flour at Italian specialty stores)
1 cup water
1/3 cup extra virgin olive oil
1/2 teaspoon salt
Wondra flour

Sauce:

8 slices pancetta (Italian bacon)
3 medium onions, chopped

3 to 4 cloves fresh garlic, chopped

2 tablespoons olive oil

chopped fresh thyme, oregano, basil, and dried
pepperoncini, to taste

8 to 10 fresh tomatoes, skins removed (see Step #3),
chopped coarsely

1 cup Half and Half or coffee cream

1 6-ounce can tomato paste, to thicken sauce

1 tablespoon sugar, to balance bitterness if needed

Garnish: grated Parmiggiano Reggiano cheese

1. Make the pasta dough: Put all dough ingredients
in the bowl of an electric mixer and using the paddle
attachment mix until the dough comes together. Change
to the dough hook and knead for 5 minutes at medium
speed. The dough should be silky smooth and resilient.
Set it on a lightly floured work surface, flatten with your
palm, oil the top with some more olive oil and wrap in
plastic wrap. Cover with a damp towel and let rest for at
least 1/2 hour. (Can refrigerate for up to 5 days.)

2. When ready to make pici, cut dough into 1/2-ounce
pieces, about the size of a quarter, then stretch and roll
each piece into long snake-like pieces, 1/8 inch thick
in diameter and about 15 inches long, using Wondra
flour on the work surface, as it doesn't clump, and place
on Wondra-sprinkled cookie sheets. Cover with thin
kitchen towels. This process will take some time, so it's
fun to make this with family or friends. Or you can make
just enough for one meal and keep dough refrigerated,
covered, for another session later on, up to 5 days later.

3. Make the sauce: Cut an x in the bottom of each fresh
tomato. Bring a pot of water to a boil and drop tomatoes
in for about 30 seconds, or until peel starts to come off.
Immediately remove from water and run under cold
water, and use a knife to remove skin and stems. Chop
coarsely. Reserve.

4. In a large skillet heat the olive oil and sauté the
pancetta until crisp. Remove, drain and crumble. Reserve.
In same skillet sauté the onions in the olive oil for
about 5 minutes, then add the garlic and sauté briefly.
Add the chopped tomatoes and herbs, the cream and
tomato paste and continue to cook until sauce is a fairly
thick consistency. If too thick add a few tablespoons of
water you are using to cook the pici. Add the crumbled
pancetta just before serving, to keep it crisp. Taste and
add salt and pepper if needed. (Leftover sauce reheats
very well.)

5. When ready to serve, bring a large pot of salted water
to a boil and add half the pici. Cook al dente (still some
resistance to the tooth) and drain. Add the second half
of the pici to the water and cook. Add one half of the
sauce to the pici in a large bowl and mix well. Serve rest
of sauce in another bowl. Pass a bowl of grated cheese to
happy guests.

PROSCIUTTO AND PARMIGGIANO REGGIANO SALAD WITH BALSAMIC VINAIGRETTE
SERVES 8

*The success of this simple but delicious salad depends on
the quality and freshness of your ingredients. Splurge and
buy the best quality you can find—it will be worth it.*

1 12-ounce package arugula

1 head of radiccio

8 very thin slices or more (depending on your budget)
of Prosciutto de Parma

shavings of Parmiggiano Reggiano cheese, from a
room-temperature chunk, using a potato peeler

Dressing:

extra virgin olive oil

balsamic vinegar

salt and freshly grated black pepper

1. On individual plates build salads, starting with a bed of
the arugula, torn leaves of the radiccio, and then cutting
each slice of prosciutto into halves or thirds, arranging it
on the greens, then laying shavings (made with a potato
peeler) of the Parmesan over that. Drizzle with olive oil
and balsamic vinegar and salt and a grinding of fresh
black pepper. Serve right away.

FRUIT CROSTATA—MAKES 2

Easy and impressive—I like to have several crusts in the freezer to be ready to make a quick dessert for spontaneous gatherings.

Dough:

2 cups all-purpose flour
1/4 cup granulated sugar
1/2 teaspoon kosher salt
1 cup (2 sticks) cold unsalted butter, diced
6 tablespoons (3 ounces) ice water

Filling:

2 cups best quality chunky preserves or jam, your choice
    of fruit—cherry, peach, apricot, raspberry—a great
    <u>brand is St. Dalfour Golden Peach made in France</u>

1. <u>Make the dough</u>: In the bowl of a food processor place the flour, sugar and salt. Pulse a few times to combine. Add the cubed butter and toss quickly with your fingers (being careful of the blade) to coat each cube of butter with flour. Pulse 12 to 15 times, or until butter is the size of peas. With the motor running add the ice water all at once through the feed tube. Keep hitting the pulse button to combine, but stop the machine just when the dough comes together. Turn dough out onto a well-floured board, roll it into a ball, cut it in half and form it into 2 flat disks. Wrap the disks in plastic wrap and refrigerate for at least one hour. If you only want to make one crostata, the other disk can be frozen, well wrapped.

2. When ready to bake crostatas, preheat the oven to 400°F. Line 2 baking sheets or pizza pans with parchment paper. Roll each disk into an 11-inch circle on a lightly floured surface. Transfer to the baking sheets. Spread the preserves on the dough, leaving a 1 1/2 inch border. Gently fold the border of pastry over the filling, pleating it to make a rustic edge, leaving the center open to show the jam. Bake crostata for about 40 minutes, or until crust is golden brown. Remove to racks to cool, leaving parchment paper on. There will be some leakage of the filling—don't worry about it. When cool enough to cut, cut into wedges and serve warm or at room temperature, leaving paper on the baking sheet.

ITALIAN IMMIGRANT COOKING

Many Italians immigrated to the United States in the late 1800s and early 1900s in search of a better life. We are richer for their contributions to our cuisine. You'll love this menu.

> Chicken Cacciatore
> Patate Arroste
> Tomato Salad Neapolitan Style
> Cannoli

CHICKEN CACCIATORE—SERVES 8

This recipe freezes beautifully. The cooking term julienne means to cut into long thin strips.

5 pound whole chicken, cut into 10 to 12 pieces
1 cup all purpose flour
1/4 cup olive oil, or more as needed

1 cup <u>each</u> chopped onions, quartered mushrooms,
    julienned carrots and julienned green pepper
2 tablespoons minced fresh garlic
2 15-ounce cans chopped tomatoes with their juice
1 6-ounce can tomato paste
3/4 cup Marsala wine or dry red wine
1 teaspoon <u>each</u> dried oregano and dried basil
1 1/2 teaspoons salt
1 teaspoon black pepper
<u>freshly grated Parmesan cheese</u>

1. Heat a large deep skillet (or use two if you don't have a large one), add oil and heat. Season the flour with the salt and pepper and roll and coat each chicken piece in the flour, then brown each piece on all sides to a golden brown, in two batches. Drain chicken on paper towels.

2. In the same skillet sauté the onions, mushrooms, carrots, green pepper and garlic for 5 minutes. Add the tomatoes and tomato paste and sauté for another 5 minutes. Add the wine, herbs, salt and pepper and cook over medium heat for another 5 minutes.

3. Return the chicken pieces back to the skillet and mix well with the sauce. Turn heat down to very low and

simmer, covered, for 1 hour. Adjust the salt and pepper to taste. Serve with some freshly grated cheese and warm Italian bread to dip in the sauce.

PATATE ARROSTE-COUNTRY-STYLE ROASTED POTATOES—SERVES 8

A standard at our house!

3 pounds Idaho (Russet) potatoes, peeled and thickly sliced
1 1/2 large heads garlic, unpeeled, cloves separated (this is not a typo error—the garlic mellows as it cooks
1 white onion, thinly sliced

1 teaspoon salt
1/2 teaspoon black pepper
2 tablespoons chopped fresh rosemary, or 2 teaspoons dried
7 tablespoons olive oil

1. Preheat oven to 425°F.

2. Place the potatoes and garlic in a large pot and cover with cold water. Bring to a boil, reduce heat to medium and cook for 5 to 7 minutes. Potatoes should still be a bit hard. Drain. Transfer the garlic cloves to a measuring cup of cold water. When they are cool enough to handle, peel by cutting off a bit at the root end and squeezing them out of their skins.

3. Place the potatoes, garlic and onions in a large bowl. Sprinkle with salt, pepper, rosemary and 5 tablespoons of the olive oil and mix well. Grease the bottom of a large baking sheet with 2 more tablespoons of the olive oil and place the potatoes, garlic and sliced onions on the sheet and roast for 20 minutes, turning once and adding the rest of the olive oil. If you like them extra crispy, roast for 10 minutes or so more.

TOMATO SALAD NEAPOLITAN STYLE
SERVES 8

Wonderful when tomato season provides the flavorful fruit. You did know that tomatoes are classified as fruit, didn't you…

6 large fresh tomatoes
1/2 red onion, peeled
1 yellow onion, peeled
2 cucumbers, peeled

Dressing:

1 cup extra virgin olive oil
1/4 cup imported red wine vinegar
1 teaspoon sugar
1 tablespoon minced garlic
2 teaspoons chopped fresh oregano, or 1 teaspoon dried
salt and black pepper to taste
1 head romaine lettuce, coarsely sliced

Garnish: 4 large hardboiled eggs, sliced

1. Cut the tomatoes and onions into small wedges. Take the onion layers apart. Place tomatoes and onions in a large bowl. Dice the cucumbers and add to the mixture. Toss well.

2. Make the dressing: In a medium bowl whisk the vinegar, sugar, garlic, oregano, salt and pepper. Whisk in the olive oil slowly. Pour over chopped salad. Marinate for 1 hour up to overnight in the refrigerator.

3. When ready to serve, make a bed of the romaine lettuce on a serving platter. Arrange the marinated tomato salad over lettuce, and garnish with slices of the hardboiled egg.

CANNOLI—MAKES 16 OR MORE

Thin (7/8-inch diameter) cannoli molds are available from Lehman's Hardware in Amish country in Ohio. You can order them online. But I prefer 1 1/4-inch in diameter molds, which are difficult to find but make a much bigger cannoli that is easier to fill. If you or someone you know is handy, like my wonderfully talented handyman, Fred Moore, you can get the job done. Buy 1 1/4-inch chrome-plated brass extension tubes from the plumbing department of a hardware store such as Lowe's, which will be 12 inches long with some threads at one end. With a pipe cutter cut off this end, and then cut the pipe into 2 1/2-inch long cannoli molds. File the cut end with sandpaper to smooth sharp edges, and you'll have perfect large cannoli molds to use over and over again.

Pastry:

2 cups all-purpose flour
2 tablespoons solid Crisco
1 teaspoon sugar
1/4 teaspoon salt
3/4 cup (6 ounces) Marsala wine (or 1/2 cup Madeira
    mixed with 1/4 cup water)
Crisco solid shortening for frying shells
1 egg white (to seal shells before frying)
confectioners' sugar, to dust finished pastries

Filling:

1 1/2 pounds Ricotta cheese
1 cup confectioners' sugar
1/4 teaspoon <u>each</u> cinnamon and vanilla
1/2 cup each mini chocolate chips and maraschino
    <u>cherries, chopped and drained</u>

1. <u>Make the pastry</u>: In the bowl of a food processor, combine flour, Crisco, sugar and salt. Mix, then gradually add the wine and blend well until a ball of dough forms. Cut the ball in two and work with one half at a time. Lightly flour a flat surface and roll one half of the dough into a thin sheet, about 1/8 inch thick. Cut into 4-inch squares, using a dough scraper to remove squares, and wrap each square around a cannoli form (see note above for sources) diagonally, overlapping the two points and sealing with a dab of egg white.

2. <u>Make Filling</u>: With a hand mixer whip the Ricotta, confectioners' sugar, cinnamon and vanilla until smooth and creamy. Fold in the mini chocolate chips and well-drained maraschino cherries. Mixture will turn a light pink—very pretty. Refrigerate for at least one hour or up to overnight.

3. Meanwhile, heat Crisco solid oil in a deep fryer to 375°F. Drop 2 or 3 tubes at a time into the hot oil and fry shells, turning once or twice until they are golden brown. Using a slotted spoon transfer shells to a paper-towel lined plate to drain and cool slightly (1 to 2 minutes), then gently remove shells from their tubes. Repeat process until all shells are made. Reserve. Can make ahead and keep at room temperature in Tupperware for a day or two.

4. <u>When ready to serve</u>: Fill a pastry bag fitted with a fluted tip with the filling <u>half-way only</u>, so filling doesn't come out of the top of the pastry bag. Fill each shell with about 1/4 cup filling, and sprinkle with some confectioners' sugar just before serving. These are best eaten soon after filling.

A TRATTORIA MENU

Ribollita
Risotto with Porcini Mushrooms
Grilled Sausages with Tricolor Peppers
Squash and Zucchini Tian
Tiramisù

RIBOLLITA—TUSCAN BEAN SOUP
SERVES 8 TO 10

This soup is justifiably famous as the perfect comfort food.

2 tablespoons olive oil, plus more for garnish
2 each medium-size stalks of celery and carrots, peeled and chopped
1 medium onion, chopped
1 medium zucchini (about 8 ounces), chopped
2 15-ounce cans white kidney beans (cannelloni) rinsed and drained
1/4 to 1/2 head of Savoy or regular cabbage, core removed and cabbage coarsely chopped
4 cloves garlic, peeled and chopped
1 tablespoon each chopped fresh parsley and basil
3 ounces fresh spinach, stems removed and coarsely chopped
1 15-ounce can diced tomatoes with their juice
6 cups chicken stock
salt and pepper to taste
heel of a chunk of Parmiggiano Reggiano, plus grated Parmiggiano to garnish each bowl of soup

Garnish: slices of crusty Italian bread

1. In a 5-quart stockpot over medium-high heat, heat the olive oil. Cook the onions, carrots and celery until tender, about 10 minutes, then add the cabbage, garlic, fresh herbs, spinach, tomatoes, zucchini and chicken stock. Mash one can of the beans with a potato masher (to thicken stock) and add. Add salt and pepper to taste, along with the heel of the cheese, which adds a wonderful depth of flavor to the soup. Bring to a boil, lower heat and simmer for about 1 hour for flavors to marry.

2. Add the other can of drained beans and heat until warmed, or you can refrigerate and reheat the next day.

Garnish each bowl with some good Parmesan cheese and a drizzle of olive oil and serve with slices of the bread.

WILD MUSHROOM RISOTTO
SERVES 8

Star Chef Wolfgang Puck's no-fail recipe is faster than the classic risotto, but doesn't lose flavor or texture.

7 or more cups chicken stock (homemade if you can) or good-quality broth
1/2 pound wild mushrooms—cremini, Portobello, shiitake or oyster, stems reserved, cut bite-size
1/3 cup vegetable oil
1 large onion, peeled and chopped
1 large garlic clove, peeled and minced
2 cups Arborio rice (this type of rice should not be washed)
1 cup dry white wine
3 tablespoons extra virgin olive oil
4 tablespoons (1/2 stick) unsalted butter, chilled and cut into small pieces
1/2 cup good quality grated Parmesan cheese
1 tablespoon chopped Italian (flatleaf) parsley
salt and freshly ground black pepper to taste

1. Put stock into a saucepan and add the reserved mushroom stems. Bring to a boil, reduce heat to maintain a bare simmer.

2. In a heavy medium saucepan heat the oil over medium-high heat and add the onions and garlic. Sauté stirring constantly with a wooden spoon just until softened, 3 to 4 minutes. Add the Arborio rice and continue to stir for 1 to 2 minutes more, until the rice is thoroughly coated with the oil.

3. Add the white wine and cook, stirring frequently, until the rice has absorbed the liquid. Pour in enough of the hot stock to cover the rice, about 3 cups, and continue to cook, stirring frequently, until all the liquid has been absorbed, about 15 minutes.

4. Meanwhile, in a medium skillet, heat the olive oil over medium-high heat and add the mushrooms. Sauté just until mushrooms have softened, 3 to 4 minutes. Reserve.

5. Pour 3 more cups of the hot stock into the rice, raise the heat to high and continue to cook, stirring frequently, until rice is almost al dente, tender but still fairly chewy, about 15 minutes more. Stir in the mushrooms. Stir in enough of the remaining stock to make the risotto creamy but not runny. Remove the risotto from the heat and, with a wooden spoon, vigorously beat in the chilled butter and 1/4 cup of the Parmesan cheese until completely incorporated. Stir in the parsley and season with salt and pepper to taste. Pour into serving bowl and serve immediately, passing the remaining 1/4 cup Parmesan.

GRILLED SAUSAGES WITH TRICOLOR PEPPERS AND ONIONS—SERVES 8

A fast meal with no compromises on flavor!

2 pounds sweet or hot (or a combination of both) Italian
　　sausages
2 tablespoons extra virgin olive oil
1 <u>each</u> large red, green and yellow pepper, seeded and
　　sliced into 1/4-inch strips
1 large onion, thinly sliced
1 teaspoon <u>each</u> dried oregano and thyme, OR 2
　　teaspoons mixed Italian seasoning
<u>salt and freshly ground black pepper to taste</u>

1. Grill sausages on an outdoor grill, OR broil them in the oven, OR you can cook them in a skillet on top of the stove with 1 cup of water, bringing to a boil, then covering until done. Whatever method you use, test doneness of sausages by cutting into the center of one sausage to be sure it is no longer pink. Cut on the diagonal into 1 inch pieces, and reserve.

2. Meanwhile, in a large skillet place the olive oil and add the peppers, onions, dried herbs, salt and pepper and sauté until peppers are golden and onion is soft. Stir in the sausages, mix well and serve hot. This dish rewarms well.

SQUASH AND ZUCCHINI TIAN—SERVES 8

Wonderful when squash is in season.

2 <u>each</u> yellow squash and green zucchini, about 2
　　pounds total, cut into 1/4-inch pieces on the
　　diagonal
1 cup fresh breadcrumbs (whirl fresh torn pieces sturdy
　　white bread such as Pepperidge Farm in processor)
2/3 cup <u>each</u> grated mozzarella and Asiago cheese
1/4 cup <u>each</u> minced fresh parsley and basil leaves
zest of 1 small lemon
1/8 teaspoon black pepper
1 teaspoon salt
<u>4 to 5 tablespoons extra virgin olive oil, DIVIDED, plus</u>
　　<u>extra to oil casserole</u>

1. Preheat oven to 350°F. Oil a 9" x 13"ovenproof casserole with olive oil.

2. In a medium bowl mix together the breadcrumbs, cheeses, herbs, zest and salt and pepper with 1 tablespoon olive oil.

3. In a large bowl toss the squash and zucchini with 2 tablespoons of the olive oil.

4. Sprinkle the greased casserole with 1/2 cup of the crumb mixture. Shingle the squash and zucchini in a circular pattern in one layer, then cover the 1/2 cup of the crumb mixture. Make another layer of the squash and zucchini as above and sprinkle with 1/2 cup more of the crumb mixture. Continue making another layer until all vegetables are used. Sprinkle any remaining breadcrumb mixture on top, then drizzle with more olive oil.

5. Bake in a preheated 375°F. oven for about 45 to 55 minutes, until browned on top. Cool for about 6 to 8 minutes, then cut into equal portions and serve.

TIRAMISÙ—SERVES 8 TO 10

Literally translated as "Lift me up" or "Pick me up." If you cannot find mascarpone cheese, you can substitute 1/2 pound ricotta cheese mixed with 1 cup heavy cream, and a tablespoon of sugar, blending in a food processor until a light cream forms. Be aware that this recipe uses raw eggs. If this is a concern for you, substitute pasteurized eggs, which are widely available at supermarkets today.

1 cup strong espresso coffee, cooled, or strong regular coffee, cooled
2 tablespoons Amaretto, Frangelica or brandy
24 Italian ladyfingers (Savoiardi crisp biscuits)

6 large eggs, <u>separated</u> into yolks and whites
7 tablespoons sugar
1 pound marscarpone cheese, at room temperature
4 ounces bittersweet or semisweet chocolate, chopped coarsely
<u>2 to 3 tablespoons Dutch process cocoa</u>

1. Mix the espresso and liquor of your choice and dip 1/2 of the ladyfingers into this mixture. Layer these on the bottom of a 9" x 13" rectangular ceramic casserole.

2. In a mixer, beat the egg yolks at low speed. Add sugar and beat on high speed until airy. Add mascarpone cheese one tablespoon at a time slowly until the mixture thickens slightly. Do not overbeat. In another bowl whip the egg whites until stiff and gently fold them into the mascarpone mixture.

3. Spread 1/2 of this mixture on the ladyfinger layer evenly, then sprinkle with the 4 ounces of chopped chocolate.

4. Dip the remaining 12 ladyfingers into the espresso mixture and arrange them over the top. Spread the remaining mascarpone mixture over this evenly over the top and then sprinkle with the cocoa.

5. Cover with aluminum foil and refrigerate for at least 1 hour or up to overnight before cutting into squares and serving. Enjoy!

PASTA AND PIZZA PARTY TIME

Here are some essentials of Italian cooking you need to add to your cooking repertoire to round out your Italian experience.

Homemade Pasta
Classic Marinara Sauce
Open Raviolo with Wild Mushrooms
"Faux" Gnocchi
Pizza Two Ways

HOMEMADE PASTA ROLLED TWO WAYS
SERVES 8

It is much easier to roll out pasta if you have a pasta machine. They are fairly inexpensive, and if you purchase one you will find it's a snap to whip up a batch of homemade pasta. Remind your loved ones of this at birthday and holiday time…

4 large eggs
2 tablespoons olive oil
4 tablespoons cold water
<u>4 cups all-purpose flour</u>

1. <u>In Processor</u>: Break the eggs directly into the work bowl of the food processor fitted with the metal blade. Add the olive oil and water and blend lightly by turning the motor on and off twice. Add 1 cup of the flour, turn the motor on and let run 5 seconds nonstop. Add the remaining flour, reserving 1/2 cup (you may or may not need it depending on the conditions of the flour and how you've stored it) and buzz the motor for 10 seconds nonstop. The dough will churn into a ball and ride up on the processor's central spindle. Remove from processor, shape into 4 even round balls and set them aside on a lightly-floured board covered with a large bowl, turned upside down, for 40 minutes, to let the gluten in the dough rest. (Or, you can wrap and refrigerate balls, or freeze them.)

2. When dough has rested, make spaghetti or fettuccine noodles as follows:

3. <u>TO ROLL OUT DOUGH WITH PASTA MACHINE:</u>

Set the dial for the largest opening on machine. After inserting one ball of flattened dough, crank the machine and roll dough out. Fold like an envelope and roll 2 to 4 times more, adding a bit of flour if sticky, until dough becomes soft and flexible.

4. Set dial for next thickness and repeat rolling. Keep setting dial and rolling until you get to the thinnest setting, which will give you very thin pasta. This is the thickness I prefer. Experiment with your pasta maker to decide your personal preference.

5. Cut the pasta by using the cutting head to make spaghetti or fettuccine. As you cut each piece of pasta dough, toss it with flour, twirl it into a mound and place on kitchen towel-lined cookie sheets, or dry it on a pasta-drying rack. You can use the pasta immediately, dry it for use up to a week, or freeze it, wrapped well for up to one month. When you are ready to cook pasta, place it into a pot of boiling water. There is no need to defrost the frozen pasta. Homemade pasta cooks quickly.

6. TO ROLL PASTA BY HAND: Divide the dough into four balls, as above. Give one pasta ball a few slaps to flatten it, then roll it out on a lightly floured surface by pushing the rolling pin *away from you* rather than into the work surface. This will stretch the dough instead of compressing it. The dough should be rolled paper thin. This is hard work!

7. Cut the dough by lightly flouring it and then gently rolling each sheet of thin dough into a very loose tube. Cut across the tube with a sharp knife, to make strips as thin as you want them. Dry as above.

DOM'S MOM'S MARINARA SAUCE
MAKES 2 QUARTS

In addition to being a very funny comedian, Dom DeLuise was a gifted cook. Here is his mother's marinara sauce. Sun dried tomatoes add an intense and delicious flavor to this sauce. They come packed in olive oil, and can be very expensive, or packaged dry, which is a much better buy. To prepare and use them if purchased this way, put the whole package of dried tomatoes in 2 cups of water and bring to a boil in a large pot. Boil for a few minutes until tomatoes become soft. Cool, drain and put tomatoes in a jar and fill with olive oil. These keep indefinitely in the refrigerator and are a wonderful addition to many dishes.

4 tablespoons olive oil
5 garlic cloves, minced
2 28-ounce cans peeled Italian tomatoes (San Marzano is the premier brand), coarsely chopped, juice reserved, (or 5 pounds fresh tomatoes, peeled and sliced)
1 6-ounce can tomato paste
4 tablespoons sun-dried tomatoes, chopped (see note)
10 fresh basil leaves, or 1 teaspoon dried basil
1/2 teaspoon freshly ground pepper
1 teaspoon salt

grated Parmesan cheese

1 pound homemade or store-bought spaghetti

1. In a 4-quart Dutch oven or large pot, heat the olive oil and on medium heat gently sauté the garlic. Do not brown it, as it will impart a bitter taste to the sauce. Add the tomatoes, roughly chopped, the tomato paste and the sun-dried tomatoes. Chop basil leaves and add, or add dried basil if you are using it. Add salt and pepper to taste.

2. Cook on medium heat for 20 to 30 minutes, stirring occasionally and adding reserved juice from canned tomatoes gradually as needed.

3. Cook pasta al dente (still has some bite to the tooth). Drain and save some of the pasta cooking water to toss with pasta if it sits several minutes to "unstick" it. Serve with sauce. Pass the Parmesan cheese. Mama Mia!

OPEN RAVIOLO WITH WILD MUSHROOMS
SERVES 8 ⏱ 👨‍🍳 👨‍🍳 👨‍🍳

A restaurant quality dish that is both impressive and mouth watering.

1 pound homemade egg pasta dough (above)
12 ounces wild fresh mushrooms such as porcini or shitake, or use a mixture with domestic mushrooms added, or add some dried mushrooms, reconstituted in boiling water and drained, reserving soaking water
2 tomatoes, blanched, skinned, seeds removed, and chopped finely
2 shallots, peeled and chopped very fine
6 ounces (1 1/2 sticks) unsalted butter
1 cup chicken stock
salt and pepper to taste
1/2 cup mushroom juice (from dried mushrooms), or red or white wine

Garnish: julienned basil, black pepper

1. Roll out pasta to thinnest setting. Cut into 16 large squares with fluted cutter. Set onto parchment paper lined cookie sheets, dust with flour, cover with a towel and set aside.

2. Melt butter in large sauté pan and add shallots. Add sliced mushrooms and sauté for about 3 to 5 minutes. Taste and add salt and pepper. Add chicken stock and mushroom juice or wine to taste. Keep warm.

3. Cook pasta squares in a large pot of salted boiling water until very flexible but still al dente. Drain and arrange eight squares out flat on each of 8 plates.

4. Spoon mushroom-shallot mixture evenly onto squares with a slotted spoon. Bring juices in pan to a boil and add tomatoes and more butter if needed. Cover pasta squares and mushroom-shallot mixture with top square. Spoon tomatoes and sauce over sides and top of finished ravioli. Garnish with julienned basil and black pepper. Serve immediately.

"FAUX" GNOCCHI (PRONOUNCED NYAWKEE)
ALLA ROMANA—SERVES 8 TO 10 ⏱ 👨‍🍳 👨‍🍳

These are not the classic work-intensive potato and flour gnocchi, but rather polenta rounds napped (lightly covered) with melted butter and sprinkled with Parmesan cheese. They are ethereally light and delicious, and can be made ahead, then popped into the oven before company comes.

5 cups whole milk
1 teaspoon salt, grinds of black pepper
1 1/2 teaspoons dried sage, or more to taste
6 tablespoons unsalted butter, DIVIDED
1 cup cornmeal (Quaker is a good brand)
1/2 cup good-quality Parmesan cheese, freshly grated

1. In a 5-quart saucepan bring the milk to a boil over medium-high heat. Add the salt, pepper, sage and one tablespoon of the butter. Hold the cup of cornmeal in one hand and pour very slowly into the pot, stirring the milk rapidly with a long wooden spoon or a wire whisk. Lower heat to medium low and stir constantly, to minimize lumps, until cornmeal is absorbed. Don't worry about a few lumps, as it is almost impossible to avoid some. Continue stirring and whisking for 10 minutes. Mixture should be very smooth and quite thick. Wet a jellyroll pan (10" x 15") with cold water and pour the cornmeal mixture into it, smoothing the top with a wet knife. Refrigerate until completely cooled and quite firm.

2. Use one tablespoon of the butter to coat an oblong or oval ovenproof dish about 9" x 13". With a cookie cutter or small glass about 2 to 2 1/2 inches in diameter cut cornmeal into about 24 rounds. Make a row of gnocchi, slightly overlapping the edges horizontally. Fill in the center of the casserole with a row overlapping slightly over the first and so on until all the rounds have been used. Reserve scraps for a cook's treat.

3. Melt the remaining 4 tablespoons of butter in microwave or small saucepan and distribute evenly over gnocchi with small spoon. Sprinkle the Parmesan cheese evenly over top. At this point you can refrigerate up to overnight, covered with plastic wrap, or proceed to bake gnocchi.

4. When ready to bake, preheat oven to 375°F. and bake for about 30 minutes, or until golden and butter is bubbly. Remove from oven and let stand at least 5 minutes before serving. Gnocchi need to rest, as if they are still bubbling, they will be too soft to serve.

HOMEMADE PIZZA TWO WAYS

When Austrian chef Wolfgang Puck created "gourmet pizzas" in California in the 1970s, he started a revolution that everyone wanted to try at home. Following is a made-from-scratch pizza dough with great toppings, as well as a marvelous pizza made from a hot roll mix.

GOURMET MINI-PIZZAS WITH SMOKED CHICKEN, BACON, CARAMELIZED ONIONS AND HERBS—SERVES 4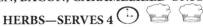

These pizzas can be made ahead up to the baking stage and held in the refrigerator for hours. Feel free to experiment with other toppings. Pizza stones, which are available at many cooking stores today, give your pizza a crispy crust and make crispy crusts on homemade bread too. After using a pizza stone, let it cool in the oven, as it gets incredibly hot and can break easily. A pizza peel sprinkled with cornmeal makes removing the baked pizza from the oven much easier.

Homemade Pizza Dough—Makes four 7 to 8-inch
    pizzas

1 package active dry yeast
1 teaspoon honey or sugar
3/4 cup warm water (110°F. to 115°F.)
2 3/4 cups all-purpose flour (approximately)
1 teaspoon salt
2 tablespoons olive oil (can add a drop of chili oil for
    flavor)

Toppings:

1 whole boneless, skinless smoked chicken breast from
    deli, or a marinated and grilled chicken breast,
    cubed into 1/2-inch cubes
6 ounces bacon, cut into 1-inch pieces

3/4 pound onions, thinly sliced
1 pound Mozzarella cheese
several good pinches thyme
black pepper

1. Make the dough: In a small bowl dissolve the yeast and honey in 1/4 cup of the warm water.

2. In a mixer bowl fitted with a dough hook, combine the flour and salt. Pour in 2 tablespoons of the oil and when absorbed, scrape in the dissolved yeast. Add the remaining water and knead on low speed about 5 minutes. If dough doesn't form a ball, add a bit more water.

3. Turn out onto a board and knead 2 to 3 minutes. Dough should be smooth and firm. Let rise in a warm spot, covered with a damp towel, about 30 minutes. (Dough will stretch when lightly pulled.)

4. Divide the dough into 4 balls, about 6 ounces each. Work each ball by pulling down the sides and tucking under the bottom of the ball. Repeat 4 or 5 times. Then on a smooth unfloured surface, roll the dough with the palm of your hand until the dough is smooth and firm, about 1 minute. Cover with a damp towel and let rest 15 to 20 minutes. At this point, the balls can be loosely covered with plastic wrap and refrigerated 1 to 2 days.

5. Prepare the toppings: To make the bacon and caramelized onions, sauté the bacon in a large skillet until crisp. Remove with a slotted spoon and set aside. Discard 1/2 of the bacon fat. In the remaining fat, cook the sliced onions over medium heat, stirring frequently, until wilted and golden, 20 to 25 minutes. Remove them with a slotted spoon and keep warm. Or, you can prepare them ahead and rewarm them briefly in microwave.

6. To Assemble the Mini-Pizzas: Preheat oven to 500°F. If you have a pizza stone, place in oven and preheat for at least 25 minutes. Or you can use a rimless baking sheet and just preheat the oven 10 minutes. Sprinkle with cornmeal.

7. Place each ball of dough on a lightly floured surface. Press down on the center, spreading the dough, or roll with a rolling pin, into a 7 to 8-inch circle, with the outer border a little thicker than the inner circle. Brush lightly with olive oil. When all balls are rolled out, arrange the

toppings as follows: first scatter the smoked chicken and bacon evenly over pizzas, then spread caramelized onions evenly over the top. Next, sprinkle on the grated cheese and top with the thyme and black pepper.

8. Sprinkle a pizza peel lightly with cornmeal, so pizzas won't stick, or you can use a large spatula. Place pizzas, one at a time, in hot oven. If you don't want to use a peel, just dust a cookie sheet, preferably rimless, with cornmeal. Bake 12 to 15 minutes, watching closely, as ovens vary. Remove pizzas from oven carefully (very hot!), cut in half and serve.

GIANT STUFFED PIZZA
SERVES 8 TO 10

The crust for this easy pizza uses a Hot Roll Mix available at the supermarket. With its ease of preparation and marvelous taste you'll be putting this one on the table for your family often!

Crust:

1 package Pillsbury Hot Roll Mix
1 cup hot tap water (110°F. to 115°F. when measured
    with an instant-read thermometer)
2 tablespoons unsalted butter, softened
1 large egg

Filling:

8 ounces bulk Italian sausage, hot or mild, your choice
1 cup (4 ounces) shredded provolone cheese
1/2 cup (2 1/2 ounces) sliced pepperoni, quartered
3/4 cup prepared pizza sauce
1 1/2 cups (6 ounces) shredded mozzarella cheese

Topping:

1 tablespoon <u>each</u> olive oil and chopped fresh rosemary
    (or 1 teaspoon dried rosemary)

<u>Crisco to grease a 12-inch pizza pan</u>

1. Grease the 12-inch pizza pan or large cookie sheet. Preheat oven to 400°F. if baking the pizzas right away.

2. In a large bowl, combine the hot roll flour mixture and yeast from the foil packet. Mix well. Stir in the hot water, butter and egg until the dough pulls away from the sides of the bowl. Turn the dough out onto a lightly floured surface and with greased or floured hands shape it into a ball. Knead dough 5 minutes or until smooth. Cover with the bowl and let rest 5 minutes.

3. In a medium skillet brown the sausage and drain.

4. Divide the dough in half. Roll one half into a 12-inch circle and fit it onto the prepared pizza pan. Top with the provolone, sausage, pepperoni, pizza sauce and mozzarella, in that order. Roll out the second half of the dough into a 12-inch circle and place over filling. Press edges together well to seal. Cut 3 slits in the top of the pizza to let steam escape when baking. Drizzle oil evenly over the top and sprinkle with the rosemary. At this point you can either bake right away for 18 to 28 minutes or until golden brown on top and bottom, OR refrigerate for several hours until ready to bake. Let stand 10 minutes before slicing and serving. Cut into 8 to 10 wedges.

COOK'S TIP

You will only get out of a recipe what you are willing to put into it, so use the BEST QUALITY ingredients you can afford. If the recipe calls for extra virgin olive oil, Parmiggiano-Reggiano cheese, aged balsamic vinegar from Modena or San Marzano tomatoes, use them and you will really see that *there is a difference.*

8

FRENCH CUISINE

I was newly married and teaching middle school French when Julia Child burst onto the American culinary scene. There was a French chef in the White House, Jacqueline Kennedy was charming the president of France, and French restaurants were mushrooming in New York City and other big cities across America. I cut my cooking teeth on Julia's iconic *Mastering the Art of French Cooking* and her ground-breaking PBS show *The French Chef,* and have been in love with this great cuisine ever since. In this chapter you will find the classic dishes that have continued to keep us coming back for more. As Julia would say, "Bon Appétit!" Menus include: French Brasserie Fare, An Homage to Julia Child, A French Meal from Provence, L' Amour, Toujours L' Amour—A Valentine's Day Meal, and Classic French Dishes.

Salade Niçoise (page 129)

FRENCH BRASSERIE FARE

Potage St. Germain—Green Pea Soup
Croque Monsieur
Salade Niçoise
Cherry Clafouti

POTAGE ST. GERMAIN-GREEN PEA SOUP
SERVES 8

Soup:

1/4 pound (1 stick) unsalted butter
1 leek, white part only, thoroughly rinsed of dirt,
    chopped
1 large onion, chopped coarsely
1 shallot, coarsely chopped
pinch of dried thyme
2 pounds fresh peas (in season) approximately 2 cups,
    OR 2 10-ounce boxes frozen baby peas
1 rib celery, chopped coarsely
1 carrot, chopped coarsely
1 to 2 potatoes, coarsely cubed
1 to 2 large cloves garlic, crushed
2 to 3 parsley stems or fresh mint stems (stems have the
    most flavor)
generous pinches or marjoram, allspice, cloves and
    sugar
freshly ground pepper to taste
1 quart (4 cups) chicken stock, preferably homemade or
    boxed
1/2 to 1 cup dry white wine
1 Honey Baked ham bone (or 1/4 pound bacon, sliced
    into 1-inch pieces, blanched and drained)
2 cups heavy cream (or less, to your taste)

Buttered Croutons

1 1/2 cups French bread, cut into 1/2-inch cubes
2 tablespoons unsalted butter, melted

1. Make the Soup: In a large stockpot (not Calphalon or
aluminum, as it can give the soup a bad taste) melt the
butter. Add the leeks, onion and shallot with a pinch of
thyme and cook 5 minutes on medium. Add the peas,
celery, carrots, potatoes and garlic, and cook 5 minutes
more.

2. Add chicken stock, ham bone, seasonings and wine.
Bring to a simmer and cook until the meat on the hock is
tender and the vegetables are quite soft, about 45 minutes.
Remove ham bone from pot. Carefully remove meat from
bone and discard bone. Return meat to the pot.

3. In blender, thoroughly blend soup in small batches,
being careful not to overload blender (it will splash up
and make a mess). Add heavy cream, reheat and serve.
(Or freeze without adding the cream. Defrost, bring to a
simmer and add cream right before serving.) Serve with
buttered croutons (see below).

4. Make the buttered croutons: In a bowl drizzle the
bread cubes with the melted butter, tossing them to coat
well. Place in a shallow baking dish lined with aluminum
foil and bake them in a preheated oven (350°F.), stirring
occasionally, for 10 minutes, or until croutons are golden
and crisp. Season with salt. The croutons may be made
one day in advance and kept in an airtight container.

CROQUE MONSIEUR SANDWICHES
SERVES 8

I made these sandwiches for my grandsons' high school French Club, and they disappeared as fast as I could cook them!

softened unsalted butter
16 thin slices good-quality white bread (Pepperidge Farm Thin Sliced or Toasting Bread)
8 thin slices Gruyère cheese
8 thin slices best quality thin-sliced honey ham
Dijon mustard
5 large eggs
10 tablespoons Half and Half
<u>1/4 pound (1 stick) or more unsalted butter, to sauté sandwiches</u>

1. Butter 8 slices of bread on one side only. Place a slice of Gruyère cheese and a slice of ham on these slices.

2. Butter the remaining 8 slices on one side only and spread thinly with the Dijon mustard. Close the sandwiches with these slices, mustard side facing in.

3. In a bowl make a batter of the eggs and Half and Half and dip the sandwiches in the batter. Let soak a minute or so on each side.

4. Melt butter in a large frying pan or electric skillet. When hot, sauté 3 to 4 sandwiches at a time, turning when golden brown. Remove and sauté the rest of the sandwiches. (Cut into halves or quarters before dipping and sautéing to make smaller hors d'oeuvres.) Serve hot immediately.

SALADE NIÇOISE—SERVES 8

This is my favorite salad to eat for lunch—it is a meal in itself.

Dressing:

2 tablespoons white wine vinegar
2 tablespoons lemon juice
1/2 teaspoon dry mustard
1/2 teaspoon salt, 1/4 teaspoon black pepper
2 cloves garlic, crushed
1/2 teaspoon dried oregano
1/2 teaspoon dried thyme or marjoram
1 cup olive oil

Salad:

2 7-ounce cans water-packed tuna, drained
2 pounds new potatoes, unpeeled, cooked until tender
1 tablespoon minced scallions (green onions)
1/4 teaspoon salt, 1/8 teaspoon pepper
1/4 cup dry white wine
1 pound fresh green beans, cut into 2-inch pieces, cooked 10 to 12 minutes, until bright green, in boiling salted water, then drained and plunged into ice water to retain their color
1 head leaf or Boston lettuce
3 tomatoes, cut into wedges
4 hardboiled eggs, quartered
1 cup Niçoise or Kalamata olives
<u>3 to 4 tablespoons minced fresh parsley</u>

1. <u>Make dressing</u>: Combine vinegar, lemon juice, herbs, dry mustard, salt, pepper and garlic in a small bowl. Slowly whisk in the olive oil. Reserve. The mustard acts as an emulsifier and makes the dressing thicker and less likely to separate.

2. <u>Make the salad</u>: Peel cooked potatoes and cut in half lengthwise, then slice 3/8 inch thick. Place in a large bowl. Add scallions, salt and pepper and white wine. Toss gently. Let stand 5 minutes, tossing gently until liquid is absorbed. Pour 1/4 cup dressing over potatoes and toss. Taste and adjust seasoning. Cover and refrigerate.

3. Marinate green beans in 1/4 cup dressing in refrigerator for up to 1 hour. If marinated too long, they will turn "army green".

4. <u>To serve</u>: Arrange large leaf lettuce or Boston lettuce leaves on a large platter. Place drained tuna, broken into chunks, in center. Arrange potatoes, green beans, tomatoes and eggs attractively at intervals. Garnish with olives. Sprinkle with parsley. Drizzle more dressing over the whole salad.

CHERRY CLAFOUTI—SERVES 8

This custardy dessert is addictive! You can substitute blueberries for the cherries if you prefer.

1 1/4 cup whole milk
1/3 cup sugar
3 large eggs
1 tablespoon pure vanilla extract
1/8 teaspoon salt
2/3 cup sifted all-purpose flour
3 cups pitted fresh black cherries OR 1 16-ounce bag of frozen dark, sweet, pitted cherries, thawed and drained
1/3 cup additional sugar

powdered sugar
1 cup heavy whipping cream, lightly whipped with <u>powdered sugar and vanilla to taste</u>

1. Preheat oven to 350°F. Lightly butter a 9-inch ovenproof Pyrex pie pan or quiche tart pan, about 1 1/2 inches deep.

2. Place the milk, sugar, eggs, vanilla, salt and flour in the jar of a blender in the order they are listed. Cover and blend for 1 minute.

3. Pour a 1/4-inch layer of this batter into the baking dish. Cover and microwave for 20 to 30 seconds or until a film of batter has set in the bottom of the dish. Sprinkle the cherries over the batter, then sprinkle with the 1/3 cup of additional sugar. Pour on the rest of the batter.

4. Bake for about 50 minutes to 1 hour. The clafouti is done when puffed and browned, and a knife put into the center comes out clean. Sprinkle top with powdered sugar just before bringing to the table. Serve warm, with the flavored whipped cream.

AN HOMAGE TO JULIA CHILD

Cheese Gougères
Boeuf Bourgignon
Pommes À La Vapeur
Reine de Saba Chocolate Cake

CHEESE GOUGÈRES
MAKES ABOUT 3 DOZEN

These savory cheese puffs are based on pâte à choux— French cream puff batter. They are a traditional accompaniment to a glass of red Burgundy wine. You can also make them larger, omit the cheese and, after baking, split them all the way through, scrape out any uncooked dough inside and fill them with chicken salad for an elegant hors d'oeuvre or luncheon dish, or go the dessert route and fill them with vanilla bean ice cream and drizzle chocolate sauce on them…scrumptious!

Batter:

1 cup water
6 tablespoons (3/4 stick) unsalted butter, cut into pieces
1/2 teaspoon salt
1/8 teaspoon black pepper
1 cup sifted all purpose flour
4 large eggs
1 cup (4 ounces) grated Gruyère or Swiss cheese (Jarlsberg is a good choice)

Glaze:

1 large egg beaten with 1/2 teaspoon water in a small bowl

<u>Optional garnish: 4 tablespoons additional grated cheese for topping</u>

1. In a heavy-bottomed 1 1/2 quart saucepan bring the 1 cup water to a boil on high heat with the butter, salt and pepper.

2. Remove the pan from heat and immediately pour in all the flour at once. Beat vigorously with a wooden spoon to

blend thoroughly. Then return pan to moderate heat and beat the batter with the spoon until the mixture leaves the sides of the pan, 1 to 2 minutes. The mixture will form a mass and begin to film the bottom of the pan.

3. Remove the saucepan from the heat and make a well in the center of the dough. Immediately break one egg into the well. Beat it into the dough with the wooden spoon for several seconds until it has been absorbed. Continue with the other eggs, beating them in one at a time and mixing well. The last 2 eggs will be absorbed more slowly. Beat for a moment more to be sure the dough is well blended and smooth.

4. Beat the grated cheese into the warm dough. Spoon into circular walnut sized mounds on sheets of parchment paper on 2 baking sheets. Or you can put the batter into a pastry bag fitted with a 1/2-inch round plain tip and squeeze out more uniform-size puffs. You can also improvise by filling a plastic bag with a small diagonal cut off one corner with the batter.

5. Dip a pastry brush into the egg glaze and flatten each puff very slightly with the side of the brush. Try not to drip glaze on the parchment paper, or the puffs won't rise nicely. If you wish, you can sprinkle each puff with a pinch of grated cheese. The puffs can be refrigerated several hours before baking. Set the sheets in the upper and lower thirds of a preheated 425°F. oven and bake for about 20 minutes, or until they have doubled in size, are golden brown and firm and crusty to the touch. Remove them from the oven and pierce the side of each puff with a sharp knife, to release steam. Then return the sheets to the turned-off oven and leave the door slightly open for 10 minutes. Cool the puffs on a rack and serve warm or at room temperature. The puffs can be stored in an airtight container when they are cooled, but are best served right away.

BOEUF BOURGIGNON
SERVES 8

One of Julia's signature dishes and worth the time.

6 ounces thick sliced bacon, cut into 1 1/2-inch pieces, blanched (simmered in 1 quart water for 10 minutes), then dried on paper towels
2 tablespoons olive oil plus more as needed
3 pounds stewing beef (from a chuck roast) cut into 2-inch cubes, leaving some fat on the pieces
1 each sliced carrot and onion
1 teaspoon salt, 1/4 teaspoon pepper
2 tablespoons flour
3 cups full-bodied young red wine, such as Beaujolais, Côtes du Rhône, Burgundy or Chianti
2 to 3 cups beef stock (More Than Gourmet is a very good quality product)
1 tablespoon tomato paste
2 cloves garlic, peeled and mashed with a Chef's knife
1/2 teaspoon dried thyme plus 1 bay leaf
18 to 24 small white onions, about 1 inch in diameter, peeled and an x cut in root end
3 tablespoons each butter and oil (to sauté onions)
1 pound quartered fresh mushrooms
3 tablespoons each butter and olive oil

Garnish: chopped parsley leaves

1. Preheat oven to 450°F.

2. In a large 3-inch deep fireproof casserole sauté the bacon over moderate heat for 3 minutes, to brown lightly. Remove to a dish with slotted spoon. Dry the beef cubes with paper towels, as it will not brown if it is damp. Reheat the casserole until the oil is almost smoking and sauté beef a few pieces at a time in the hot oil and bacon fat until nicely browned on all sides. You may need to add more oil. Remove and add to bacon.

3. In the same oil, brown the sliced vegetables over medium heat for 3 to 4 minutes and add to beef. Pour out the sautéing fat. Return beef, bacon and vegetables to the casserole and toss with salt and pepper. Then sprinkle on the flour and toss to coat lightly. Set casserole uncovered in the middle rack of preheated oven for 4 minutes. Toss meat and return to oven for 4 minutes more. This browns the flour and covers meat with a light crust. Remove

casserole and turn oven down to 325°F. Stir in the wine and enough stock to barely cover meat. Add the tomato paste, garlic, thyme and bay leaf. Bring to a simmer on top of the stove then cover the casserole and set in lower third of the preheated oven. Check heat so liquid simmers very slowly for 3 to 4 hours. Meat is done when a fork pierces it easily.

4. While beef is cooking, <u>Prepare the onions and mushrooms</u>: To prepare the onions, place 3 tablespoons <u>each</u> unsalted butter and vegetable oil in a 10-inch skillet and add the onions. Sauté over moderate heat for about 5 minutes rolling the onions about so they will brown as evenly as possible. Take care not to break their skin. Then pour in 1/2 cup beef stock, season to taste, and add 1/2 teaspoon thyme, 3 sprigs of parsley and a bay leaf. Cover and simmer slowly for 40 minutes, until onions are perfectly tender but still retain their shape and liquid has evaporated. Remove and discard parsley and bay leaf and add onions to meat. In a separate skillet, melt 3 tablespoons each unsalted butter and vegetable oil and sauté the mushrooms until golden brown on all sides, stirring frequently. Reserve onions and mushrooms in a large bowl.

5. When meat is tender, remove it from the pan and add it to the onions and sautéed mushrooms. Strain sauce through a fine sieve and return sauce to casserole and simmer a few minutes, skimming off any fat. You should have about 2 1/2 cups sauce thick enough to coat a spoon lightly. If sauce is too thin, you can thicken by boiling it down rapidly. If it is too thick, add more beef stock. Return meat, bacon, mushrooms and onions to sauce in casserole. Stir gently, taste and adjust seasonings. Can serve hot at this point, or cool down, refrigerate and reheat next day. This also freezes well. Sprinkle some chopped parsley over casserole just before serving.

POMMES DE TERRE À LA VAPEUR-STEAMED POTATOES—SERVES 8

A classic pairing with Boeuf Bourgignon. It is the perfect accompaniment to the rich meat.

32 small new potatoes
6 tablespoons unsalted butter, melted
salt and freshly ground black pepper to taste
<u>chopped parsley</u>

1. Cut a band of the peeling all around the middle of each potato and discard. Place potatoes in a steamer basket set over simmering water and cover with a lid.

2. Steam them until tender, 20 to 30 minutes, testing by inserting a small knife into one potato—if the potato falls off the knife easily, it is done. (If cooked ahead, reheat for several minutes in the steamer before serving.)

3. Transfer the potatoes to a warm bowl. Coat with the melted butter and sprinkle lightly with salt, pepper and parsley.

REINE DE SABA (QUEEN OF SHEBA) CAKE
SERVES 8 TO 10 ⏱ 👨‍🍳 👨‍🍳 👨‍🍳

This truly is the "Queen" of chocolate desserts, from the Queen of French Cooking, Julia Child.

Cake:

8-inch round cake pan, 1 1/2 inches deep
butter and flour to prepare cake pan
4 ounces best quality semi-sweet or bittersweet
    chocolate, chopped, melted
2 tablespoons dark rum or coffee
1/4 pound (1 stick) unsalted softened butter
2/3 cup granulated sugar
3 large egg yolks
3 large egg whites
pinch of salt
1/4 teaspoon cream of tartar
1 tablespoon granulated sugar
1/3 cup toasted ground almonds (in processor or
    blender)
1/4 teaspoon. pure almond extract
3/4 cup sifted cake flour

Glaze:

1 ounce semi-sweet or bittersweet chocolate, chopped
1 tablespoon rum or coffee
3 tablespoons unsalted butter, softened to room
    temperature
water to thin if needed, or 2 to 3 tablespoons sifted
    confectioners' sugar if too thin

Garnish: almond slices, toasted on foil-lined cookie
    sheet at 350°F. for 10 minutes until golden

1. Preheat oven to 350°F. Butter and flour the cake pan. Melt the chocolate with the rum or coffee over almost simmering water.

2. Cream the butter and sugar together in an electric mixer until they form a pale yellow, fluffy mixture. Beat in the egg yolks until well blended. Transfer to a large bowl.

3. In another bowl beat the egg whites with the salt and cream of tartar until soft peaks form. (The cream of tartar adds volume and stability to the whites.) Sprinkle on the 1 tablespoon of sugar and beat until stiff peaks form, but not until they are too dry. Reserve.

4. With a rubber spatula blend the melted chocolate mixture into the butter-sugar mixture. Stir in the ground almonds and almond extract. Immediately stir in 1/4 of the beaten egg whites with a clean spatula, to lighten the batter. Then gently fold in one-third of the remaining whites until partially blended, then gently add one-third of the flour and continue folding. Alternate rapidly with more egg whites and more flour until all are incorporated.

5. Turn the batter into the prepared cake pan, using an offset spatula or rubber spatula to spread the batter slightly up sides of pan. Bake in middle rack of the preheated oven for about 25 minutes. Cake is done when it has puffed, and 2 1/2 to 3 inches around the top of the cake are set. A cake tester plunged into that area should come out clean. The center should move slightly if pan is shaken and the tester will come out oily.

6. Allow cake to cool in the pan for 10 minutes on a cake rack. Run a knife around the edge of the pan and reverse cake carefully onto another rack. Allow to cool for an hour or till thoroughly cool before glazing.

7. Prepare glaze: In a bowl set over a saucepan with hot water stir chocolate and rum or coffee until chocolate has melted into very smooth cream. Remove from hot water pan and beat the butter into the chocolate, one tablespoon at a time. Then beat over cold water until chocolate mixture is cool and of spreading consistency. Immediately spread it over your cake with an offset spatula or knife. Press sliced toasted almonds around the sides of the cake.

A FRENCH MEAL FROM PROVENCE

Veal Marengo
Oven Roasted Potatoes Provençale
Ratatouille
Tarte Aux Amandes et Au Citron

VEAL MARENGO—SERVES 8

*One of my husband's very favorite dishes! It was
supposedly created by Napoleon's chef after the 1800 Battle
of Marengo to please the Emperor.*

3 pounds veal stew meat, all fat removed, cut into
    2-inch pieces
3 to 4 tablespoons olive oil, more if needed
1 cup minced onions
1 1-pound can chopped tomatoes, juices discarded
2 tablespoons flour
1 teaspoon salt
1/4 teaspoon black pepper
2 cups dry white wine or dry white vermouth
1/2 teaspoon dried basil or tarragon
1/2 teaspoon dried thyme
a 3 inch strip of orange peel (no white pith), about 1/2
    inch wide, cut using a very sharp paring knife
2 cloves garlic, mashed
salt and pepper to taste
1/2 pound fresh mushrooms, quartered if large
1/2 tablespoon cornstarch mixed with 1 tablespoon
    water for thickening sauce if needed

Garnish: 2 to 3 tablespoons chopped fresh basil,
    tarragon or parsley leaves

1. Dry the veal on paper towels or it will not brown. Heat
the olive oil on high heat in a heavy 12-inch skillet until
almost smoking. Brown the meat a few pieces at a time,
being careful not to crowd meat in the skillet or it will not
brown. Place in a 4-quart ovenproof casserole. In a skillet
on medium heat brown the onions lightly for 5 minutes.

2. While onions are browning, on medium heat toss the
veal in the casserole with the flour and salt to brown
flour lightly. Remove casserole from heat. Preheat oven to
325°F.

3. To the onions in skillet add the wine and boil for 1
minute, scraping up sauté juices. Pour wine and onions
into casserole and bring to a simmer, shaking and stirring
to mix. Stir tomatoes into casserole. Add herbs, orange
peel and garlic. Bring again to the simmer and season to
taste. Cover and set in preheated oven to simmer slowly
for 1 1/4 to 1 1/2 hours, or until meat is almost tender
when pierced with a fork. Add mushrooms to casserole,
cover and return to oven for 15 minutes.

4. Remove casserole from oven and pour contents into
strainer over a saucepan. Remove orange peel and return
meat and vegetables to casserole. Boil the sauce down
rapidly in the saucepan until it has reduced to about 2
1/2 cups. It should be lightly thickened and a rich reddish
brown. If too thin, blend in the cornstarch and water
mixture and simmer for 2 minutes. Correct seasoning
and pour the sauce back into the casserole over the veal
and vegetables. (May be done ahead to this point. Set
aside, or refrigerate till up to next day, or freeze.)

5. Shortly before serving, cover and bring casserole to a
simmer on top of stove for 5 to 10 minutes. Serve in its
casserole, or on a platter surrounded by noodles, rice or
parsleyed potatoes. Decorate with fresh chopped herbs if
desired.

POTATOES PROVENÇALES AUX HERBES
SERVES 8

This recipe calls for Herbes de Provence, an herb mixture readily available in grocery stores, which consists of herbs most often used in Provençale cooking, such as thyme, savory and bay leaves. When using this herb, be sure to strain out the crumbled bay leaves from the dish before serving, as they have very sharp edges that don't soften when cooked and can cut the esophagus.

3 pounds white or red all-purpose potatoes
2/3 cup oil (half olive oil, half vegetable oil)
1 tablespoon dried herbs total: Herbes de Provence,
    thyme, savory, or a mixture of these
1 teaspoon salt
<u>1/2 teaspoon freshly ground black pepper</u>

1. Preheat oven to 425°F.

2. Peel potatoes and slice them thinly (Use the slicing disk on a food processor or mandolin or slice by hand.) Dry slices on paper towels and place them in a large bowl. Add the oils, herbs, salt and pepper and mix thoroughly with your hands or large spoon to be sure each slice of potato is coated.

3. Spread the slices in two or three layers in a shallow baking dish and bake about 30 minutes, or until crisp and brown. Remove from pan with a spatula. Check seasoning and serve.

RATATOUILLE—SERVES 8 TO 10

Although it takes more time to cook the vegetables separately, the flavor is much better using this method. You can try it both ways and see if you agree with me or if it's not worth your time.

2 medium eggplants, about 1 1/2 pounds total, unpeeled
2 medium zucchini (1 pound total)
1/2 cup extra virgin olive oil
3 cloves garlic, peeled and coarsely chopped
1 large onion, sliced
1 green or red bell pepper, cubed
3 pounds or more ripe tomatoes, about 4 medium,
    peeled, seeded and sliced
1 teaspoon sea salt
1/2 teaspoon freshly ground black pepper
1 bay leaf
1 tablespoon fresh oregano and basil or thyme OR 1
    teaspoon dried oregano
3 tablespoons minced fresh parsley leaves
<u>1/4 cup white wine or chicken stock</u>

1. Preheat oven to 350°F.

2. Cut the eggplants and zucchini into 1-inch chunks. In a large skillet heat 2 tablespoons of the oil. Sauté the eggplants until lightly browned, about 3 minutes on each side. Remove and reserve. Add 2 more tablespoons oil and sauté zucchini until lightly browned, about 2 minutes. Reserve.

3. In the same skillet, add the rest of the olive oil and sauté the onion, pepper and garlic until tender but not brown, about 5 minutes. Add tomatoes and season with salt, pepper, bay leaf and oregano. Pour into a large bowl and add the wine or stock, then mix all together with the reserved eggplant, zucchini and parsley

4. Spray a large ovenproof rectangular or oval casserole with cooking spray and pour in the vegetable mixture. Bake, basting occasionally with vegetable juices, until most of the liquid has evaporated, about 30 minutes. Remove bay leaf before serving. Serve hot or cold. Rewarms well.

TARTE AUX AMANDES ET AU CITRON—ALMOND AND LEMON TART—SERVES 8

Classic and classy!

Sweet Short Pastry:

2 large eggs
1/2 cup sugar
Pinch of salt
1 1/2 cups sifted flour
1/2 cup (1 stick) cold unsalted butter, cut into small
  pieces

Filling:

2 large eggs
1/2 cup sugar
grated rind of one lemon
6 1/2 tablespoons fresh lemon juice
1/2 cup unsalted butter, melted
1/2 cup ground toasted almonds
12 whole blanched almonds, toasted at 350°F. for 10
  minutes

1. Make pastry: In a large bowl beat together the eggs, sugar and salt by hand. Add flour in small amounts and mix well. Turn out onto a work surface and work in the cut up butter with hands, until absorbed. Using the ball of the palm of the hand, smear the dough to distribute the butter evenly. This French technique is called fraisage. Roll into a ball and wrap in plastic wrap and refrigerate for at least one hour or up to overnight.

2. Roll pastry out on lightly floured surface and place in a 10-inch tart pan with a removable bottom. Cover with heavy duty foil and fill with raw beans, rice or pie weights. This method is called blind baking. Place on cookie sheet or pizza pan and bake in preheated 400°F. oven for 15 minutes. Remove foil and beans and cook 5 minutes more. Let shell cool slightly.

3. Make filling: Beat eggs and sugar until light and creamy in mixer. Mix in lemon rind and juice, then the melted butter and ground toasted almonds. Pour into partly baked pastry shell and bake for 10 minutes. Turn oven temperature down to 375°F., carefully open oven and remove tart and arrange toasted whole blanched almonds about 1 inch from rim in a circle. Return tart to oven, cover loosely with foil to prevent overbrowning, and continue to bake for 20 minutes or until set and golden. Serve slightly warm or at room temperature.

L' AMOUR, TOUJOURS L' AMOUR—A VALENTINE'S DAY MENU

Chicken Liver Terrine
Coq Au Vin
Potato Gratin
Crème Brûlée

CHICKEN LIVER TERRINE (MOUSSE DE FOIE DE VOLAILLE)—MAKES 3 1/2 CUPS

Yes, this is decadent, but it is surprisingly easy to make and one of the most delicious things you can eat. Just try to practice moderation in the portion you eat. This marvelous recipe is my version of one from French Star Chef Jacques Pépin.

1 1/2 cups (3 sticks) unsalted butter, softened to room temperature
1 cup coarsely chopped onions or shallots
1 pound chicken livers, drained of any liquid and dried
2 tablespoons Dijon mustard
3 tablespoons brandy or cognac
pinch of nutmeg
1/2 to 1 teaspoon salt and 1/4 to 1/2 teaspoon pepper, to taste

<u>Garnish</u>: chopped parsley, French bread, thinly sliced, <u>buttered and toasted in a 350°F. oven, or crackers</u>

1. In a medium saucepan melt 1/4 cup (1/2 stick) of the butter and sauté the onions or shallots over medium heat until translucent. Add chicken livers and sauté until cooked through and no longer pink inside but not overdone, about 8 minutes. Cool to room temperature.

2. Put this mixture into the food processor with the mustard, brandy and seasonings. Process until thoroughly puréed. Add the remaining butter one fourth at a time, pulsing briefly after each addition. Spoon this mousse into an attractive small tureen or ramekin and chill until solid (at least 1 hour) before serving. If made a longer time ahead, make sure to bring mousse to spreadable consistency before serving. Sprinkle with chopped parsley if desired and serve with the toasted bread or crackers.

COQ AU VIN—SERVES 8

The depth of flavor in this dish belies the fact that it is simply perfectly stewed chicken. If you don't have time to make the homemade brown chicken stock, use a puck of More Than Gourmet reconstituted, or boxed stock.

<u>Homemade Brown Chicken Stock:</u>

3 to 4 pounds chicken backs, necks, wings and other trimmings from whole chicken
2 <u>each</u> cut-up onions and carrots

8 slices thick-cut bacon
2 tablespoons unsalted butter
3 1/2 to 4 pounds cut up frying chicken
1/2 teaspoon salt, 1/4 teaspoon pepper
1/4 cup good-quality Cognac
3 cups full-bodied red wine, such as a Burgundy
1 to 2 cups brown chicken stock (recipe below), More Than Gourmet or boxed chicken stock
2 tablespoons tomato paste
2 cloves fresh garlic, mashed in garlic press
1/2 teaspoon dried thyme
1 bay leaf
24 pearl onions (small onions 1 inch in diameter)
Bouquet garni (herb bouquet): 2 sprigs of parsley, 1 sprig of thyme and a bay leaf tied in cheesecloth
1/2 pound mushrooms, cleaned and halved if very large
2 tablespoons <u>each</u> unsalted butter and oil to brown onions and mushrooms
3 tablespoons flour mixed with 2 tablespoons softened butter (beurre manié)

<u>Garnish: chopped fresh parsley</u>

1. <u>Make Homemade Brown Chicken Stock</u>: Place the 3 to 4 pounds chicken backs, necks, wings and other trimmings in large rectangular baking pan along with 2 cut-up onions and 2 cut-up carrots. Brown in oven at 400°F. for 45 minutes, then transfer to large stockpot and cover with cold water. Bring to a boil, reduce heat to simmer and cook, partially covered for 2 hours or more until any meat has fallen off bones and stock has rich golden color. Strain, discard all solids, and refrigerate overnight. Next day remove solid layer of fat. You can reduce this stock by boiling, for richer stock, since you didn't add any salt to the stock. Freezes well, so you can double the recipe and have some on hand for other recipes.

2. In large heavy ovenproof casserole melt the butter and sauté the bacon slowly until it is lightly browned. Remove bacon, cut into 1-inch pieces, and reserve. Dry the chicken pieces and brown in hot butter in the casserole. Season chicken with salt and pepper and cover casserole. Reduce heat and cook slowly for 10 minutes, turning chicken once.

3. Uncover casserole and pour in the cognac. Avert your face and ignite the cognac with a lighted long fireplace match. Shake casserole back and forth a few seconds until flames subside. Add the wine. Alternately if you do not want to ignite the cognac, wait until you pour the wine into casserole and bring liquid to a boil to dissipate some of the alcohol in the cognac. Add just enough stock to cover the chicken. Stir in the tomato paste, garlic and herbs. Bring to a simmer. Return bacon to skillet, cover and simmer slowly 30 minutes, or until juices of chicken run clear yellow when pierced with a fork. Remove chicken and bacon from sauce to a platter and reserve. Discard bay leaf.

4. While chicken is cooking, prepare the onions and mushrooms. Peel the pearl onions and cut a small x in root end (to keep them together while cooking). Melt 1 1/2 tablespoons each butter and oil in large skillet with 1 1/2 inch sides. Sauté onions until golden, reduce heat to simmer, and add the bouquet garni. Add 1/2 cup brown chicken stock or beef stock, cover and simmer slowly for about 30 minutes until onions are tender but retain their shape. Discard bouquet garni, reserving onions. In another medium skillet melt 2 tablespoons butter and 2 tablespoons oil and sauté mushrooms on high heat about 5 minutes. Reserve. Sautéeing in a mixture of butter and oil allows you to cook on higher heat than if you used butter alone, which has a higher smoke point than oil. (The smoke point is the point at which heated fat begins to smoke and impart an unpleasant flavor to foods.)

5. Finish the dish by blending the butter and flour together into a smooth paste, which in French is called beurre manié. Stir the paste into the hot sauce in the casserole with a wire whip. Bring to a simmer, stirring, and simmer for 2 minutes, or until sauce is thick enough to coat a spoon. Return chicken and bacon to pot, along with the cooked onions with their liquid and the mushrooms. Garnish with parsley if desired and serve.

POTATO GRATIN—GRATIN DE POMMES DAUPHINOIS—SERVES 8

2 1/2 pounds baking potatoes, peeled and sliced thinly (in processor is fine)
1 large clove garlic, peeled and halved
softened butter to butter the casserole
1 cup (4 ounces) grated Gruyère or other Swiss cheese
1 teaspoon salt, 1/2 teaspoon freshly ground black pepper
2 cups whole milk or Half and Half, boiling

1. Preheat oven to 400°F. Rub the inside of a large oval gratin dish or 9" x 13" rectangular ceramic casserole with the cut sides of the garlic. Slice garlic into slivers and reserve. Butter the casserole.

2. Spread half of the potatoes in casserole, sprinkle with half of the cheese and sprinkle with half of the salt and pepper. Scatter with reserved slivers of garlic. Add the rest of the potatoes, top with the rest of the cheese and salt and pepper. Pour the boiling milk over top and bake for 45 minutes to 1 hour, or until potatoes are tender and top of casserole is brown. Can serve right away or keep warm for up to half an hour, loosely covered with foil.

CRÈME BRÛLÉE—SERVES 8

This is the original recipe created in the kitchens of the legendary French restaurant Paul Bocuse outside of Lyon, France. We are incredibly lucky to have fabulous French chef Richard Blondin, who was the pastry chef there, as Chef de Cuisine at our outstanding French restaurant The Refectory, owned by the great restaurateur Kamal Boulos, in Columbus, Ohio, where this non plus ultra dessert is always on the menu. Now you can create it at home!

1 fresh vanilla bean (supple, fragrant and soft)
1 quart (4 cups) heavy cream
1/2 cup vanilla sugar (recipe follows) or regular sugar
6 large egg yolks
1/2 cup sugar
<u>8 oven-proof ramekins or custard cups</u>

1. Preheat oven to 300°F.

2. Cut the vanilla bean in half lengthwise with a sharp knife, and using the back of the knife scrape out the tiny black seeds. In a large heavy saucepan combine the heavy cream, vanilla bean seeds and vanilla pod halves. Bring mixture to a boil. Remove from the heat, cover the pan and let mixture steep for 15 minutes. Remove the vanilla pods, which can be washed, dried and used to prepare vanilla sugar (see below).

3. In a medium size bowl, combine the vanilla sugar or regular sugar and the egg yolks, and using a whisk blend well. Add the warm cream with the vanilla seeds slowly, whisking constantly to "temper" the yolks so they won't curdle. Transfer to a large glass measuring cup that has a pouring spout.

4. Place the ramekins in a roasting pan and carry to top of the stove. Carefully pour the cream mixture into the ramekins. Slowly add enough boiling water to the roasting pan to reach halfway up the sides of the ramekins. This is known in French cooking as using a Bain Marie or water bath, which cooks the custard mixture gently. Carefully transfer the roasting pan to the preheated oven and bake just until the mixture is set in the center, about 35 to 45 minutes. Test by poking a butter knife into the center of a ramekin—if it comes out clean it is done. The mixture will still "tremble" when shaken.

5. Refrigerate for at least 1 hour or up to 24 hours. When ready to serve, remove from the refrigerator, spoon about 1 tablespoon of the sugar in an even layer over the top of each baked ramekin. Put under a preheated broiler, watching carefully, until the sugar melts into a golden crust. Alternately, you can use a small cooking blow torch, available at cooking stores, which actually gives you more control over the amount of browning and melting and is very dramatic. Be careful not to let the crust burn. Can return custards to the refrigerator for up to one hour until ready to serve. This dessert will wow your guests!

6. <u>To make vanilla sugar:</u> In a large glass jar with a tight lid place 2 cups sugar. Split one fresh vanilla bean and scrape out the tiny black seeds. Add the bean halves and the vanilla seeds to the 2 cups of sugar. Cover tightly and let sit for at least two weeks, or up to 1 year, to flavor the sugar. Use this vanilla sugar in place of regular sugar whenever you are baking desserts that call for vanilla, to add extra flavor. Alternately, whenever you use a vanilla bean in other recipes, such as above, dry the bean pod <u>thoroughly</u> , add it to 2 cups of sugar and make more vanilla sugar.

CLASSIC FRENCH DISHES

Soupe À L' Oignon Gratinée, with a Master
Recipe for Beef Stock
Coquilles St. Jacques
Classic Composed Salad with Vinaigrette
Tarte Tatin

SOUPE À L' OIGNON GRATINÉE—FRENCH ONION SOUP—SERVES 8

You'll rarely find this quality of onion soup at a restaurant, since so many of them do not make their own stock anymore, and unfortunately use a stock that is usually too salty and off-tasting. Take my word for it, you will be proud to present this to your guests.

3 tablespoons unsalted butter
4 medium onions, thinly sliced
2 tablespoon flour
8 cups beef stock, preferably homemade (recipe follows) OR a puck of More Than Gourmet Beef Stock, diluted with 8 cups hot water
1/2 cup boiling whole milk
1/3 pound grated Swiss cheese
8 slices French bread, dried in 350°F. oven
<u>melted butter</u>

1. In a Dutch oven or 5-quart stockpot melt butter and cook onions until <u>slightly</u> browned and translucent. Sprinkle with flour and cook over low heat until golden, never allowing onions to become dark brown, as this will impart a bitter taste to the soup. Caramelizing the onions will take up to 30 minutes of careful stirring, which will bring out the sweet taste of the onions. Whisk in the stock and bring to a boil, stirring constantly with a wooden spoon, then simmer gently uncovered 20 minutes. Whisk in the boiling milk, taste and add salt and pepper as needed.

2. Pour into a large ovenproof casserole or individual ovenproof bowls. Place slices of the dried bread on top, sprinkle generously with the grated cheese and spoon a bit of melted butter over the top of each slice of bread. Brown quickly under preheated broiler, watching closely so the bread doesn't burn. Serve immediately.

HOMEMADE BEEF STOCK—MAKES ABOUT 8 CUPS

Admittedly time-intensive, but you will be thrilled with the results.

7 to 8 pounds beef or veal bones, preferably marrow and knucklebones (get friendly with your butcher!)
2 carrots, ends removed, washed and quartered
2 stalks celery, cleaned and quartered
2 onions, peeled and halved
Bouquet Garni: 1 bay leaf, 2 cloves garlic, 3 sprigs parsley,
1 sprig thyme or 1 teaspoon dried thyme, 8 whole
black peppercorns, tied in a cheesecloth bundle
1 bottle dry red wine (never use "cooking" wine, which is a salty inferior product. Cook with a wine you would enjoy drinking. It doesn't have to be super expensive)
1 1-pound can tomatoes with their juice
<u>16 cups cold water</u>

1. Place bones and vegetables in large foil-lined roasting pan and roast in a 450°F oven until brown, about 45 minutes, turning occasionally to make sure bones and vegetables don't burn.

2. Carefully (they will be hot) transfer to large stockpot with a slotted spoon, discarding any fat in pan. Add the bouquet garni, wine, tomatoes and water and bring to a boil. Skim off any scum that has risen to the top and reduce to a simmer. Cook uncovered at least 6 hours, or preferably all day.

3. Strain into a large strainer or Chinoise, discarding bones and pressing on any marrow and the vegetables to extract juices. Discard vegetables. Refrigerate the stock overnight.

4. Next day, remove and discard the top layer of solidified fat. Reduce stock to 8 cups for soup by boiling at high heat. This stock freezes very well and also can be further reduced to make a wonderful base for sauces (glace de viande) by continuing to boil until reduced to 1/2 cup or so of very syrupy glaze. As it has no salt, there is no danger of it becoming too salty in the reduction process. (Stock can be prepared and refrigerated up to 4 days ahead of using, or frozen for several months. Divide it

into 1 or 2 cup containers and you can always have great stock available when you need it, from one commitment of your time!)

COQUILLES ST. JACQUES (PRONOUNCED COKEE SAN JAAK)—SERVES 8

This is my friend Peggy's slightly simplified rendition of Julia Child's classic recipe. Coquilles St. Jacques is actually the French word for scallops.

2 cups dry white wine
1 teaspoon salt
pinch of white pepper
1 bay leaf
4 tablespoons minced shallots
1 1/2 to 2 pounds fresh sea scallops
1 pound sliced fresh mushrooms

Sauce:

6 tablespoons unsalted butter
1/2 cup flour
1 1/2 cups whole milk, warmed
1 cup whipping cream, warmed
4 large egg yolks
salt and white pepper to taste
optional: a few drops of fresh lemon juice to taste

1 to 2 tablespoons butter, cut into tiny cubes
12 tablespoons grated Swiss cheese (Jarlsberg is a good choice)
12 scallop shells or a 9" x 13" casserole, lightly buttered
French bread slices, warmed

1. In a large saucepan or skillet bring the wine, salt, pepper, bay leaf and shallots to a boil, then reduce heat and simmer for 5 minutes. Add the scallops and mushrooms to the wine mixture and pour in enough water to barely cover ingredients. Bring to a simmer again and cook, covered, for 4 to 5 minutes. Remove scallops and mushrooms with a slotted spoon or into a sieve over a bowl and reserve. Rapidly boil down the cooking liquid until it has reduced to 2 cups.

2. Make sauce: In a large saucepan melt the butter until bubbly but not brown, then add the flour and stir with a wooden spoon, cooking for 2 minutes. Add the boiling reserved liquid from cooking the scallops, stirring with a whisk, then add the milk and cream. Boil, stirring constantly for one minute. Whisk ladlefuls of this mixture into the egg yolks slowly, being careful to warm them gently and avoid making scrambled eggs! This technique is called *tempering* the yolks. Then whisk the egg yolk mixture into the mixture on the stove and boil stirring for 1 minute. Season to taste with salt, pepper and optional lemon juice.

3. Cut the scallops in half lengthwise, then blend the sauce with the sliced scallops and mushrooms gently.

4. Using a slotted spoon, spoon scallop-mushroom mixture into shells, then cover them with some of the remaining sauce. Arrange the shells on 2 baking sheets. Sprinkle with grated cheese and dot with butter. You can prepare this recipe to this point and refrigerate until ready to broil. Alternately, you can put the mixture into the buttered casserole. You may have extra sauce—it is delicious over pasta!

5. When ready to heat, preheat broiler and set rack 8 to 9 inches from heat source. Brown shells 5 minutes if mixture is warmed, or up to 10 minutes if it has been refrigerated (Check by tasting sauce.) Serve at once with some slices of crusty French bread to sop up the luscious sauce!

CLASSIC GREEN COMPOSED SALAD WITH FRENCH VINAIGRETTE—SERVES 8

Vinaigrette—Makes 1 cup:

4 tablespoons best quality wine vinegar
1/4 teaspoon salt
1 teaspoon Dijon mustard
1 cup best quality olive oil
freshly ground black pepper
Optional: 1/2 teaspoon dried herbs such as tarragon or basil

Salad:

2 1/2 to 3 quarts salad greens, part mesclun mix, part romaine, washed and dried
fresh minced herbs of your choice, such as parsley, chives or tarragon

Optional additions:

1 can sliced or julienned beets, tossed with a few tablespoonfuls of the above vinaigrette
1 can sliced hearts of palm, drained, marinated in a few tablespoons of the vinaigrette
enoki mushrooms, cleaned and marinated as above
1 can drained and rinsed kidney beans, marinated as above
toasted pine nuts (toast in a small skillet on top of stove, watching carefully so they won't burn

1. Make the Vinaigrette: In a medium bowl beat the vinegar, salt and mustard to dissolve the salt. Whisk in the olive oil slowly, and add your seasonings of choice. Refrigerate until needed.

2. Marinate your ingredients of choice—beets, hearts of palm, enoki mushrooms, kidney beans, etc. for about 10 minutes or up to overnight, each ingredient in its own separate bowl of marinade.

3. Just before serving, toss greens lightly with some of the vinaigrette and place on a large platter. Place the beets and other ingredients artfully on the salad greens, sprinkling with pine nuts last to keep them crisp, and serve immediately, passing extra vinaigrette.

TARTE TATIN—UPSIDE DOWN APPLE TART SERVES 8 TO 10

This famous dessert was created by two French sisters living in the Loire Valley, who supported themselves by making and selling it.

Pâte brisée sucrée—Sweet short pastry

1 cup all-purpose flour
1 tablespoon sugar
1/8 teaspoon salt
4 tablespoons chilled unsalted butter plus 1 1/2 tablespoons chilled solid Crisco
2 1/2 to 3 tablespoons ice water

Filling:

3 1/2 pounds Granny Smith or other tart crisp apple
1/3 cup granulated sugar
1 teaspoon cinnamon
1/2 cup sugar
6 tablespoons melted unsalted butter

3 tablespoons sugar (optional if needed, to brown finished tart)
1 cup heavy cream, lightly whipped with 1 tablespoon sugar

1. Make the pâte brisée: Place the flour in a bowl, mix in the sugar and salt. Cut butter and shortening into small dice and add to bowl. Rub together rapidly between the tips of your fingers until the fat is broken into pieces the size of oatmeal flakes. Do not overdo this step as the fat will be blended more thoroughly later. Add the ice water and blend quickly with one hand, fingers held together and slightly cupped as you rapidly gather the dough into a mass. Press the dough firmly into a roughly shaped circle. Wrap in plastic wrap and refrigerate until needed.

2. Make the Filling: Quarter, core and peel the apples. Cut into lengthwise slices 1/8 inch thick. Toss in a bowl with the 1/3 cup sugar and cinnamon. You should have about 10 cups of apples. Reserve.

3. Heavily butter a 9-inch or 10-inch cast iron skillet or pyrex dish that is 2 to 2 1/2 inches deep. Sprinkle 1/4 cup

of the sugar in the bottom of the dish and arrange one half of the apples in the bottom of the pan. Sprinkle with one half of the melted butter. Make another layer with the rest of the apples and butter and sprinkle the rest of the sugar over the apples. Preheat oven to 375°F.

4. Roll out the pastry (pâte brisée) into a 1/8-inch thick circle. Place it over the apples, tucking in extra pastry against the inside edge of dish. Cut 5 or 6 slits in the top of pastry to allow steam to escape. Bake 50 minutes, then test a slice of apple that you can spear out with a fork to check for tenderness. If pastry is getting too brown, cover with foil. Liquid in the bottom of pan when tilted should be a thick brown syrup.

5. Immediately unmold the tart by placing a heatproof serving dish over the pastry and <u>carefully</u> but quickly turning them both upside down. Do this over the sink or several layers of newspaper on your counter in case of spills. Remove the baking dish carefully. If apples are not a light caramel brown, which is often the case, sprinkle with 3 tablespoons sugar and either put under broiler or use a propane torch to caramelize the sugar. Serve warm with lightly whipped sweetened heavy cream. If you let the tart cool before removing it from the dish, you will need to reheat it to get it out of the dish, so plan your timing accordingly.

COOK'S TIP

"FAT EQUALS FLAVOR" is my mantra. When you substitute no-fat ingredients in a recipe, you not only compromise the flavor but the texture of the dish. Choose small portions of rich foods, and savor every bite. Eating should be a pleasurable experience, not a science experiment or a guilt trip.

9

EXPLORING ASIAN FOOD

Asian food doesn't have to mean ordering Chinese takeout anymore! In this chapter we'll explore recipes for a Dim Sum Party with a variety of luscious small bites; check out different Oriental noodle recipes; learn about the fascinating customs for celebrating Chinese New Year; experience Thai food; and have fun exploring, various Asian cuisines, highlighting specialties from several different regions in the Orient. Get into the spirit… bring out the chopsticks, rice bowls and a pot of Jasmine tea. Menus include: Dim Sum Party, Oodles of Asian Noodles, Celebrating Chinese New Year, A Taste of Thai Cuisine and Asian Accents.

Singapore Fried Noodles (page 151)

DIM SUM PARTY

Steamed Dumplings
Fried Rice Family Style
Spring Rolls
Shrimp Toast
Barbequed Pork Buns

STEAMED DUMPLINGS (NORTHERN CHINA) SERVES 8

These dumplings can also be deep-fried, gently boiled, or made into pot stickers, by putting them in a skillet with 1/2 inch of water, covering and cooking on medium high. Have guests help shape them, and eat each batch as it is done. I have had people who can eat up to 20 of them at a sitting!

Filling:

3 cups cabbage, finely chopped
1 pound raw ground pork
8 chopped scallions
2 tablespoons dry sherry
1 tablespoon <u>each</u> cornstarch, hot fried oil, oriental sesame oil, minced fresh ginger root and salt
2 10-ounce packages dumpling wrappers

Dipping Sauce

1/2 teaspoon hot pepper oil
3 tablespoons soy sauce
1 tablespoon <u>each</u> white vinegar, oriental sesame oil, <u>fresh chopped garlic and fresh chopped ginger</u>

1. <u>Make Filling</u>: In a large bowl mix all filling ingredients together, except dumpling wrappers. Place 1 teaspoon of this filling in center of each dumpling wrapper. Using water to seal edges, bring up the edges of the dough and pinch together firmly in the center, forming a filled crescent-shaped dumpling. Make a ripple or pleat on one side, gather up the rest of the side and make two more pleats toward the center. Do the same on the other side. This gives the dumpling a broad bottom to keep upright better when steaming. Place each finished dumpling on a lightly oiled plate that can fit in your Chinese steamer as it is finished. Cover plate with a damp cloth while making rest of dumplings. Can refrigerate plates as you finish them.

2. <u>Prepare steamer</u>: Using a wok or large pot with rack, fill bottom with boiling water, place steamer on top. Place one plate of dumplings in steamer and cover. Steam 10 minutes, or until dough looks transparent. Keep warm while preparing rest of dumplings in same manner.

3. <u>Prepare dipping sauce</u>: Combine all dipping sauce ingredients together in a medium bowl. Serve with dumplings.

FRIED RICE FAMILY STYLE—SERVES 8

Note that the cooked rice MUST BE cold. This is a great use for leftover rice.

5 cups cold cooked rice (cooked day before) long-grain
1 cup good baked ham, cut 1/2-inch thick into julienne slices
1/2 cup frozen green peas, defrosted but not cooked
1/2 cup chopped scallions, green part included
3 large eggs, slightly beaten
1 teaspoon salt, or more to taste
soy sauce to taste
<u>4 tablespoons vegetable oil</u>

1. Heat oil in large skillet. Sauté ham and scallions 3 to 4 minutes. Add cold rice, stirring constantly to separate grains. Cook till heated through but not browned.

2. Quickly add eggs, stirring constantly to blend in. Add peas, salt and soy sauce to taste. Serve immediately.

SPRING ROLLS (NORTHERN CHINA)
MAKES ABOUT 20

Traditionally, no sweet and sour sauce is served in China with these rolls, which are eaten in the spring, hence the name. You may be more familiar with them as egg rolls. I have included two fabulous and easy dipping sauces to accompany them.

Filling:

1 pound ground beef or ground pork
1 tablespoon dry sherry
2 pounds cabbage, cored, cut into strips, then coarsely chopped
1 tablespoon <u>each</u> salt, black pepper and oriental sesame oil
1/2 tablespoon cornstarch

16 egg roll skins (find them in the produce section at the supermarket)
Beaten egg
Crisco solid shortening for deep frying

Dipping Sauce #1:

9 tablespoons soy sauce (1/2 cup plus 1 tablespoon)
3 tablespoons white vinegar

Dipping Sauce #2:

6 tablespoons dry mustard
<u>5 tablespoons water, to make a smooth paste</u>

1. In a large skillet cook ground meat with sherry until brown. Drain well in colander, discard fat and cool the meat.

2. Bring large pot of salted water to a boil and blanch cabbage 3 minutes, timing from when water returns to a boil. Immediately drain and rinse in cold water. Squeeze <u>very hard</u> with hands to remove as much water as possible and cabbage is very dry. Cool.

3. <u>Make Filling</u>: Mix cooled meat, cabbage, salt, pepper, sesame oil and cornstarch together in a large bowl.

4. Place 3 tablespoons filling on the lower third of an egg roll skin. Fold bottom flap over filling, fold in both sides, sealing with the beaten egg, then roll up, sealing the edges also with the egg. Can be prepared to this point and refrigerated on a cookie sheet lined with parchment paper that has been dusted with cornstarch so the egg rolls don't stick, for several hours until ready to fry.

5. <u>Make Dipping Sauces</u>: Make each sauce by combining ingredients for each in 2 separate bowls. Can make a day ahead and reserve, refrigerated.

6. When ready to serve, heat 6 cups of oil in deep fryer or heavy pot to 375°F. Fry 3 to 4 egg rolls at a time, turning once or twice so they brown evenly. Wrap a napkin around the end of each spring roll and serve immediately with the 2 dipping sauces.

SHRIMP TOAST—MAKES ABOUT 24

When my niece Debbie tested this recipe for me, her family devoured them as quickly as she could make them! She says they'll become regulars at their house from now on.

1 pound raw shrimp, (45 to 59 count to the pound size), peeled and deveined, <u>DIVIDED</u>
8 thin slices good quality bread (such as Pepperidge Farm, not Wonder Bread)

Marinade for whole shrimp:

1/8 teaspoon salt
2 teaspoons <u>each</u> dry sherry and soy sauce
1 egg white, lightly beaten
3 tablespoons minced scallion, white part only

Shrimp Paste Mixture:

8 canned water chestnuts, minced
1 teaspoon <u>each</u> Oriental sesame oil, fresh ginger root, minced, oyster sauce, and dry sherry
1/8 teaspoon white pepper
1/2 teaspoon light soy sauce
1 egg white, lightly beaten
4 teaspoons cornstarch

<u>6 cups Crisco solid shortening OR canola oil, for deep frying</u>

1. <u>Prepare toasts</u>: Heat oven to 240°F. or lowest temperature. Cut the crusts from the bread. Cut bread into 32 squares, 1 1/2 x 2 inches each. Put crusts and bread squares on a cookie sheet and toast for 30 minutes, turning pieces half way through baking time. Reserve.

2. Set aside half (24) of the shrimp. Slice remaining 24 shrimp almost in half lengthwise, so they may be opened and flattened out. Place them in a bowl with the marinade. Cover and refrigerate 1/2 hour.

3. Mince the remaining 24 shrimp with a Chinese cleaver, knife or in food processor until it is a mashed paste. Mix with remaining ingredients. Cover and refrigerate if not using immediately.

4. Place dried crusts in a plastic bag and roll with a rolling pin to make fine breadcrumbs. Reserve.

5. When ready to fry, pat the marinated whole shrimp dry with a paper towel. Spread the mashed shrimp paste mixture onto each dried bread square, covering the surface. Press a butterflied shrimp onto the paste. Sprinkle with breadcrumbs. Continue until you have used up all 24 whole shrimp. If you have leftover paste, spread it on the extra bread squares.

6. <u>Fry Shrimp Toasts</u>: Heat 6 cups of your choice of oil in wok or deep fryer to temperature of 350°F. Gently add a shrimp toast, shrimp side down, to the oil with a slotted spoon and fry until golden brown, about 30 to 40 seconds, then turn carefully and continue to fry for 30 seconds more, or until golden brown—a total frying time of 1 1/2 to 2 minutes. The shrimp should be cooked and the bread square golden, not oily. Remove and sample. If done, add other shrimp, 4 to 5 at a time, and fry until all are done. Drain on paper towels and serve immediately. Or make ahead and reheat in a preheated 350°F. oven for 5 minutes. Makes 24 squares with whole shrimp and up to 8 extra toasts with just shrimp paste.

BARBEQUED PORK BUNS—MAKES 24 LARGE OR 48 COCKTAIL-SIZE

This recipe seems very complicated, but basically it consists of three separate parts.
Each one can be started ahead and then assembled when ready to eat. Or, the buns can be made completely ahead and refrigerated, or frozen and reheated at 250°F. for 30 minutes. You can also just make half the recipe, but as long as you're doing all the work, why not have goodies in your freezer? These are so good!

Bun Dough (Makes 24 large buns or 48 smaller buns)

1 package dry yeast
1 1/4 cups warm water, 110°F.
6 cups all-purpose flour
2 teaspoons baking powder
1/3 cup sugar
1/2 teaspoon salt
3 tablespoons Crisco shortening OR unsalted butter, room temperature
<u>1/2 cup whole milk</u>

1. In a small bowl mix yeast and 1/2 cup warm water. Let stand until mixtures begins to bubble, about 5 minutes.

2. In a large bowl mix flour, baking powder, sugar and salt together by hand. Add Crisco, dissolved yeast, milk and the remaining 3/4 cup water. Mix with a wooden spoon into a smooth dough.

3. Turn dough out onto a lightly floured board. Add baking powder and knead until it becomes flexible and loses most of its stickiness. Return to a large bowl which has been washed and oiled, and cover with plastic wrap. Let rise for 1 hour or until doubled in volume OR you can refrigerate the dough overnight at this point and use when ready to continue with recipe.

Barbecued Pork

1 pound pork loin, all fat removed, cut in half
   lengthwise

Marinade:

1 1/2 tablespoons minced scallion, white part only
1/2 medium onion, minced
4 canned water chestnuts, minced
1/2 teaspoon each minced fresh ginger and Oriental
   sesame oil
1/2 cup light soy sauce (or 1/4 cup regular soy sauce and
   1/4 cup water)
1/2 cup water
1 teaspoon oyster sauce
1/2 tablespoon dry sherry
1/8 teaspoon white pepper
1/2 teaspoon cornstarch

1. Make marinade: Mix marinade ingredients and pour
into a resealable plastic bag or into a bowl. Add the pork
and mix well, then seal bag or cover bowl and refrigerate
overnight or for at least 4 hours.

2. Preheat oven to 450°F. Remove pork from marinade
and lay in one layer on a rack, which has been sprayed
with cooking spray and placed on cookie sheet. Cook
meat for 15 minutes, turning once. Reduce oven
temperature to 350°F. Bring marinade to a boil and brush
meat with the marinade, then roast 15 minutes more.
Discard remaining marinade. Using two forks, shred
pork. If it gets too difficult to do by the time you get to
the middle of the pieces of meat, you can drop them in
the food processor and pulse a few times.

Dipping Sauce:

1 tablespoon hoisin sauce
2 tablespoons each oyster sauce and ketchup
1/3 cup brown sugar (packed)
1/4 teaspoon white pepper
1 teaspoon cornstarch
1/2 cup chicken stock
1 tablespoon dry sherry
hot chili oil to taste

For baking:

1 egg beaten with 1 tablespoon water
4 tablespoons butter, melted

1. Make dipping sauce: Combine sauce ingredients in a
small pan, bring to a boil, stirring, then transfer to a bowl
and refrigerate until needed.

2. Assemble the Pork Buns: Punch the bun dough down
and divide into 24 equal portions., or 48 portions if you
want to make cocktail size buns. Keep covered under
a damp cloth. Roll them out, one at a time, into 4-inch
disks, separating rolled disks with parchment paper.
Take one disk in your hand and place one tablespoon of
filling in the center for large buns, and 1 1/2 teaspoons
filling for the smaller ones. Bring sides of circle up to the
middle, gently guiding the filling into the pocket with
your thumb, then twist in the shape of a drawstring purse
(without the strings). Place twisted side down on two (or
more if making the smaller buns) greased cookie sheets.
Continue filling until all buns are formed. Cover with a
towel and let rise for 45 minutes.

3. Preheat oven to 350°F. Brush buns with the egg beaten
with the water and bake for 20 minutes, or less for smaller
buns, until golden brown. Remove from oven and brush
with melted butter. Cool on racks. Serve with reserved
dipping sauce. It would be fun to serve the smaller buns
on fancy toothpicks with mixed drinks you create with
names like *Zombies* and *Dragons* to wash them down.

OODLES OF ASIAN NOODLES

It can be really confusing when you venture into an Asian market and see the variety of Asian noodles available. Here are four recipes using four different types of noodles, to guide you through some of the choices. Remember to have fun exploring when you go into an Asian market. You will find the owners and clerks eager to help you succeed!

Thai Spring Rolls
Japanese Beef Udon Noodles
Singapore Fried Noodles
Chinese Ginger Scallion Noodles

THAI SPRING ROLLS
MAKES 16 ROLLS

These differ from Chinese Spring rolls, as the filling uses bean thread noodles and has distinctive Thai flavors.

3 ounces bean thread vermicelli noodles
6 dried black mushrooms, soaked in cold water 25
    minutes
4 ounces firm tofu (bean curd)
1 cup shredded bamboo shoots (shred in processor)
1/2 cup <u>each</u> shredded carrots and celery or jicama (in
    processor)
3/4 cup fresh bean sprouts, pods and roots removed,
    washed
1/4 cup loosely packed cilantro (Chinese parsley) leaves
1/3 cup finely chopped scallions
3 tablespoons nam pla (Thai fish sauce)
1/2 teaspoon white pepper
1 tablespoon mashed fresh garlic
2 quarts solid Crisco oil for deep frying
16 Spring roll wrappers (8 1/2 inch square)
beaten egg (to "glue" seams of spring rolls)

Dipping Sauces:

Purchased sweet and sour sauce, hoisin sauce, sweet or
<u>hot chili sauce</u>

1. Soak the vermicelli in hot water for 15 minutes. Drain in a fine strainer, then cut with kitchen shears into 1-1/2 inch pieces and reserve. Drain the mushrooms, squeezing out excess water, and remove and discard the stems (or save for soup). Cut the caps into fine shreds. Slice the tofu thin, then stack slices and cut them into fine shreds. Prepare the other vegetables and combine all well in a large bowl, adding the cilantro, scallions, nam pla, white pepper and garlic.

2. Soak each spring roll wrapper in a large dish of warm water for about 1 1/2 minutes, or until it softens enough to be pliable, handling carefully, as they are very brittle and fragile at first. Use two softened wrappers per roll, piling one on top of the other, to insure tight wrap even with tears in one wrapper. Position the wrappers in front of you and place a generous 1/3 cup filling slightly above center. Fold the top over the filling and press to moisten. Fold in the two sides, then roll toward you. Moisten end with egg and fold, squeezing gently to make it adhere. Place on rectangular tray that has been sprayed with cooking spray and continue until all rolls and filling are used. Spray some plastic wrap with cooking spray and cover rolls. At this point you can refrigerate them for several hours, or fry and eat.

3. <u>To fry:</u> Heat the oil in a deep fryer or large deep pot to 375°F., using a deep fat frying thermometer. Gently lower the rolls, two at a time, into the oil and fry about 4 minutes a side, or until golden brown. Drain on absorbent paper. Be sure to keep oil at 375°F. to keep rolls crisp. Serve with your choices of the dipping sauces.

JAPANESE BEEF UDON NOODLES—SERVES 8

Always prep all your ingredients before beginning to cook Asian dishes—then you can put them together quickly with no last-minute nerves.

2 tablespoons <u>each</u> soy sauce, oyster sauce and dry
    sherry
1/2 to 3/4 cup chicken broth
2 teaspoons minced garlic

1 teaspoon sugar
3 scallions, cut into 2-inch long julienne strips
1/4 cup water
1 stalk broccoli, cut into florets, discarding stems, to
    measure 1 cup

1/4 head Napa cabbage, very thinly sliced, to measure 1
    cup
2 large eggs, beaten in a small bowl
1/2 pound beef tenderloin, sliced into 1/4-inch slices
    and then into 1/2-inch wide strips
12 ounces dried udon (Japanese wheat noodles)
2 tablespoons vegetable oil
1/4 cup sliced onions
1 can rinsed and drained canned straw mushroons
<u>1 cup fresh bean sprouts</u>

1. In a small bowl stir together the soy and oyster sauces,
dry sherry, chicken broth, garlic and sugar.

2. In a 5-quart large stockpot bring 3 1/2 quarts of salted
water to a boil and cook noodles 12 to 14 minutes, until
just tender. Rinse noodles in a colander under cold water
and drain well. Reserve.

3. Heat a wok or large heavy skillet over high heat until a
bead of water dropped on cooking surface immediately
evaporates. Add 1/2 tablespoon oil, swirling wok to coat
evenly, and heat until just smoking. Stir-fry the eggs until
scrambled, about 30 seconds and transfer to a bowl. Wipe
out the wok with a paper towel.

4. Add 1 tablespoon oil to wok and stir-fry the onion and
beef in batches on high heat until beef is browned but
still pink inside, about 1 minute. Season with salt and
pepper. Transfer to a bowl. Add the last 1/2 tablespoon of
oil to wok and stir-fry the broccoli 30 seconds. Add the
water and cook broccoli, stirring, until crisp-tender. Add
the sauce mixture, noodles and mushrooms and cook,
stirring until heated through, adding up to another 1/4
cup broth, if needed to prevent noodles from sticking.
Stir in scallions, cabbage, sprouts, beef, eggs, salt and
pepper to taste until well combined. Transfer to bowl and
serve right away.

SINGAPORE FRIED NOODLES—SERVES 8

Curry Paste:

2 tablespoons oil
1 tablespoon curry powder
1 teaspoon turmeric
1/2 cup chicken stock

8 ounces rice vermicelli, soaked in lukewarm water 20
    minutes, drained
2 cups <u>each</u> broccoli and cauliflower florets
2 carrots, shredded (in processor)
1 onion, chopped
2 tablespoons chopped shallots
2 cloves garlic, chopped
2 cups Napa cabbage, shredded
1/4 teaspoon pure chili powder
1 large egg
4 green onions, sliced

1 cup chicken stock
2 tablespoons cilantro leaves, coarsely chopped

<u>Optional: Sambal Oelek chili sauce or Sriracha hot chili
sauce (careful-very spicy!)</u>

1. Place 2 tablespoons of oil in a medium skillet and add
the curry powder and turmeric. Stir to roast spices to
bring out their flavor. Add the 1/2 cup chicken stock,
stirring to make a paste. This will add flavor and color to
dish. Reserve.

2. In a wok put 2 to 3 tablespoons of oil and sweat the
onions, garlic and shallots on Medium heat. Add the
broccoli and cauliflower florets, carrots, salt and pepper.
Steam them with 1/4 cup water, covered. Add the cabbage
and the chili powder. Clear a space in the center of this
mixture, add another tablespoon of oil and scramble the
egg in the center, then mix it into the vegetables. Add in
handfuls of the noodles, stirring, until all are in the wok,
then add the curry paste. Stir in the green onions and 1
cup of chicken broth. Garnish with the cilantro leaves
and serve right away, with Sambal Oelek or other hot
sauce if desired.

GINGER-SCALLION NOODLES—SERVES 8

To make homemade Chinese chicken broth: in a large pot combine 3 1/2 pounds chicken bones—necks, backs, wings, etc. with 9 cups water, 1 cup Chinese rice wine or sake, and 6 slices of fresh ginger, each about the size of a quarter and lightly smashed with the flat side of a knife. Either bring to a boil on top of the stove in a large pot, reduce heat to low and simmer uncovered for 1 1/2 hours, skimming the foam from time to time, OR put into a large bowl, cover with plastic wrap and microwave for 45 minutes. Using either method, strain the broth through a fine strainer and skim off any fat when cooked, or cool and refrigerate, then remove solidified fat layer. Makes 6 cups of Chinese stock. The advantages of making your own stock are that there is no MSG in it, which is unfortunately found in many canned products, and homemade always has a much better flavor. This stock freezes well, too. You can take 1/2 pound chicken breasts cut into thin strips or 1/2 pound peeled raw shrimp and stir-fry them in 2 tablespoons oil in a hot wok and add to finished dish to make this dish non-vegetarian.

Sesame Sauce:

3/4 cup Chinese chicken broth, homemade (directions above) or canned
1 1/2 tablespoons Oriental toasted sesame oil
1 1/2 teaspoons salt, or to taste
1/2 teaspoon freshly ground black pepper
1 teaspoon cornstarch

1 1/2 tablespoons vegetable oil
2 cups finely chopped scallions
1/2 cup finely shredded fresh ginger (peeled, chopped in processor)
1/2 cup Chinese rice wine or sake
3 cups fresh bean sprouts, rinsed and drained

1/2 pound thin Chinese egg noodles, or angel hair pasta, cooked just until tender, rinsed under cold water, drained

Optional: 1/2 pound boneless, skinless chicken breasts, thinly sliced plus
1/2 pound raw shelled shrimp.
2 tablespoons oil

1. Make sesame sauce: Mix all ingredients well and reserve.

2. Heat a wok or heavy skillet over high heat. Add the oil and heat until very hot but not smoking, about 30 seconds. Add scallions and ginger and stir-fry until fragrant, about 30 seconds. Add the rice wine and bean sprouts and toss lightly for about 1 minute.

3. Add sesame sauce to above mixture in wok along with the noodles. Stir-fry until sauce is thickened, about 2 minutes. At this point you can add the optional stir-fried chicken and shrimp if desired, then transfer to a bowl or platter and serve right away.

CELEBRATING THE CHINESE NEW YEAR

Every year a different sign of the zodiac in the Chinese calendar is celebrated. Get a group of your friends together to make this marvelous meal.

Prosperity Tray
Savory Chicken Soup with Shrimp Balls and Straw Mushrooms
Rainbow Peanut Noodles
Spicy Chicken Stir-Fry with Cashews
Steamed Lemon Sponge Cakes with Asian Fruits

PROSPERITY TRAY

During the Chinese New Year each food served from a prosperity tray carries a symbolic meaning. Traditionally, the tray is laden with some of the following items, which can be purchased at many Asian markets. Lay the ingredients out on a Chinese red lacquered tray or a bamboo tray if you can find one (although any tray will do), and explain the symbols to your guests, to enhance their dining experience.

Red-dyed melon seeds, to symbolize joy, happiness and sincerity
Lychee nuts to symbolize strong family relationships
Kumquats and coconuts for togetherness
Peanuts for long life
Lotus seeds to insure a large family
Longan Fruit for good and dutiful sons
Tangerines and oranges to symbolize good luck

During Chinese New Year, each person's birthday is celebrated, and noodles, which symbolize longevity, are as important as our Western birthday cake. By eating noodles, it is hoped one will be assured of a long and prosperous life.

A whole fish is often served at the New Year's Feast, to symbolize bounty. Many vegetables are eaten also, often cut in the shape of coins for prosperity.

During the Feast, red envelopes which contain money (a coin and a bill) are passed out to the children, and firecracker displays are common everywhere. Everyone stays up to welcome in the New Year, believing that if the children stay up it will make their parents live longer. On New Year's Day there is a huge Dragon Parade, as the dragon is the most important and powerful animal of the Chinese zodiac. Its appearance once a year at the New Year brings good fortune to everyone.

SAVORY CHICKEN SOUP WITH SHRIMP BALLS AND STRAW MUSHROOMS—SERVES 8

Shrimp Balls

6 ounces raw, shelled deveined shrimp
1 ounce pork suet or fat from a pork chop
1/2 teaspoon cornstarch
1/2 teaspoon salt
1/4 teaspoon black pepper
1/2 teaspoon sesame oil
1 egg white

1 tablespoon peanut or other vegetable oil
6 cups chicken stock
1 1/2 teaspoons dry white wine or dry sherry
2 teaspoons salt, or to taste
1 1/2 cups canned straw mushrooms, drained

Garnish: 6 green onions, cut into thin diagonal slices

1. Pat shrimp dry and chop into a fine paste with pork suet. Mix with salt, pepper, sesame oil, cornstarch and egg white. Form into small balls.

2. In large wok or stockpot heat 1 tablespoon oil. Add stock, wine and salt. Bring to a boil and add mushrooms and shrimp balls and cook over high heat until shrimp balls float to top. Ladle soup into serving bowls and garnish with the green onion shreds.

SPICY CHICKEN STIR-FRY WITH CASHEWS
SERVES 8

Marinade:

1/2 cup low-sodium soy sauce (or 1/4 cup regular with
    1/4 cup water)
1/4 cup dry sherry
2 tablespoons cornstarch
2 cloves garlic, crushed
1 1/2 teaspoons finely chopped fresh gingerroot

1 1/2 pounds skinless, boneless chicken breasts, cut into
    1/2 inch strips

2 tablespoons peanut or vegetable oil
1 head broccoli, cut into florets, about 4 cups
3 medium carrots, peeled and cut into 1/4 inch slices,
    about 1 1/2 cups
6 scallions with green tops, cut into 1/2 inch pieces
    diagonally
1 can of straw mushrooms, drained
1 jar or can of baby corn, drained
1 cup (4 ounces) cashew nuts, roasted in 350°F. oven 10
    minutes
1 cup low-sodium chicken broth
1/2 to 1 teaspoon Kitchen Bouquet or Chinese brown
    gravy (for color)
1 to 2 teaspoons sesame oil, and chili oil to taste

1. In medium bowl mix soy sauce, sherry, cornstarch,
garlic and ginger well. Add chicken, tossing to coat
thoroughly and refrigerate for at least 20 minutes or up to
one hour.

2. Drain chicken, reserving marinade. In wok or large
heavy skillet over high heat, heat 1 tablespoon of the oil.
Add chicken, 1/4 at a time and cook, stirring constantly
until lightly browned and cooked through. Remove to
plate and keep adding more chicken to the wok until all
meat is browned. Wipe out wok.

3. Add remaining tablespoon oil and heat to High.
Add broccoli and carrots and cook 2 to 4 minutes,
stirring constantly, until vegetables are crisp-tender.
Add scallions, mushrooms and baby corn and stir-fry 2
minutes to heat through.

4. Return chicken with any accumulated juices to wok.
Add cashews, chili oil, reserved marinade, chicken broth,
sesame oil to taste and Kitchen Bouquet for color. Cook,
stirring constantly, until mixture boils and thickens,
thoroughly coating chicken and vegetables. Remove to a
serving bowl and serve with freshly cooked rice.

RAINBOW PEANUT NOODLES
SERVES 8 TO 10

This dish is a very popular choice at Asian restaurants today.

Chinese Peanut Dressing:

2 slices 1/2-inch thick fresh gingerroot, peeled and
    sliced in half
8 large cloves garlic, peeled
2 to 3 teaspoons hot chili paste, or Thai garlic sauce, or
    more to taste
1 cup smooth peanut butter, or more if necessary
7 tablespoons each sugar and Chinese black vinegar or
    Worchestershire sauce
6 tablespoons toasted sesame oil
6 to 8 tablespoons chicken broth or water, or more if
    necessary
3/4 cup chopped peanuts

1 pound thin noodles, such as linguine, cooked until
    just tender, rinsed under cold water, drained and
    tossed with 2 teaspoons toasted sesame oil
3 carrots, peeled and grated
2 English cucumbers (seedless), peeled and halved
    lengthwise, then shredded and squeezed dry
3 cups fresh bean sprouts, rinsed and drained
1 red bell pepper, cored, seeded, and julienned into thin
    strips
3 tablespoons minced scallion, green and white parts

1. Make the Peanut Dressing: In the food processor
fitted with the metal blade or in a blender, finely chop
the ginger and garlic. Add remaining ingredients except
chopped peanuts in the order listed and process until
smooth. The dressing should be the consistency of heavy
cream. If too thick, add more water or chicken broth.
If too thin add more peanut butter. Add the chopped
peanuts. Refrigerated in a covered container, this dressing
will keep for 2 to 3 weeks.

2. Place cooked warm noodles and sesame oil in a large
serving bowl. Toss well with all the vegetables. Mix in the
peanut dressing, coating the noodles well.

3. Serve at room temperature or chilled.

STEAMED LEMON SPONGE CAKES
MAKES 6

A light way to finish an Asian meal. This dessert is not too sweet.

2 large eggs, separated
1/2 cup light brown sugar
2 teaspoons grated lemon zest
2 tablespoons fresh lemon juice
1/2 teaspoon pure vanilla extract

2/3 cup sifted flour, measured after sifting
1/4 teaspoon each baking powder and salt

canned Chinese fruits, such as lychees, kumquats,
    mandarin oranges, drained, chilled

1. Beat the egg yolks in an electric mixer until light and
lemon-colored, about 4 to 5 minutes. Add the brown
sugar and beat 2 to 3 minutes more, stirring several
times. Add the lemon zest, lemon juice and the vanilla.

2. Combine the flour, baking powder and salt. Fold into
the yolk mixture gently but thoroughly. Transfer to a
bowl with a wide top, for ease in folding, below.

3. Beat the egg whites with an electric mixer until stiff
peaks form. Fold into batter gently with a clean rubber
spatula.

4. Divide the mixture among six 2-inch midget foil or
ceramic muffin cups and place on the racks of a Chinese
steamer, then place into a large wok or saucepan. If you
do not have a steamer use a large saucepan with a foil pie
plate overturned, which you have pierced with a skewer
to make several holes for steam to escape. Add water to
just below the level of the rack or top of foil pan. Cover,
bring water to a boil and let steam on high heat for 10
minutes, or until cakes are set. Serve warm or cold with
chilled Chinese fruits.

A TASTE OF THAI CUISINE

Classic Pad Thai
Panko Shrimp with Thai Dipping Sauce
Stir-Fry Beef with Mint
Ginger Lychee Sorbet

CLASSIC PAD THAI—SERVES 8

One of my favorite dishes. Now you can recreate it at home.

8 ounces dried rice stick noodles (1/8 inch wide, like linguine), cut in half with kitchen scissors

2 eggs
1/4 teaspoon sea salt

2 tablespoons tamarind paste rehydrated in 3/4 cup boiling water, then puréed
OR 1 cup dried apricots puréed in blender with 1 cup cherry juice
1/2 cup palm sugar (tropical sugar made from coconut or date sap and processed in cones) OR packed light brown sugar
1/2 teaspoon sea salt
1/4 cup fish sauce (nam pla)
1 tablespoon rice vinegar (seasoned or plain)
1 tablespoon or more chili paste (to taste)
2 tablespoons vegetable oil

2 tablespoons vegetable oil, <u>DIVIDED</u>
12 ounces medium shrimp (31/35 count), peeled and deveined
1 tablespoon (3 garlic cloves pressed through garlic press)
1 medium shallot, minced (about 3 tablespoons)

2 tablespoons dried shrimp, chopped fine (optional but authentic)
6 tablespoons chopped roasted unsalted peanuts
3 cups (6 ounces) fresh bean sprouts
5 medium scallions, green parts only, sliced thin on sharp bias
<u>lime wedges</u>

1. In large bowl cover the rice sticks with very hot tap water. Soak until softened, pliable and limp but not fully tender, about 30 minutes or more. Drain noodles and set aside. Beat eggs and salt in small bowl and set aside.

2. In large bowl place either the tamarind paste which has been rehydrated in the water OR the dried apricots with cherry juice. Stir in palm sugar, sea salt, fish sauce, rice vinegar, chili paste and 2 tablespoons vegetable oil. Can be made several days ahead and refrigerated.

3. In a large wok heat 1 tablespoon oil over high heat until just beginning to smoke, about 2 minutes. Add shrimp and sprinkle with 1/4 teaspoon salt. Stir-fry until shrimp are opaque and browned around the edges, about 2 to 3 minutes. Transfer shrimp to plate and set aside. Off heat, add remaining 1 tablespoon oil to wok and swirl to coat. Add garlic and shallot and return to medium heat and cook, stirring constantly, until light golden brown, about 1 minute. Add reserved eggs and salt and stir vigorously until eggs are scrambled and barely moist, about 20 seconds. Add drained noodles and dried shrimp and toss with two large spoons to coat. Gradually add fish sauce and tamarind or apricot mixture to wok, tossing constantly, until noodles are evenly coated. Scatter 1/4 cup of the peanuts, the bean sprouts, all but 1/4 cup of the scallions and cooked shrimp over the noodles and continue to cook, tossing constantly, until noodles are tender, about 3 minutes more, adding a bit of water to wok if needed for noodles to get tender.

4. Transfer noodle mixture to large serving platter, garnish with remaining scallions, peanuts and lime wedges and serve right away.

PANKO SHRIMP WITH THAI DIPPING SAUCE
SERVES 8

Panko is Japanese breadcrumbs that are coarser and crisper than regular bread crumbs. They are available at all supermarkets today, so do not substitute regular bread crumbs in this dish if you want it to be authentic.

Thai Dipping Sauce:

1 cup fresh lime juice
5 teaspoons light brown sugar
4 teaspoons fresh ginger, minced
2 teaspoons <u>each</u> fish sauce and chopped cilantro
4 teaspoons dry roasted peanuts, chopped
2 green onions, minced

32 large shrimp, peeled and deveined, tails still attached if desired
salt and freshly ground black pepper
1 1/3 cups all purpose flour
4 eggs, thoroughly beaten
3 cups Panko
<u>vegetable oil, for deep frying</u>

1. <u>Prepare the dipping sauce:</u> In a medium saucepan heat the lime juice, brown sugar, ginger and fish sauce to 180°F. to dissolve sugar. Remove from heat and cool. Add the peanuts, cilantro and green onion. Reserve.

2. <u>Prepare the shrimp:</u> Place the flour and Panko on separate pieces of parchment or waxed paper, and break the eggs into a shallow bowl like a pie plate, and stir with a fork. Dust each shrimp with flour, then coat with egg. Return shrimp to the flour, dip in egg again, and then coat with the Panko breadcrumbs. Place on parchment paper or waxed paper and use right away, or refrigerate covered, up to an hour if necessary.

3. <u>When ready to serve:</u> In a heavy pot, heat 3 inches of oil to 325°F. to 350°F. Cook 3 to 4 shrimp at a time for about 3 to 4 minutes or until golden and crispy. Drain on rack and serve with sauce.

STIR-FRY BEEF WITH MINT—SERVES 8

Remember to prep all of your ingredients before you start cooking, (mise en place) so you can stir-fry quickly. This insures that the meat and vegetables will cook evenly.

1 ounce (about 7) finely chopped Serrano chilis (use rubber gloves to handle them)
2 tablespoons finely chopped garlic
1/2 cup finely chopped yellow onion

2 tablespoons vegetable oil
2 pounds flank steak, sliced across grain into 1/8-inch thick strips

3 tablespoons fish sauce
1 tablespoon granulated sugar
1/2 cup water
1/2 cup loosely packed fresh mint or basil leaves
2 cucumbers, peeled and thinly sliced, and fresh mint sprigs

<u>Garnish for platter: green leaf lettuce</u>

1. In blender or using a mortar and pestle grind the chilis, garlic and onion to a coarse paste. You may need to add a bit of vegetable oil to the blender to aid in grinding.

2. Heat a wok, add the 2 tablespoons oil and swirl it over the surface of the pan. Add the paste and stir-fry until it is light golden. Add the beef in several batches and stir-fry until beef is light brown, but do not overcook it.

3. Add the fish sauce, sugar, water and mint leaves. More water may be added if the sauce is too dry.

4. Arrange a single layer of lettuce on serving platter and put the beef mixture on it. Garnish with cucumber slices (to cut the heat of this dish) and mint sprigs if desired.

GINGER LYCHEE SORBET—SERVES 8

Cool, simple and refreshing.

2 20-ounce cans pitted lychees in heavy syrup
<u>2 tablespoons pickled sushi ginger</u>

1. Purée the lychees with their syrup and the ginger in a food processor or blender until completely smooth.

2. Pour into a shallow pan and freeze until solid, about 4 hours or longer.

3. Cut or break the frozen mixture into very small cubes and purée in a food processor in two batches until creamy.

4. Store in the freezer in a tightly closed container for up to 1 week. If the mixture should become solid, cut it into cubes and purée it again in food processor before serving.

ASIAN ACCENTS

Pho-Vietnamese Chicken Noodle Soup
Skewered Pork Satay
Baby Bok Choy with Chinese Mushrooms
Citrus Fried Rice
Fried Bananas with Coconut Milk and Sesame Seeds

PHO (PRONOUNCED FUH)—VIETNAMESE CHICKEN NOODLE SOUP—SERVES 8

This is the national dish of Vietnam. Pho restaurants are popping up all over America. Try it once and you'll be addicted to its savory flavors.

8 ounces dried rice noodles (flat, fettuccine-shaped)

12 ounces boneless chicken breast, cut into julienne (long, thin) strips
1 teaspoon salt
4 teaspoons cornstarch
2 teaspoons sesame oil

12 cups chicken stock, homemade, More Than Gourmet, or boxed
12 thin slices peeled fresh ginger root
2 garlic cloves, smashed
2 stalks of lemongrass (bottom third only, smashed with flat side of Chef's knife, then sliced thinly)
1 teaspoon coriander seeds OR 1 whole star anise
2 tablespoons fish sauce
1 tablespoon sugar
1/2 cup Asian basil leaves if possible, or if not available, regular basil leaves, coarsely chopped
4 tablespoons (1/4 cup) freshly squeezed lime juice
1/4 cup fresh cilantro leaves
2 teaspoons freshly ground black pepper
1 cup fresh bean sprouts
julienned fresh red or green chili peppers to taste
<u>lime wedges</u>

1. Soak noodles in boiling water to cover, about 30 minutes or until soft, then drain well and reserve.

2. Toss julienned chicken strips with the 1 teaspoon of

salt, the cornstarch and the sesame oil. Refrigerate 30 minutes.

3. Bring the chicken stock to a boil with the ginger, garlic, lemongrass and coriander seeds or star anise. Turn heat to low, cover and simmer for 30 minutes. Strain stock, discarding the lemongrass, garlic and ginger. Bring back to a boil and add the fish sauce and the sugar. Lower to medium heat and add the julienned chicken, basil and lime juice. Continue to simmer a few minutes.

4. Meanwhile, divide drained noodles among 8 serving bowls. Ladle soup into bowls, sprinkle with the cilantro leaves and black pepper. Taste and adjust seasoning. Serve with the bean sprouts, chilis and lime wedges arranged on small plates, to be added by each diner according to their taste.

2. In large non-metallic casserole marinate pork cubes in marinade for at least 2 hours or up to overnight in refrigerator.

3. Soak wooden skewers for 1/2 hour in water so they won't burn when broiling meat.

4. Thread marinated pork cubes on 8 skewers and broil or grill for up to 10 minutes, basting with oil and watching carefully. Do not overcook or they will be dry. Cut into one cube half way through grilling to see if it is no longer pink and is cooked through.

5. Meanwhile, bring marinade to boil on stove or in microwave and put into a serving bowl.

6. When pork is cooked, serve right away with the peanut sauce and the cooked rice.

SKEWERED PORK SATAYS WITH PEANUT SAUCE—SERVES 8

Marinade/Sauce:

1 tablespoon coriander seeds
1 cup unsalted peanuts
1/2 cup creamy peanut butter
1/8 teaspoon cayenne pepper
1/4 teaspoon freshly ground black pepper
1 clove garlic, crushed
1 small onion, finely chopped
1 tablespoon brown sugar
3 tablespoons fresh lemon juice
1/4 cup each soy sauce and water
1/2 cup dry sherry

1 1/2 pounds boneless pork tenderloin, fat removed, cut into 1/2-inch cubes

vegetable oil to brush kebabs

2 cups rice, rinsed well in a strainer, then cooked in 4 cups water

1. Make marinade/sauce: In blender or processor grind coriander seeds with peanuts until finely chopped. Add rest of ingredients up to pork.

BABY BOKCHOY WITH CHINESE MUSHROOMS SERVES 8

10 large dried Chinese mushrooms

20 heads baby bokchoy or 1 large head bokchoy, washed well, as they can be sandy
3 cloves garlic, finely minced
1 large shallot, finely minced

Hot Wok Sauce:

1/4 cup each chicken stock and rice wine or dry sherry
2 tablespoons oyster sauce
1 tablespoon each dark sesame oil and cornstarch
1/2 teaspoon sugar
freshly ground black pepper to taste

2 tablespoons or more cooking oil

1. Place dried mushrooms in a bowl and cover with boiling water. Place a small plate on top of them to keep them submerged. Soak until softened, about 30 minutes. Gently squeeze out most of the water, cut off and discard tough mushroom stems, then cut mushrooms in half.

2. Cut the baby bokchoy in half lengthwise. If using the large head, cut off and discard bottom end. Separate head

into stalks and then cut each stalk on a sharp diagonal, then turn and cut again, making diamond shapes if you wish. You will need 4 to 5 cups of bokchoy in all. Mix with the mushrooms and set aside, or refrigerate if not ready to make the stir-fry.

3. Combine the garlic and shallots in a small bowl.

4. Combine the <u>Hot Wok Sauce</u> ingredients and reserve.

5. When ready to cook, place wok over highest heat. When it is very hot, add the cooking oil in the center. Roll oil around the wok, and when it gives off a wisp of smoke the wok is ready. Add the garlic and shallot and sauté for 1 minute, then add the vegetables. Stir and toss vegetables until leaves begin to wilt and turn bright green, about 3 minutes. Stir in the Hot Wok Sauce and toss until vegetables are glazed with the sauce, about 1 minute. Taste and adjust seasonings. Immediately transfer to heated platter and serve.

CITRUS FRIED RICE—SERVES 8

This is a lovely variation on the standard fried rice.

3 large eggs

1 red bell pepper, cut into 1/4-inch cubes
2 small carrots, peeled and cut on the diagonal
4 whole green onions, cut on the diagonal
10 stalks asparagus, tough ends snapped off, peeled, cut on the diagonal into 1/8-inch pieces

4 cups <u>cold</u> cooked rice (see directions for cooking below)
1/4 cup white sesame seeds
1/4 cup rice wine or dry sherry

Hot Wok Sauce:

2 teaspoons minced orange zest
1/3 cup orange juice, freshly squeezed if possible
2 tablespoons <u>each</u> rice wine or dry sherry and dark sesame oil

3 tablespoons oyster sauce
1/2 teaspoon Asian chili sauce

3 tablespoons cooking oil
3 cloves garlic, finely minced
<u>**2 shallots, finely minced**</u>

1. In a small bowl beat eggs with a fork and reserve.

2. Combine bell pepper, carrots, green onions and asparagus in a bowl and reserve.

3. Place sesame seeds in a small sauté pan and toast them over medium heat until they turn golden, then transfer to a small dish and reserve.

4. <u>To cook rice:</u> Do NOT use instant rice. Put 1 1/2 cups raw rice in a fine sieve and run cold water over until water runs clear, to remove gluten and any powder or dirt. Place in a large saucepan and add 3 cups of cold water. Bring to a boil on high heat, then reduce heat to low, cover and cook until rice has absorbed all the water, about 20 to 25 minutes. Transfer to a bowl and cool. When cool you can refrigerate for several days or freeze it in a plastic bag. This will yield 4 cups cooked rice.

5. <u>Make Hot Wok Sauce:</u> In a small bowl combine ingredients. Reserve.

6. <u>When ready to cook:</u> Place wok over highest heat and when it is very hot add 1 tablespoon of the oil to the center. Roll oil around wok and when it gives off a wisp of smoke add the eggs. Stir and toss eggs until they become lightly scrambled, then immediately slide onto a plate and reserve. Immediately return wok to heat and add the remaining 2 tablespoons oil and the garlic and shallots. As soon as they turn white, about 5 seconds, add the vegetables and stir and toss until asparagus and carrots brighten in color, about 3 minutes. During the cooking, add the 1/4 cup rice wine to prevent scorching if needed.

7. Add the cold rice and scrambled eggs to the wok. Stir in the Hot Wok Sauce and sesame seeds. Stir and toss until all ingredients are mixed evenly and rice is thoroughly heated. Taste and adjusts seasonings, then transfer to heated platter and serve.

FRIED BANANAS WITH COCONUT MILK AND SESAME SEEDS—SERVES 8

1/4 cup cornstarch
3/4 cup all-purpose flour
1/2 teaspoon salt
1 teaspoon baking powder

1 egg, lightly beaten
1/2 cup heavy cream or Half and Half
1/4 cup cream of coconut (Coco Lopez) or more to thin batter to correct consistency
1 tablespoon melted butter
3 tablespoons sesame seeds

5 to 6 firm bananas (about 3 pounds)

Crisco solid shortening for deep frying

1. In a medium bowl mix together cornstarch, flour, salt and baking powder. In another bowl mix together egg, cream, coconut milk, butter and sesame seeds. Add this mixture to dry ingredients, stirring only until moistened.

2. Peel bananas and cut into 1 1/2-inch lengths on the diagonal.

3. Heat Crisco to 375°F. Using a slotted spoon, dip pieces of banana in batter, spreading batter evenly over bananas, draining excess, and working quickly, fry for about 3 minutes or until golden brown. Drain on paper towel and serve right away.

COOK'S TIP

You may not be familiar with several of the ingredients featured in the recipes in this chapter. Before attempting to cook these recipes, read each recipe thoroughly, then visit an Asian market in your city to familiarize yourself with these new ingredients. Bring a list so that you can build an Asian pantry, as many of the same ingredients are used in multiple recipes, and have a long shelf life if stored properly. All red spices should always be refrigerated, as should sesame oil and any opened sauces.

10

RECIPES FROM THE MELTING POT

Throughout America's history, we have welcomed many people who came seeking freedom in this glorious land of opportunity. They have enriched our cuisine with their native foods and made our country a rich melting pot of great culinary diversity. Starting when I was very young I had the opportunity to experience first hand the smells and tastes of exotic foods in the windows of the various neighborhoods in Cleveland, Ohio—from Hungarian paprika rubbed bacon to plump purple Greek olives to Jewish breads and pastries at ethnic bakeries. What fun it has been to share these foods with my family and introduce them to my friends and students! This cookbook has entire chapters featuring Italian, French and Asian cooking, and in this chapter we offer unique dishes brought by several other major waves of immigrants. Many of these recipes have become integrated into our food scenes, and we welcome them as part of our national cuisine. We take it for granted that on every corner there is a Mexican grocery, an Indian restaurant, and Jewish delis today. Here is your chance to become a world traveler *in your own kitchen* and cook some of these foods. Come experience and experiment fearlessly. Don't be intimidated—I'll walk you through the new techniques and ingredients to ensure that you'll be a hit with your "audience." Your adventures will include recipes from Jewish, Irish, Mexican, Middle Eastern, Greek and Indian cooking! Menus include: Jewish Classics, Irish Fare, Mexican Fiesta, Middle Eastern Delights, Greek Cuisine and Indian Adventure.

Schwarma Kebabs (pages 172-173) and Saffron Rice Pilaf with Toasted Pine Nuts (page 173)

JEWISH CLASSICS

This is the food I grew up with. As any Jewish mother would say, "Try It, You'll Like it!"

Golden Chicken Soup with Matzoh Balls
Classic Savory Brisket
Potato Latkes
Cinnamon-Nut Sour Cream Kuchen (Coffeecake)

GOLDEN CHICKEN SOUP WITH MATZOH BALLS—SERVES 8 TO 10

In my house this was known as Jewish penicillin, but you don't have to be Jewish to enjoy this savory comfort food. As a newlywed, at the first Passover Seder meal I prepared for another couple, I mistakenly boiled the matzoh balls in the chicken soup. When I removed the lid from the pot I found that the matzoh balls had soaked up almost all the soup! Luckily, I had just enough for the four bowls we needed that night, but it taught me to cook the matzoh balls in salted water ever since.

Chicken Soup:

4 to 5-pound roasting chicken, cut up, excess fat
   removed
3 1/2 to 4 quarts water to cover
2 medium onions, peeled
2 to 3 carrots, peeled and cut into 1-inch pieces
2 stalks celery, cut into 1-inch pieces
1 parsnip, peeled
1 tablespoon salt, or to taste
2 sprigs fresh parsley, plus 2 tablespoons chopped
   parsley

Matzoh Balls:

4 tablespoons rendered chicken fat (schmaltz) or
   margarine
4 large eggs, slightly beaten
1 cup matzoh meal
<u>1 teaspoon salt</u>

1. <u>Make Soup</u>: In large pot combine chicken, water, onions, carrots, celery, , parsnip salt and sprigs of parsley.

Bring to a boil and skim off any scum that rises to the top. Lower heat to a simmer and cook until chicken and vegetables are tender, 2 1/2 to 3 hours. Strain soup into a shallow pan if possible, (to speed the chilling process), reserving vegetables and chicken, and put in refrigerator uncovered to cool completely, at least 4 hours or up to overnight.

2. <u>Meanwhile, Make Matzoh Balls</u>: In a medium bowl blend chicken fat or margarine and eggs together. In another bowl mix matzoh meal and salt together, then add the matzoh meal mixture to eggs and mix well. Add soup and mix till well blended. Cover bowl and refrigerate for 15 minutes. Bring a large pot of salted water to a boil. Reduce to slightly boiling. Form matzoh balls from above mixture and drop into pot. Cover pot and cook 30 to 40 minutes, until balls are tender when tested with a knife. Remove balls with a slotted spoon to a large bowl and reserve.

3. Remove chicken meat from bones and discard bones and skin. Cut meat into bite-size pieces and refrigerate, along with the onion, celery, parsnip and carrots, discarding the parsley sprigs.

4. When soup is completely cooled, remove fat layer that has formed on the top (discard or save some to make matzoh balls or potato pancakes, below) and return meat and vegetables to pot. Season to taste with more salt and black pepper and sprinkle with chopped parsley. Serve hot with a matzoh ball and some of the cooked vegetables in each bowl.

CLASSIC SAVORY BRISKET—SERVES 8

Brisket is one of the easiest roasts to make. For a variation of this recipe, instead of water, place 1 cup prepared chili sauce, a 12-ounce bottle of beer (not dark), 1/2 cup of water, a one-ounce package of dry onion soup mix, 3 thinly sliced onions, and 2 ribs of chopped celery in a bowl. Mix together and pour over seasoned brisket in pan. Cover and proceed as below. Serve sliced meat with vegetables and sauce.

garlic powder, onion powder, salt, pepper and sweet
   paprika
<u>3-pound brisket, with a good layer of fat on top</u>

1. Preheat oven to 350°F.

2. Mix spices together and sprinkle liberally on both sides of the brisket. Rub in well.

3. Place in roaster pan and add 1 to 2 cups water to come up halfway up the brisket. Cover and roast for about three hours, or until fork-tender. Cool. Put gravy in a separate gravy boat and refrigerate, so that fat will form a layer that can be discarded. Slice meat thinly and reheat. Serve with warmed gravy.

POTATO LATKES (PANCAKES)
SERVES 8

This is my husband's grandmother's recipe. I've never found one to top it. This is a traditional dish eaten at the Jewish holiday of Chanukah.

6 large Idaho (Russet) potatoes (about 3 pounds) peeled and cut into cubes
3 medium onions, peeled and quartered
3 large eggs
salt and pepper to taste
2 teaspoons chicken fat (schmaltz) or margarine
about 1/2 to 1 cup flour to make batter like pancake batter
vegetable oil for frying

Optional: sour cream and applesauce

1. In blender or food processor place potatoes, onions and eggs and process until finely chopped. Transfer to a bowl and add salt, pepper, chicken fat or margarine and flour.

2. Put 3 to 4 tablespoons of the oil in an electric skillet or other skillet . Heat on High and fry a small quantity of the batter and adjust seasonings. (Do not taste batter, as it has raw eggs in it.) Then use a coffee cup measure (2 tablespoons) for each latke. Fry until golden, turn over and fry until golden and crisp, adding more oil as needed. Drain on absorbent paper and serve immediately with sour cream and applesauce, or keep warm on racks placed on cookie sheets in one layer in low oven (250°F.) while frying rest of batter.

MOM'S CINNAMON-NUT SOUR CREAM KUCHEN (COFFEECAKE)

A family treasure from my beloved mother-in-law, Ruth Litvak. My daughter Diane thinks this is the definitive coffeecake and doesn't bother to taste any others.

Filling:

1 cup chopped walnuts
1/2 cup sugar
1 teaspoon cinnamon

Batter:

2 cups flour
1 teaspoon each baking powder and baking soda
1/4 pound(1 stick) unsalted butter
1 cup sugar
2 large eggs
1 teaspoon vanilla
1/2 pint (8 ounces) sour cream

1. Preheat oven to 350°F. Grease a 9" x 13" pan well with Crisco.

2. In small bowl combine filling ingredients. Set aside.

3. In a medium bowl combine flour, baking powder and baking soda. Set aside.

4. In a mixer cream the butter. Add the sugar and continue to beat. Add the eggs, one at a time. Add vanilla. Add combined dry ingredients alternately with the sour cream, starting and ending with dry ingredients, which ensures a better texture to the cake.

5. Spread half of the batter in pan. Sprinkle with half of the filling mixture. Spoon on the rest of batter. Don't worry if the batter doesn't cover the whole filling. Sprinkle rest of filling over the top. Bake for 30 minutes. Cool and cut into about 24 squares.

IRISH FARE—A ST. PATRICK'S DAY MEAL

Corned Beef and Cabbage Pot Pies
Oven-Roasted Herbed Carrots and Parsnips
Irish Soda Bread
Bailey's Irish Cream Chocolate Cake with Bailey's-
Spiked Whipped Cream

CORNED BEEF AND CABBAGE POT PIES
MAKES 9

A great company dish, which I adapted from a recipe from cooking teacher Betty Rosbottom.

8 ounces best-quality cooked corned beef, very thinly
     sliced
1/2 small head of cabbage (about 3/4 pound)
6 tablespoons <u>each</u> unsalted butter and all-purpose flour
3 cups whole milk, warmed
1/2 cup chopped onion, sautéed in 2 tablespoons
     unsalted butter
1 cup grated Swiss cheese
1/4 teaspoon freshly grated nutmeg
generous sprinkling of cayenne pepper
1 teaspoon fresh dill or 1/4 teaspoon dried dill
1 1/2 tablespoons stone-ground mustard
1 1/2 packages (3 sheets) frozen puff pastry, defrosted
1 large egg
<u>1 teaspoon cold water</u>

1. Chop the corned beef into large dice. Cut out the tough inner core from the cabbage and cut cabbage into large dice. Cook the cabbage in lightly salted boiling water to cover until tender, 5 to 8 minutes. Remove from heat and drain, then dry the cabbage well. Reserve.

2. <u>Make the sauce and filling</u>: In a medium-size heavy saucepan over medium heat melt the butter. Stir in the flour and cook, stirring, 2 minutes. Whisk in the warmed milk and whisk constantly until mixture is smooth and thick. Stir in the sautéed onions, then gradually stir in the cheese. Stir in the nutmeg, cayenne pepper, dill and mustard. Add the corned beef and cabbage and mix well. Taste the mixture and adjust as needed. Cool the mixture. Can use at once or cover with plastic wrap and refrigerate until needed.

3. <u>Make the Crusts</u>: Roll out the first sheet of puff pastry on a lightly floured board into a 12" x 14" square. Cut out 4 circles, about 6 1/2 inches each, using a round bowl or a piece of cardboard you have prepared. Place on parchment paper on a cookie sheet and refrigerate while cutting out other pastry circles. Roll out second sheet of pastry and cut 4 more circles. If making 9 pies, cut out another circle from the third sheet. Cut out shapes from the remaining puff pastry, either scalloped circles or diamonds or maple leaves. I tried cutting shamrocks, but by the time they rose when baked, they didn't look like shamrocks.

4. <u>Assemble Pies</u>: Put 2/3 cup chilled filling in each of 9 4-inch (1 cup) ramekins or custard cups. Blend the egg and cold water and brush edges of each ramekin and down 1/2 inch on the outer rim. Place a pastry round on top and press down against the sides of the ramekins so pastry will stick. Brush top with more egg wash. You can press all along the sides with the tines of a fork for decoration if you wish. Brush the tops and sides with egg glaze. Place in the refrigerator for at least one hour. You can do this up to a day ahead, covering the pies loosely with foil and refrigerate.

5. When you are ready to bake, preheat oven to 400°F. Place cut out decorations on parchment-lined baking sheets. Bake until golden brown, about 25 minutes. Remove ramekins from oven and serve on heat-proof plates, with a pastry cut-out to the side as decoration.

OVEN-ROASTED HERBED CARROTS AND
PARSNIPS—SERVES 8

You can substitute other root vegetables such as potatoes, turnips or rutabaga if you prefer.

8 fresh young carrots, peeled and cut in halves or
     quarters, depending on size
8 fresh young parsnips, peeled and cut in halves or
     quarters, depending on size
4 tablespoons <u>each </u>honey and extra virgin olive oil
sprigs of thyme
2 tablespoons balsamic vinegar
<u>salt and pepper to taste</u>

1. Preheat oven to 375°F.

2. Bring a large pot of water to a boil. Reduce heat to a simmer and blanch the carrots and parsnips for about 5 minutes, until slightly tender but not cooked through. Drain.

3. Mix the olive oil and honey and put half of this mixture on a baking sheet. Arrange the vegetables on the sheet, drizzle on rest of oil/ honey mixture and add salt and pepper. Add sprigs of thyme and bake for about 45 minutes, or until golden brown and tender, stirring once or twice. Remove from oven to a serving dish, drizzle with balsamic vinegar and serve.

IRISH SODA BREAD—MAKES ONE LOAF

A great quick bread to add to your baking repertoire.

3 1/4 cups all-purpose <u>sifted</u> flour
1 tablespoon baking powder
1 teaspoon baking soda
1 teaspoon salt
1/4 cup firmly packed light brown sugar
3 tablespoons vegetable oil
1 cup raisins (optional)
2 large eggs, lightly beaten
1 cup buttermilk
1 tablespoon butter, melted
<u>1 tablespoon granulated sugar</u>

1. Preheat oven to 375°F. Grease a 9-inch round layer cake pan, 1 1/2 inches deep

2. Resift flour with the baking powder, baking soda and salt into a large bowl. Add the brown sugar. Add the oil and mix with a fork or pastry blender until fine crumbs form. Stir in the optional raisins.

3. Combine eggs and buttermilk in a liquid measuring cup. Gradually add to the flour mixture, stirring until a soft dough forms. Dough will be sticky. Turn out onto a floured board and knead gently about 10 times, adding a bit more flour as needed.

4. Shape dough into a round and fit into the pan. Flatten slightly. With a sharp knife cut loaf crosswise into

quarters about 2/3 of the way through the dough. Brush top with melted butter and sprinkle with granulated sugar.

5. Bake in preheated oven for 30 to 40 minutes, or until cake tester or wooden pick inserted in center comes out clean. Another test of doneness is to remove the bread from the pan and insert an instant read thermometer in the bottom of the loaf. It should read 190°F. When baked to the right temperature, remove bread from pan and place on a rack to cool, or serve hot out of the oven with butter.

BAILEY'S IRISH CREAM CHOCOLATE CAKE WITH FLAVORED WHIPPED CREAM
MAKES 1 CAKE

Although there are a lot of steps to this cake, it is a make ahead recipe, and a unique and delicious dessert.

6 ounces bittersweet chocolate or dark chocolate, 60% strength if possible, chopped into small pieces
1/2 cup (1 stick) unsalted butter
3 tablespoons Bailey's Irish Cream Liqueur
1/2 cup sifted and then measured cake flour
3/4 cup finely ground almonds (in processor) packed
3 large eggs, separated
2/3 cup sugar

Glaze:

6 ounces bittersweet chocolate
4 ounces unsalted butter
1 tablespoon light corn syrup

1 cup whipping cream
1 tablespoon Bailey's Irish Cream Liqueur
<u>1 teaspoon confectioners' sugar</u>

1. Preheat oven to 350°F. Butter one 9-inch round cake pan. Line it with a parchment paper circle, butter and flour the paper and sides of pan.

2. Melt chocolate in double boiler over barely simmering water, stirring occasionally. Add butter and 3 tablespoons of the Bailey's. Set aside.

3. Mix the flour and ground almonds and set aside.

4. Beat the egg whites with l/3 cup of the sugar until they keep their shape, set aside.

5. Beat the egg yolks with the remaining l/3 cup of sugar until thick and they form a ribbon-like drizzle when dropped from a spoon. Fold the chocolate mixture into the beaten egg yolks. Fold the flour/almond mixture alternately with the beaten egg whites gently into the chocolate mixture until smooth, but do not overbeat, as it will deflate the whites.

6. Pour the batter into the prepared pan and bake until knife inserted into the center of the cake comes out clean, about 25 minutes. Cool in pan l0 minutes and then gently invert onto cake rack. Remove pan and let cake cool completely. When cool, you can wrap and freeze, or glaze and serve.

7. To make glaze: place the remaining 6 ounces bittersweet chocolate, along with the 1/4 pound unsalted butter and l tablespoon corn syrup in top of a double boiler and melt, stirring frequently until smooth, but do not heat over l20°F.

8. To glaze cake: Place the cake on a cardboard cake circle and place on a rack over a plate. Have ready a clean, dry metal icing spatula. Pour all the glaze in a puddle in the center of the top of the cake. Working quickly, use just 2 or 3 spatula strokes to spread the glaze over the top of the cake so that it runs over all sides of the cake. Fill in any unfrosted spots carefully.

9. Whip the cream to soft mounds, add the last tablespoon of Bailey's and serve separately in a pretty crystal bowl.

MEXICAN FIESTA

Roasted Poblano and Garlic Guacamole with House-Made Chips
Christmas Tamales
Orange, Avocado and Onion Salad
Mexican Flan

ROASTED POBLANO AND GARLIC GUACAMOLE WITH HOUSEMADE TORTILLA CHIPS
SERVES 8 TO 10

Nothing makes your guests feel more pampered that your own freshly made guacamole and housemade chips!

12 ounces (about 4 medium) fresh poblano chilis
12 ounces (about 4 plum tomatoes or 2 medium round) ripe tomatoes
4 garlic cloves, unpeeled
6 tablespoons chopped fresh flat-leaf parsley
6 medium-large (about 2 1/2 pounds total) ripe avocados
1 to 2 teaspoons salt, to taste
2 to 4 tablespoons fresh lime juice, to taste
4 tablespoons grated Mexican queso anejo cheese, or other dry grating cheese, such as Parmesan or Romano

Tortilla Chips:

1 package (10 count) flour tortillas
Crisco solid shortening for deep frying, if you choose to fry chips
coarse sea salt

1. Roast the poblanos, tomatoes and garlic: Use either on a baking sheet, set 4 inches under a very hot broiler, or grill them on your outdoor grill. Roast, turning every couple of minutes, until chilis and tomatoes are soft, blistered and blackened in spots and garlic is soft, 12 to 13 minutes. Place chilis in a paper bag and close top for 5 minutes, then wipe off blackened skin, pull or cut out the stems and seeds. Rinse quickly to remove any stray seeds and bits of char. Peel tomatoes and discard skins. Slip papery skins off garlic. (This can all be done the day before you make the guacamole, just cover and

refrigerate.) In a mortar (the Mexican one is a called a molcajete, the pestle is called a metlapil) or with a food processor, make a coarse purée of the roasted garlic and poblanos, and place in a large bowl. Chop the roasted tomatoes, discarding any juice from the baking sheet, and add to the poblano mixture with the chopped parsley.

2. Cut the avocados lengthwise in half around the pit, twist the halves apart and remove pits. Scoop out the flesh into the bowl. Using a potato masher or back of a large spoon, coarsely mash together with the garlic, poblanos, tomatoes and parsley. Taste and season with salt, then add enough lime juice to brighten the flavors. Cover with plastic wrap, directly on the surface of the guacamole, and refrigerate until ready to eat, up to several hours ahead. When ready to serve, uncover, top with cheese and serve with Tortilla chips.

3. To make the Tortilla chips: Using kitchen scissors cut each flour tortilla into 6 or 8 wedges, depending on how big you want them to be. Heat a deep fryer with a good 3 inches of Crisco to 375°F., or if you prefer, line several rimmed cookie sheets with foil and preheat oven to 375°F. Fry or bake chips in batches until golden and crisp, then salt them and serve with the guacamole.

CORN TAMALES—MAKES ABOUT 2 DOZEN

A traditional Christmas preparation. Do as the Mexicans do and get a group together and have a tamale-making party. Although this is not a low fat dish, the flavors make it worth it! As a bonus, the tamales freeze well.

corn husks (from Hispanic stores)

1 3/4 cups Masa Harina
5 ounces lard (found at grocery store or more flavorful
    type from Hispanic stores) or solid Crisco
chicken stock or water, amount depending on
    consistency
1 14 1/2-ounce can creamed corn
salt to taste
3 slices of bacon, diced and fried, with their drippings
grated Monterey Jack cheese
4-ounce can chopped mild green chilis, not drained

red or green salsa (or both) to serve with finished tamales

1. Separate corn husks from package, and soak in very warm water, completely submerged, for at least 1 hour and up to overnight. Trim any ragged edges and soak more than the 2 dozen husks you'll need to wrap tamales, to line the steamer. Husks can be soaked ahead, shaken of any excess water, wrapped in plastic wrap and refrigerated the day before forming tamales. The most perfect husks will be used to wrap tamales, with the irregular and smaller ones used to line steamer and to cut strips to tie tamales.

2. Make the Masa dough: In a food processor combine the lard (or solid Crisco), Masa, creamed corn, bacon and drippings, and salt and process to a consistency that sticks to your fingers but is not runny. Add chicken stock if needed.

3. Make Tamales: Lay one corn husk on a work surface, rough side down. Put 1 to 2 tablespoons of the masa mixture in center, flatten, then add one teaspoon each of the Monterey Jack cheese and chopped green chilis, and fold Masa over to cover, then fold, wrapping to make rectangular packages, using strips of husk to tie. Continue with rest of filling and husks.

4. Steam Tamales: Prepare a steamer, using a collapsible steamer rack or a Chinese bamboo steamer inside a large pot with about 2 inches of water on the bottom. Make a bed of broken or other husks, then line up the finished tamales around the pot, standing them up. If you have any extra room, ball up some aluminum foil and place it in center to keep tamales upright. Cover with more husks, put on lid, bring water to a boil, then lower heat to medium and steam for 40 to 45 minutes, adding water once or twice if needed. Take out one tamale, unwrap it to see if it is still too moist; if so, steam 5 minutes more. When done, remove tamales from pot and either serve right away with a side of salsa, or cool and wrap. Can freeze, or store them in refrigerator and gently rewarm in microwave later.

ORANGE, AVOCADO AND ONION SALAD— ENSALADA DE NARANJA, AGUACATE Y CEBOLLA—SERVES 8

A classic Mexican salad.

Dressing:

1/2 teaspoon <u>each</u> sugar and dry mustard
scant 1/8 teaspoon cayenne pepper
2 tablespoons <u>each</u> fresh lemon juice and white vinegar
1/2 cup vegetable oil

1 large white or yellow onion, peeled and very thinly
    sliced
4 large navel or Valencia oranges
2 avocados
<u>romaine lettuce leaves or other lettuce of your choice</u>

1. <u>Make dressing</u>: Combine all ingredients in a jar with
a tight-fitting lid and shake well. Can make ahead and
refrigerate for a day or more.

2. Place sliced onions in salted ice water while you
prepare other ingredients of salad. This draws out the
bitterness and heat from the onions. Peel and slice the
avocado. Peel oranges and take off all white pith, then
slice into thin rounds.

3. Arrange lettuce leaves on shallow platter. Drain and
dry onion slices. Arrange onion slices alternately with
orange and avocado slices. Dress salad lightly with salad
dressing and serve. Serve any extra dressing in a separate
sauceboat.

MEXICAN FLAN—MAKES 8 TO 10

*A classic Mexican dessert. Be sure to take care when
making the caramel to avoid a painful burn.*

Custard:

2 1/4 cups canned evaporated milk (1 1/2 12-ounce
    cans)
1 1/2 cups sugar
3/4 cup water
6 large eggs
1/2 teaspoon vanilla

Caramel:

1 cup sugar, divided

<u>Garnish: mint sprigs</u>

1. Preheat the oven to 300°F.

2. Place the custard ingredients into the top of a double
boiler. Beat with a whisk or a hand mixer at medium
speed, for about 1 minute, or until the mixture is well
blended and begins to froth at its edges. Place the pan
over the bottom of the double boiler, which has been
filled with water and brought to a simmer. Make sure
the bottom of the pan does not touch the water. Heat the
custard mixture over medium-low heat, stirring, until it is
warm throughout, but does not boil (135°F. on an instant
read thermometer). Turn off the flame and keep custard
warm over bottom pan while preparing caramel.

3. <u>To make the caramel</u>: Set 8 to 10 6-ounce custard cups
or other heatproof cups in a shallow baking pan, large
enough to hold all the custard cups with a little room
for air circulation. Bring to the stovetop. Place half the
sugar in a 1-quart or less heavy saucepan and cook over
low heat, watching carefully, until the sugar melts into
a golden brown caramel syrup. There is no need to stir
unless the sugar is melting unevenly, then just swirl the
pan. When syrup turns a rich medium brown use an
oven mitt to hold handle of the pan and immediately
remove pan from heat, USING EXTREME CAUTION.
<u>There is no burn as bad as a sugar burn</u>. Pour about one
tablespoon into the bottom of half of the custard cups,

being very careful, tilting to coat bottoms. The caramel will harden very quickly, which is the reason for making the caramel in two batches. Repeat with the second 1/2 cup of sugar, filling the other custard cups. Boil some water in the pan you made the caramel in, to dissolve caramel and make cleanup easier.

4. Ladle the warm custard mixture equally into the caramel-lined custard cups, and place the pan in the oven. Carefully add very hot water to the pan to cover the bottom third of the cups and bake 50 to 60 minutes, or until custard is firm and top has a light golden color. Test by inserting a butter knife into center of one—it should come out clean. Remove cups from oven and water bath carefully, drying bottoms, and refrigerate, covered, for at least 3 hours or up to overnight.

5. When ready to serve, run a knife around the rim of each cup and dip bottom of cup in a bowl of <u>boiling</u> water carefully, then remove from bowl of water, cover with a serving plate and invert, giving the cup a brief shake to loosen. The custard should drop onto the plate. If it doesn't, carefully insert a knife at one edge and it should drop out. The liquid caramel should pour out over the flan. Serve, garnished with a mint sprig if desired.

MIDDLE-EASTERN DELIGHTS

Moroccan Cigars
Tabbouleh Salad
Schwarma Kebabs
Saffron Rice Pilaf with Toasted Pine Nuts
Baklava

MOROCCAN CIGARS
MAKES 24

A memorable recipe to begin an outstanding meal. Learning to work with phyllo dough gives you many options for other recipes as well.

<u>Filling:</u>

1 tablespoon melted butter
3 scallions, thinly sliced
1 10-ounce package frozen chopped spinach, thawed, squeezed dry
1/3 cup part-skim ricotta cheese
3 ounces feta cheese, crumbled
1 egg white (from 1 large egg)
1/4 cup grated Parmesan cheese
1/4 teaspoon freshly ground black pepper

Parmesan-Dill Mixture

1/4 cup Parmesan cheese
2 tablespoons minced fresh dill

1 to 2 sticks unsalted butter, melted in microwave
<u>12 sheets phyllo (pronounced feelow) dough, thawed</u>

1. In small skillet place 1 tablespoon of the melted butter over medium heat. Add scallions and cook until softened, 1 minute. Let cool.

2. <u>Make filling</u>: In medium bowl, combine scallions, spinach, ricotta and feta cheeses, egg white, 1/4 cup of the Parmesan cheese and the pepper. In a separate small bowl make Parmesan-dill mixture by combining the other 1/4 cup of the Parmesan with the dill.

3. Unroll package of phyllo dough onto a work surface, cover with plastic wrap and place a damp towel, which you have wrung out well, over plastic wrap. This is an important step, as the phyllo is very thin and can dry out and become like fragile paper that will crumble if not protected in this way. Uncover and remove one sheet of dough carefully to a large work surface, recovering the pile of phyllo. Using a pastry brush, lightly brush some of the melted butter onto the phyllo sheet to cover whole surface. Sprinkle with 2 teaspoons of Parmesan-dill mixture. Cover with another sheet of phyllo and brush with more butter. Cut in half crosswise, then lengthwise, to form 4 rectangles. This will make 4 cigars.

4. Divide filling mixture into 24 equal portions at this point. To form cigars, place about 2 teaspoons of the spinach filling in a thin log along short side of one of the phyllo squares, you have cut, above, about 3/4 inch from edges. Fold bottom edge up over filling and tuck in ends. Loosely roll up into a cigar shape, not wrapping too tightly, or they will split. Place seam side down on ungreased <u>rimmed</u> baking sheet. Continue with the other three phyllo squares, making 4 cigars. Now repeat this process with the remaining phyllo sheets and filling, to make 24 cigars in all, using more baking sheets as needed. Lightly brush tops of cigars with any remaining butter. Bake right away, or cover with a piece of plastic wrap that has been sprayed with non-stick spray, and refrigerate for up to one day, or freeze, well wrapped. If frozen, defrost in the refrigerator overnight before proceeding to bake.

5. To bake, preheat oven to 375°F. Bake cigars 18 to 20 minutes, or until phyllo is crisp and browned. Cool slightly and serve right away.

TABBOULEH SALAD—SERVES 8

A healthy, easy and refreshing salad.

1 cup bulghur wheat, fine grind
1 teaspoon salt
1 cup boiling water
1 cup <u>each</u> tomatoes, chopped (about 2 tomatoes) and flatleaf parsley leaves, finely chopped
2 tablespoons fresh mint, finely chopped
3 tablespoons <u>each</u> fresh lemon juice and extra-virgin olive oil
1 teaspoon cumin, or to taste
1 teaspoon harissa (hot sauce from a Mediterranean <u>store), or a few drops of Tabasco</u>

1. Place the bulghur wheat in a large glass bowl and cover with the boiling water. Stir in the salt and let soak 15 minutes, until the bulghur is soft but still a bit crunchy. Cool.

2. Stir in the chopped tomatoes, parsley, cumin and mint. Mix well. Add the lemon juice, olive oil and harissa or Tabasco to taste. Mix well and taste for seasoning. Cover and refrigerate until ready to serve. Can be made a day ahead.

3. Serve as a salad or have guests put some of the tabbouleh in halved pita bread.

SCHWARMA KEBABS—SERVES 8

2 to 2 1/2 pounds boneless, skinless chicken breasts, cut into 1-inch chunks

2 1/2 cups plain low-fat yogurt
2 medium onions, finely chopped
4 large cloves garlic, crushed in a garlic press
1 teaspoon <u>each</u> hot and sweet Hungarian paprika
1 teaspoon crushed saffron threads, diluted in 2 tablespoons warm water
1 teaspoon <u>each</u> dried thyme and oregano
1/2 teaspoon salt, or to taste
3 to 4 tablespoons olive oil

<u>wooden skewers</u>

1. In a large glass bowl, combine the chicken with the remaining ingredients except the skewers, and toss well. The marinade mixture will be very thick. Cover and refrigerate for at least 2 hours, or up to overnight. Soak wooden skewers in water for at least 30 minutes before planning to grill, then drain.

2. When ready to grill, heat grill until very hot, OR if you choose to broil the chicken, preheat the broiler. Oil the grill or broiler rack, using a crumpled piece of heavy-duty foil.

3. Remove chicken pieces from the marinade, saving marinade. Thread on skewers, without crowding the pieces. Put marinade into a saucepan and bring to a slow boil, thinning with some milk or water and adding powdered garlic, salt and pepper to taste. Don't worry if the sauce curdles when you boil it—you can whirl it in a blender to smooth it out if necessary.

4. Grill or broil the chicken about 10 minutes, turning several times and basting. Juices should run clear when pricked with a skewer. Remove to a platter and serve with boiled marinade in a sauceboat.

SAFFRON RICE PILAF WITH TOASTED PINE NUTS—SERVES 8

Saffron is the yellow-orange stigmas from a small purple crocus variety, and is the world's most expensive spice, since each flower has only 3 stigmas, and has to be carefully hand harvested and dried. A small amount goes a long way, and provides a lovely color and subtle flavor to the pilaf. Store it in the refrigerator or freezer to keep it fresh.

2 cups Basmati rice
1 teaspoon salt

2 tablespoons vegetable oil or butter
1 medium onion, chopped
1/2 teaspoon salt
3 1/2 cups good-quality chicken stock
1/2 teaspoon saffron threads, dissolved in 1 tablespoon
    warm water
1/2 cup pine nuts, toasted in a skillet until golden
fresh chopped parsley leaves

1. Place the rice in a fine sieve and rinse thoroughly under cold running water until the water runs clear, to remove starch. Place rice in a large bowl and add enough lukewarm water to cover it by about 1 inch. Add 1 teaspoon salt and let rice soak for 1/2 hour. Drain the rice and rinse well under cold running water.

2. In a large pot heat the oil and sauté the onion and rice until golden. Add 1/2 teaspoon salt. Pour in stock, saffron mixture and 1/2 teaspoon salt and bring to a boil uncovered. Cover, lower heat to a simmer and let cook for about 10 minutes, or until liquid is absorbed and rice is tender. Remove from heat, transfer to a serving bowl, add the pine nuts and sprinkle top with parsley. Serve or hold in low oven up to 1 hour. Reheats well.

BAKLAVA—MAKES ABOUT 24 DIAMOND-SHAPED PIECES

1 cup walnuts, ground in blender
1/2 cup almonds, ground in blender
2 tablespoons sugar
1 teaspoon cinnamon
1/2 teaspoon nutmeg
1/8 teaspoon ground cloves

1/2 package phyllo dough (found in freezer section)
   defrosted in refrigerator overnight
1 cup (2 sticks) unsalted butter, melted

Syrup

1/2 cup each sugar and water
juice of 1/2 lemon, about 1 tablespoon
2 tablespoons honey

1. Preheat oven to 350°F.

2. In a medium bowl combine walnuts, almonds, sugar, cinnamon, nutmeg and cloves.

3. Butter the bottom of an 8-inch square baking dish with some of the melted butter. Lay the defrosted phyllo on a large piece of parchment paper. Cut in half and then trim into 30 8-inch squares, keeping dough covered with plastic wrap and a damp towel as you work to prevent drying.

4. Begin to build the baklava by laying 10 sheets of phyllo in buttered pan, buttering each sheet using a pastry brush. Sprinkle 1/2 of the nut-spice mixture on this first layer of sheets, then add another 10 sheets, buttering as you go along. Sprinkle second half of nut-spice mixture on top and top with the last 10 sheets of phyllo, buttering each layer. Cut into about 24 diamonds with a sharp knife, not cutting all the way to the bottom of pan. Bake in preheated 350°F. oven until golden brown, about 45 to 55 minutes.

5. Meanwhile make the syrup: In a medium saucepan mix sugar, water and lemon juice. Bring to a boil, stirring, then boil gently 10 minutes. Stir in honey. Reserve.

6. When baklava is baked, remove to cooling rack and cut all the way through slices. Pour the warm syrup over dough and let cool. Serve warm or at room temperature, or you can freeze leftover diamonds.

GREEK CUISINE

Tiropetes
Stuffed Grape Leaves
Moussaka
Kourambiedes

TIROPETES—GREEK PHYLLO FETA CHEESE APPETIZERS—MAKES 4 DOZEN

You can prepare these savory pastries up to the baking stage, cover with plastic wrap that you have sprayed with nonstick cooking spray, then keep overnight before baking. OR you can cover them with the plastic wrap, then overwrap them with heavy-duty foil and freeze them for up to one month before baking. You can also make them cocktail size by folding each cut strip of phyllo in half, filling with 1/2 teaspoon filling and baking for 8 to 10 minutes, in which case you will get 8 dozen pastries from the recipe.

Filling:

8 ounces feta cheese
1/4 cup (3/4 ounce) grated Parmesan cheese
1/4 teaspoon ground nutmeg
1/2 teaspoon dried oregano
1 1/2 teaspoons fresh dill (or 1/2 teaspoon dried dill)
1/4 teaspoon freshly ground black pepper
2 large egg yolks

12 sheets phyllo pastry, defrosted
1 1/2 cups melted unsalted butter

1. Preheat oven to 400°F.

2. Make filling: Place all filling ingredients in a large bowl and mix well.

3. Lay one sheet of phyllo dough out on a large work surface and brush with butter. Lay a second sheet directly over the first one and brush with butter. With a sharp knife cut crosswise into 8 equal strips. Keep remaining phyllo dough covered with waxed paper and a damp cloth to keep it from drying out.

4. Place one teaspoon of filling at the short end of each strip nearest you. Fold up the packages as you would fold a flag, to form triangles, with the pastry seam at the bottom. Place on ungreased rimmed baking sheets about 1/2 inch apart. Repeat with remaining pastry and filling to make 48 pastries. Brush tops of each pastry with butter. At this point you can place them on buttered cookie sheets, cover with plastic wrap that has been sprayed with non-stick spray, refrigerate and bake the next day, or overwrap with heavy-duty foil and place in freezer for up to one month. Defrost before baking. To bake as soon as you form them, put in the center of the preheated oven for 12 minutes, or until golden brown and crisp. Remove from oven and cool on racks. Serve right away.

STUFFED GRAPE LEAVES
MAKES 40

Fun to make with a group and then divide the "riches", so everyone can take some home.

Filling:

1 large onion, grated
1/2 cup raw white or brown rice
1 1/2 tablespoons black currants
1 tablespoon pine nuts
2 tablespoons <u>each</u> fresh parsley and dill sprigs, leaves
    chopped, <u>stems reserved</u>
2 tablespoons fresh mint, chopped
1 tablespoon fresh lemon juice
1/3 cup extra virgin olive oil
1/2 teaspoon sugar
1/2 teaspoon <u>each</u> ground allspice and salt

1 8-ounce jar grape leaves, drained
6 cups boiling water

reserved stems of parsley and dill
1 cup or more chicken stock

leaf lettuce
<u>2 lemons, cut into wedges</u>

1. <u>Make filling</u>: In large bowl mix all ingredients well. Reserve.

2. Place drained, unrolled grape leaves into boiling water and boil for 2 minutes. Carefully remove with slotted spoon and drain in colander under cold running water. Carefully separate leaves and hang leaves around the rim of the colander. Remove small stem from grape leaf and discard, place about 1 teaspoon filling at the stem end and fold over. Then fold sides securely in, rolling to make a neat package.

3. In the bottom of a heavy large deep skillet or saucepan place the reserved parsley and dill stems. Arrange the grape leaves in one layer close together on top. Pour the stock slowly over the leaves and cover with parchment paper. Place a heavy plate on top and cover the pan. Cook over medium heat for about 1 hour, or until all the stock is absorbed. You may need to add a bit more stock if it evaporates too early. Cool the covered pan in the refrigerator. Can make 2 days ahead and refrigerate.

4. When ready to serve arrange grape leaves on a platter lined with leaf lettuce and decorate with lemon wedges.

MOUSSAKA—GREEK LAMB AND EGGPLANT CASSEROLE—SERVES 8

Don't let the long list of ingredients deter you from making this dish. You probably have many of them in your pantry, and even better, it can all be made ahead and refrigerated or even frozen. Although ground lamb is traditional in this dish, you may substitute ground beef if you prefer.

3 medium-sized eggplants
salt
olive oil

Meat Sauce:

2 tablespoons olive oil
2 medium onions, chopped
3 cloves garlic, mashed
2 pounds ground lamb
1/2 cup dry red wine
3 tablespoons tomato paste
salt and black pepper
1/4 cup parsley leaves, chopped
2 tablespoons water
1/2 teaspoon ground cinnamon
1/2 cup grated cheese, Parmesan or Greek kefalotyri
3 tablespoons bread crumbs
2 large eggs, beaten

Béchamel (White) Sauce:

6 tablespoons <u>each</u> unsalted butter and flour
3 cups hot whole milk
salt and pepper to taste
dash nutmeg
4 large egg yolks, lightly beaten

Topping:

<u>3 tablespoons each breadcrumbs and Parmesan cheese</u>

1. <u>Prepare eggplants</u>: Remove stems and tips, then cut off 1/2-inch wide strips of peel lengthwise from eggplants, leaving 1/2-inch peel between strips. Cut into 1/3-inch thick lengthwise slices. Sprinkle with salt and let stand for 30 minutes, to draw out any bitterness from eggplants. Rinse slices very well, drain thoroughly, and pat dry. In a large skillet heat 2 teaspoons olive oil for every two slices of eggplant on high heat and sauté slices lightly, then drain on paper towels. Reserve.

2. <u>Prepare Meat Sauce</u>: In large skillet heat the 2 tablespoons olive oil and sauté the onions until translucent. Add garlic and cook 1 minute more, then add the ground lamb and sauté till lightly browned. Add the red wine, tomato paste, parsley, salt, pepper, and a bit of water if mixture is too dry, and simmer till liquid is absorbed. Cool, then add cinnamon, eggs, cheese and the 3 tablespoons breadcrumbs. Reserve.

3. <u>Make Béchamel (White) Sauce</u>: In a saucepan melt the butter over medium heat. Whisk in the flour and stir until well blended and bubbly, then whisk in the hot milk, and continue to whisk until sauce is thick and smooth. Add salt, pepper and nutmeg to taste. Combine egg yolks with a bit of the hot sauce (this is called tempering, to keep the sauce from cooking the yolks and curdling them.) Whisk the egg mixture into the sauce and cook over very low heat for 2 minutes, stirring constantly. Reserve.

4. <u>Assemble the moussaka casserole</u>: Grease a 9" x 13" casserole and sprinkle the bottom with the 3 tablespoons of breadcrumbs. Make a layer of eggplant slices, then a layer of meat, and continue to build layers until all eggplant and meat is used, ending on the top with a layer of eggplant. Cover with the béchamel sauce and sprinkle with breadcrumbs and grated cheese. At this point you can cover casserole and refrigerate it to bake the next day. When ready to bake, preheat oven to 350°F. and bake for 1 hour. Serve hot.

KOURAMBIEDES—MAKES ABOUT 4 DOZEN

These almond shortbread cookies are traditionally served at Christmas time. Be sure to knead the finished dough to a smooth consistency for ease in shaping cookies.

10 ounces blanched almonds
2 cups (8-ounce container) whipped sweet unsalted butter
2 large egg yolks
1/4 cup sifted confectioners' sugar
1/2 teaspoon baking powder
1/2 teaspoon pure almond extract

3 tablespoons (1 1/2 ounces) of scotch whiskey or
   brandy
2 to 2 1/2 cups sifted all purpose flour

<u>about 2 cups sifted confectioners' sugar, to coat cookies</u>

1. Preheat oven to 350°F. Lightly toast the almonds either
in an ungreased skillet over low heat or in the preheated
oven until light golden brown, about 7 minutes. Watch
carefully so they don't burn. Chop finely in the processor
and set aside.

2. In a large bowl of the electric mixer set at high speed,
mix the butter, egg yolks, 1/4 cup confectioners' sugar
and baking powder, until smooth and creamy, 6 to 9
minutes. Add the almonds and alcohol and beat for
another 4 to 5 minutes, until smooth. Add 1 3/4 cups of
the sifted flour and stir in by hand. Add remaining flour
in 1/4 cup increments until just enough flour has been
added to make a silky, smooth dough that doesn't stick to
your hands. Turn mixture out onto a lightly floured work
surface and knead for 5 to 8 minutes, or until dough stays
together.

3. Take a piece of dough about the size of an unshelled
walnut and shape it into an oval or cone-shaped mound.
Place on ungreased cookie sheets about 1 inch apart.
Repeat with remaining dough. Bake in preheated oven for
18 to 20 minutes, or until cookies are a yellowish-golden
color. They should not be golden brown.

4. Remove cookie sheet from oven and remove cookies
to a wire rack. Cool slightly, then sift confectioners' sugar
over them until tops and sides are completely covered,
using a shaker if you have one. Cool completely before
storing in tins. Can repowder cookies just before serving
if needed.

INDIAN ADVENTURE

Tandoori Chicken
Moong Dal
Raita
Spiced Mango Cream

TANDOORI CHICKEN—SERVES 8

*Traditionally, tandoori chicken is made in a tandoor, a
vat-shaped clay oven, heated with charcoal or wood. The
heat inside is so intense that skewered small whole chickens
cook in 10 minutes, searing in the juices. Marinating the
meat in flavorful spices imparts a delicious flavor. This
adaptation by fabulous Indian chef (and movie actress)
Madhur Jaffrey works very well in a home oven and loses
little "in translation."*

8 chicken breasts or thighs, or combination of both,
   bone-in and with skin
1 teaspoon salt
juice from 1 large lemon

Marinade:

16 ounces plain yogurt (not fat-free), drained in
   strainer lined with cheesecloth 1 hour
1 onion, peeled and quartered
1 large clove garlic, peeled
1 1/2 teaspoons fresh ginger, peeled and coarsely
   chopped
1/2 fresh, hot green chili, roughly sliced, with seeds
2 teaspoons garam masala (an Indian spice mixture
   found at Indian groceries)
3 tablespoons yellow food coloring mixed with 1
   tablespoon red coloring

<u>Garnish: wedges of lemon and lime sliced, and 1 onion,
   lightly roasted in 350°F. oven</u>

1. Cut each breast into 4 pieces and each thigh in half.
Cut long slits in meaty part of each piece, not starting
at the edges, so meat stays together but can absorb the
marinade. Spread pieces on large work surface and lightly
rub in half the salt and half the lemon juice, then turn
and rub in remaining salt and lemon juice. Set aside
while making marinade.

2. In a blender or food processor combine yogurt, onion, garlic, ginger, green chili and garam masala and blend until you have a smooth paste. Place this mixture into a large ceramic or stainless steel bowl.

3. Brush the chicken pieces on both sides with the food coloring and place them, with any accumulated juices and remaining food coloring into the bowl with the marinade. Mix well, cover and refrigerate for 6 to 24 hours (overnight is best).

4. When ready to cook chicken, preheat oven to its maximum temperature. Remove chicken from the marinade and discard marinade. Arrange in large shallow baking sheet in single layer, with onion slices. Bake for 20 to 25 minutes or until juices run clear when meat is pricked with a fork, carefully draining off excess liquid half-way through cooking. Serve hot, with lemon and lime wedges and roasted onion slices if you wish.

MOONG DAL—SERVES 8

Find the dal, which are lentils, at an Indian grocery store. When my younger daughter Ayla was a child, she had a wonderful collection of International dolls from our travels. One day we went to an Indian grocery store in search of an addition to her collection, and when we asked the Indian gentleman behind the counter where the dolls were, he was very impressed and excited that we were familiar with the "dals" and showed us to his large assortment of many colored lentils. We were too embarrassed to tell him what we were really looking for!

2 cups yellow split moong dal
2 teaspoons ground turmeric
6 cups water
5 to 6 hot green peppers, 1/2 of the seeds discarded,
    coarsely chopped using rubber gloves
1 teaspoon salt, or to taste

8 whole cloves
2 tablespoons fresh curry leaves, coarsely chopped, or 2
    teaspoons garam masala
1 teaspoon whole cumin seeds, or ground cumin
4 cloves garlic, coarsely minced
2 tablespoons chopped fresh ginger
<u>8 tablespoons unsalted butter</u>

1. In a large pot bring the dal, turmeric, water, peppers and salt to a boil on high heat. Lower heat to medium and cook till the dal is tender. This should take about 20 minutes. Reserve.

2. Place the cloves, curry leaves, cumin seeds or powder, garlic and ginger in a mortar and use a pestle to grind it and combine (or use a blender). Heat the butter in a small saucepan on high heat and add ground spices. Stir and cook on medium high heat for 2 minutes.

3. Add these roasted spices to the cooked dal. Stir well, return to heat for 2 to 3 minutes more. Serve hot.

RAITA—MAKES 2 CUPS

This great accompaniment helps cool down spicy dishes such as the dal.

1 medium cucumber, peeled
salt

1 1/2 cups plain yogurt (not fat-free)
1 tablespoon finely chopped fresh mint leaves
1/2 teaspoon <u>each</u> salt and black pepper, or to taste
<u>1 teaspoon sugar</u>

1. Rub peeled cucumber with salt, then grate it on large holes of grater through a strainer to remove excess water.

2. Beat yogurt in a medium bowl with a whisk until smooth. Add cucumber, mint, salt, pepper and sugar and taste for seasoning. Refrigerate and serve cold.

MANGO CREAM WITH CARDAMON AND PISTACHIOS—SERVES 10 ⏲ 👨‍🍳

This dessert is very refreshing after a flavorful Indian meal.

1 30-ounce can mango purée or pulp, canned, (from an Indian grocery store), chilled
1 cup heavy whipping cream, whipped to soft peaks

4 tablespoons superfine sugar, (If you can't find it, whirl granulated sugar in a blender) or to taste
1 1/2 envelopes unflavored gelatin (Knox)
1/8 teaspoon saffron powder or 1/4 teaspoon saffron threads, dissolved in 1 tablespoon hot water
1/2 teaspoon freshly ground cardamom

Optional garnish: extra heavy whipping cream
8 to 10 pistachio nuts, shelled and coarsely chopped

1. Place mango purée in large bowl and mix in the sugar. Fold in the whipped cream gently and reserve.

2. Dissolve the gelatin in 1/2 cup of boiling water, along with the saffron and cardamom, stirring constantly until the water is clear and gelatin has dissolved. Mix this into the mango mixture and pour into individual serving dishes or one large bowl, and refrigerate for 2 hours or up to overnight before serving.

3. When ready to serve, gently whip the optional cream and place a dollop on each serving, then top with some of the chopped pistachios.

COOK'S TIP

Taste, Taste, Taste! Always check each recipe both *as it is cooking* and *before you serve it* and adjust for salt, pepper and other spices. Speaking of spices, make sure your spices and herbs are fresh, not flat or musty. For dried herbs such as oregano, basil, tarragon, etc. they will usually last one year. Before you add them rub them between your palms to activate the natural oils and get more flavor from them. For aromatic spices, such as cardamom, nutmeg, cloves and cinnamon, six months is the limit for freshness. Smell them to tell if they're still fragrant. There should never be a musty smell. It would really be a shame after all your hard work to ruin a dish with old spices! Some of these spices can be expensive, so consider splitting a jar with friends. Also, remember that no recipe is written in stone, so feel free to add or omit ingredients according to your individual taste, *with the exception of when you are baking*, when omitting or adding ingredients can throw off the recipe and spoil your results.

11

DESSERTS

Who doesn't love dessert? Here are 20 show stoppers to add to your repertoire, each one a winner—from quick and easy to more complex and fabulous. On days when nothing seems to be going right, why not eat dessert first! In this chapter we have recipes for various bars, squares and brownies, fabulous cookies, pies, cupcakes and cakes, so grab an apron, heat up the oven and get bakin'!

Easy-Time Cherry Squares (page 182)

PRIZE-WINNING PEACH BARS
MAKES 24

One of the great advantages of being a judge at the Ohio State Fair is discovering outstanding recipes, like this great blue ribbon winner.

solid Crisco to grease pan
3/4 cup (1 1/2 sticks) unsalted butter, room temperature
1 cup sugar
1 large egg
2 cups all-purpose flour
1/4 teaspoon baking powder
1/2 teaspoon pure vanilla extract
1/3 cup shredded coconut

1 jar (12 ounces) best-quality peach preserves

1. Preheat oven to 350°F. Grease a 9" x 13" rectangular pan and reserve.

2. In mixer cream the butter and sugar. Add the egg and mix well. Add the flour and baking powder to the creamed mixture and mix well. Add the vanilla and stir in the coconut.

3. Press 2/3 of the mixture (about 2 cups) into the prepared pan. Spread preserves over this mixture. Crumble remaining mixture over the preserves. It will not cover the entire top—don't worry, that's how it's supposed to look. It will look wonderful after it's baked. Bake for 30 to 35 minutes. Cool in the pan, then cut into 24 bars.

EASY-TIME CHERRY SQUARES
MAKES 20 SQUARES

This is a lifesaver when you need a fast but fabulous dessert for a crowd. I've been making it for many, many years, and it always gets rave reviews!

Crisco to grease pan
1 cup (2 sticks) unsalted butter, room temperature
1 1/2 cups granulated sugar
4 large eggs
2 cups all purpose flour
1/2 teaspoon lemon extract or 1 teaspoon fresh lemon juice

1 can (21 ounces) cherry pie filling (blueberry pie filling is good too!)
confectioners' sugar

1. Preheat oven to 350°F. Grease a jellyroll pan, 10" x 15" x 1".

2. In the large bowl of an electric mixer, cream the butter and sugar until fluffy and no longer grainy. At medium speed of the mixer, add the eggs, one at a time, beating well. Reduce speed to low and add the flour and lemon flavoring.

3. Pour the batter into the prepared pan and smooth the top with an offset spatula or butter knife. Mark off 20 equal squares (5 rows by the length of the pan and 4 by its width) with a butter knife. Place one heaping tablespoon of cherry pie filling in the center of each square, equally dividing the cherries and juice as much as possible.

4. Bake in preheated oven for 30 minutes or until golden brown. Remove from oven to a wire rack. While still warm, recut the squares with a sharp knife. Cool slightly, then sprinkle the top with confectioners' sugar. Best eaten the day you bake them.

ONE-BOWL KILLER BROWNIES
MAKES 16 ⏱ 👨‍🍳

These brownies are very easy to make and the results are excellent. They are our "house" brownies.

Crisco solid shortening, to grease pan
1/2 cup (1 stick) unsalted butter
2 ounces unsweetened baking chocolate, chopped
1 ounce semi-sweet baking chocolate, chopped
1 1/4 cups sugar
1 1/2 teaspoons pure vanilla extract
3 large eggs
1 1/4 cups all-purpose flour
1/4 teaspoon salt

Optional: 2/3 cup chopped, walnuts or pecans

1. Preheat oven to 350°F. Grease the bottom only of an 8 inch square baking pan.

2. Place the butter and two chocolates in a 2-quart microwavable bowl and put in microwave on 50% power for 2 minutes. Stir until smooth. If chocolate has not melted completely continue cooking at 50% power at 30-second intervals until mixture is melted and smooth. Remove from microwave and stir in the sugar and vanilla.

3. Add eggs, one at a time, mixing well after each addition. Stir in the flour and salt and mix just until all ingredients are moistened and mixture is smooth. Add the optional nuts if desired. Spread brownie mix evenly in the prepared pan and bake in preheated oven for from 26 to 32 minutes, depending on how fudgy or dry you like them. A cake tester should come out slightly moist when tested in the center of the pan, for my taste. Do not overbake. Cool completely on a rack, then cut into 16 pieces and enjoy!

SAN FRANCISCO FUDGE FOGGIES
MAKES 32 PIECES ⏱ 👨‍🍳 👨‍🍳

The essence of chocolate. This recipe is from an early issue of Chocolatier, the marvelous publication devoted entirely to all things chocolate. You can substitute semisweet chocolate for the bittersweet chocolate, which is slightly more intense, but do not substitute unsweetened chocolate, as it has no sugar and will not work in this recipe. Be sure to follow the instruction carefully, and you'll be rewarded with an amazing treat.

softened butter to butter the pan

1 pound bittersweet chocolate, finely chopped (easy in the processor)
1 cup (2 sticks) unsalted butter, cut into tablespoons
1/3 cup strong brewed coffee

4 large eggs, room temperature
1 1/2 cups sugar
1/2 cup all purpose flour
8 ounces (about 2 cups) walnuts, coarsely chopped

1. Preheat oven to 375°F. Line a 9" x 13" baking pan with heavy duty foil, so that the foil extends 2 inches beyond all sides of the pan. Butter the bottom and sides of the foil.

2. In the top of a double boiler set over hot, NOT boiling water, melt the chocolate, butter and coffee, stirring frequently. Remove pan from heat and cool, stirring occasionally, for 10 minutes.

3. In the large bowl of the electric mixer beat the eggs at high speed for 30 seconds or until foamy. Gradually add the sugar and continue to beat for 2 minutes or until mixture is very light and fluffy. Reduce mixer to low speed and gradually beat in chocolate mixture until just blended. Using a wooden spoon, stir in the flour. Stir in the walnuts. Do not overbeat the mixture at this point.

4. Scrape the batter into the prepared pan and spread evenly with an offset spatula or butter knife. Bake 30 minutes or until the foggies are just set around the edges. They will remain moist in the center. Cool in the pan on a wire rack for 30 minutes, then cover the pan tightly with aluminum foil and refrigerate overnight, or put into the freezer for 2 hours. Do not skip this step.

5. Remove the top foil and run a sharp knife around the edge of the foggies. Using the two ends of foil as handles, lift out of the pan. Invert onto a large cutting board and peel off foil. Invert foggies again onto a smooth cutting board with the help of the back of a baking sheet. Cut them into 32 pieces, as they are very rich. These freeze well also. Outstanding!

LUSCIOUS LEMON BARS
MAKES 32 TRIANGLES

When I was compiling recipes for this chapter, my daughter Diane said this one was a MUST!

Crust:

1/2 pound (2 sticks) unsalted butter, at room
    temperature
1/2 cup granulated sugar
2 cups all-purpose flour
1/8 teaspoon salt

Filling:

7 large eggs, room temperature
3 cups granulated sugar
2 tablespoons grated lemon zest (from about 4 lemons)
1 scant cup freshly squeezed lemon juice (about 4
    lemons)
1 cup all-purpose flour

<u>confectioners' sugar for dusting finished bars</u>

1. Preheat oven to 350°F.

2. <u>Make crust</u>: In an electric mixer with the paddle attachment cream the butter and sugar until light. On a piece of parchment paper, combine the flour and salt. With the mixer on low, add this to the creamed mixture just until mixed. Turn the dough out onto a well-floured board and gather into a ball. Flatten the dough with floured hands and press it evenly into a 9" x13" x 2" baking pan, building up a 1 inch edge on all sides. Chill for at least 15 minutes or up to an hour.

3. Bake the crust for 15 to 20 minutes, until very lightly browned. Let cool on a wire rack. Leave the oven on.

4. <u>Make the filling</u>: In a large bowl whisk the eggs, sugar, lemon zest, lemon juice and flour together. Pour over the crust and bake for 30 minutes, until filling is set. Let cool to room temperature.

5. Dust with confectioners' sugar and cut into 32 triangles, by cutting 4 rows across and 4 rows lengthwise, then halving the squares diagonally.

LINZER BARS—MAKES 16

The classic combination of almonds, lemon peel and raspberries is irresistible.

1 1/2 cups all-purpose flour
1/2 cup <u>each</u> granulated sugar and ground almonds
   (grind in processor)
1 1/2 teaspoon freshly grated lemon peel
1 teaspoon <u>each</u> baking powder, instant coffee powder
   and cinnamon
1/4 teaspoon salt
1/2 cup unsalted butter, room temperature
2 large eggs, lightly beaten

3/4 cup red raspberry preserves

<u>Glaze: yolk of 1 large egg, beaten with 1 teaspoon water</u>

1. Preheat oven to 350°F.

2. In a large bowl mix flour, sugar, almonds, lemon peel, baking powder, coffee, cinnamon and salt. Add butter and work in with a wooden spoon until mixture is crumbly. Add beaten eggs and stir until mixture clumps into a dough. Work a minute or so longer to mix well.

3. Put 3/4 cup of the dough between two sheets of wax paper and roll out to a 9 inch square. Slide onto a baking sheet and freeze firm, about 10 minutes.

4. Press remaining dough evenly in the bottom of an ungreased 9-inch square pan. Spread preserves over the dough.

5. Remove top sheet of wax paper from chilled dough and turn out onto a lightly floured wooden board. Remove other sheet of wax paper. Dough is very sticky to roll out and pick up, so use a pastry scraper and add a bit of extra flour if you need it. Cut dough into 1/2-inch wide strips. Arrange half the strips diagonally on top of preserves. Arrange other half across them to make a lattice pattern.

6. Brush yolk glaze over the top of lattice and preserves. Bake 25 to 30 minutes, or until pastry is a rich golden-brown. Remove from oven and place on wire rack to cool before cutting into 16 bars.

SNICKERDOODLES—MAKES ABOUT 5 DOZEN

Everybody's favorite cookie, and this recipe is no-fail!

1/2 cup <u>each</u> solid Crisco and unsalted butter
1 1/2 cups sugar
2 large eggs
1/2 teaspoon pure vanilla

2 3/4 cups flour
2 teaspoons cream of tartar
1 teaspoon baking soda
1/4 teaspoon salt

Coating Mixture:

4 tablespoons sugar
<u>4 teaspoons (1 tablespoon plus 1 teaspoon) cinnamon</u>

1. Preheat oven to 375°F.

2. In the bowl of an electric mixer on high speed, cream the shortening, butter and sugar. Add the eggs, one at a time, then the vanilla.

3. Meanwhile, mix the flour, cream of tartar, baking soda and salt in a medium bowl. Stir into creamed mixture on medium speed.

4. Roll this mixture into balls the size of small walnuts and roll in the sugar-cinnamon coating mixture. Place 2 inches apart on ungreased baking sheets. Bake 8 to 10 minutes. Let rest on sheet for about 3 minutes, then transfer to wire rack to cool. These cookies puff up at first, then flatten out as they cool. They freeze well!

CHOCOLATE HAZELNUT MADELEINES
MAKES 24 TO 30 COOKIES

These cookies do require special Madeleine pans, but they are so good it's worth adding them to your "batterie de cuisine". Madeleine pans have shallow shell-shaped indentations, which give the characteristic shape to these cookies. They are best served warm the day you make them.

1/2 cup hazelnuts
very soft unsalted butter and all-purpose flour, to
    prepare molds
13 tablespoons unsalted butter

8 ounces good quality bittersweet or semisweet
    chocolate, chopped

3/4 cup confectioners' sugar, sifted
1/2 cup plus 1 tablespoon flour, sifted with above
    confectioners' sugar

6 large egg whites

extra confectioners' sugar to dust completed cookies

1. Preheat oven to 350°F. and toast hazelnuts on a cookie sheet for 8 minutes, until golden. Cool and grind in food processor until fine. Reserve.

2. Prepare Madeleine molds by brushing with softened butter and dusting lightly with flour, shaking out excess flour. Reserve.

3. Make brown butter by placing the 13 tablespoons of butter in large saucepan and heating over moderately high heat, letting it change from a foamy white liquid to a clear, golden liquid with big bubbles to a light brown nutty smelling mixture, being careful not to burn it. Transfer to bowl and cool.

4. Melt chocolate in microwave at 50% power, 1 minute at a time until melted. Cool.

5. Add the reserved ground hazelnuts to the sifted confectioners' sugar and flour.

6. Whisk egg whites in electric mixer with whisk attachment until foamy. Add the hazelnut-flour mixture and whisk until thoroughly combined. Blend in the brown butter and melted chocolate. Spoon batter into prepared molds, filling them almost to the top. Refrigerate for 1 hour to firm up batter. Keep molds refrigerated until ready to bake.

7. Preheat oven to 375°F. and bake 12 to 15 minutes, until evenly brown and springy to the touch. Rap tin sharply against a flat work surface and unmold immediately, transferring to rack to cool. Can sift powdered sugar over cookies just before serving.

DRIED CHERRY-PISTACHIO BISCOTTI
MAKES ABOUT 5 DOZEN

The perfect ending to an Italian meal, or dunked in Vin Santo, the divine Italian dessert wine.

2 1/2 cups all-purpose flour
1 teaspoon baking powder
1/4 teaspoon baking soda
1/2 teaspoon salt

3/4 cup (1 1/2 sticks) unsalted butter, slightly firm
2 teaspoons each freshly grated orange zest and lemon
    zest
1 cup plus 1 tablespoon sugar, DIVIDED
2 large eggs
1 teaspoon pure vanilla extract

1 cup shelled pistachios, unskinned, toasted at 350°F.
    for 10 minutes, then coarsely chopped
5 ounces dried cherries (or dried cranberries)

Egg wash: 1 large egg, beaten with 2 teaspoons water in
    a small bowl

1. Preheat oven to 350°F.

2. On a large sheet of parchment or waxed paper sift the flour, baking powder, baking soda and salt three times using a fine strainer. Reserve.

3. In the bowl of an electric mixer with the paddle attachment, mix the butter with the two zests on medium-high speed until smooth, about 1 minute. Slowly add the one cup of sugar and beat for one minute longer. Add the eggs one at a time, then beat for one minute more. Scrape down the bowl as needed with a rubber spatula. Beat in the vanilla. Reduce speed to low and add the dry ingredients in three additions, mixing *just* until combined.

4. Remove bowl from machine and, using a large rubber spatula, fold in the pistachios and the dried cherries. Transfer dough to plastic wrap and chill for 1 hour or up to overnight.

5. Position 2 racks in upper and lower third of oven. Line 2 jellyroll pans with parchment paper, or you can butter them. Divide the chilled dough into thirds, and on a lightly floured surface press each piece into a 1/4 inch somewhat flattened log. Place 2 logs on one pan and 1 log on the other pan. Brush each log with the egg wash, then sprinkle tops with the one tablespoon of sugar. Bake for 25 minutes or until lightly browned, rotating pans from front to back and top to bottom. Remove from oven and let rest in pans for 5 minutes.

6. Meanwhile, reduce temperature of oven to 300°F. Using a serrated knife cut logs into 1/2-inch slices. Lay the slices on their sides and return to oven for 8 minutes, or until just slightly brown. Remove from oven, turn slices over and bake another 8 minutes. Let rest on pan for 5 minutes before transferring to cooling racks. These cookies freeze well.

VIENNESE WALNUT-CARDAMOM CRESCENTS
MAKES 2 DOZEN

My wonderful culinary assistant and friend Pam Workman presented these melt-in-your-mouth cookies to me on a gorgeous china serving dish for my birthday one year. What a fabulous way to make someone feel special! Mixing the dough in the food processor makes these cookies a snap to prepare.

1 cup all-purpose flour
3/4 cup walnuts
1/2 cup (1 stick) unsalted butter, chilled, cut into 1/2-inch pieces
1/4 cup granulated sugar
1/2 teaspoon <u>each</u> ground cardamom and grated orange zest
pinch of salt

<u>vanilla sugar or confectioners' sugar</u>

1. Preheat oven to 325°F.

2. In the bowl of a food processor fitted with the metal blade combine all ingredients except the vanilla sugar or confectioners' sugar. Using rapid on-off pulses, process until the mixture resembles coarse meal, then process continuously until the dough begins to gather together. Empty onto a work surface and knead a few minutes till the dough comes together nicely.

3. Roll 2 teaspoons of dough between your palms to form a rope 2 1/2 inches long, slightly tapering it at the ends. Arrange the rope on parchment-lined cookie sheets in a crescent shape. Repeat with the remaining dough, spacing the cookies 1 inch apart.

4. Bake until just firm to the touch, about 20 minutes. Let cool on the baking sheet for 5 minutes, and then transfer cookies to a wire rack. Sprinkle the warm cookies with the vanilla sugar or shake the confectioners' sugar over cooled cookies with a fine sieve. Freeze very well. Store in an airtight container at room temperature for up to 5 days, if they last that long! These cookies also freeze well.

<u>NOTE</u>: There are two ways to make vanilla sugar. If you are using a fresh vanilla bean, split it lengthwise, scrape out the seeds and place the bean pod and seeds in 2

cups of granulated sugar in a glass jar or other airtight container for at least one week. Alternately, when you have used a vanilla bean in a recipe, wash it and let it dry out *thoroughly* for several days, then insert it into a jar of granulated sugar, again using the formula of one bean for every 2 cups of granulated sugar. In both cases, remove the vanilla bean from the vanilla sugar before using the sugar. The vanilla sugar can be used in any baking project that calls for vanilla.

MOMMA'S BUTTER COOKIES
MAKES ABOUT 60 COOKIES

My mother was truly a gifted cookie baker, but sadly she never wrote down her recipes. As with many women of her generation, the cookies were her specialty and she preferred to make them herself, to share with everyone from the postman to lucky neighbors, and, of course our family (she shared the cookies but not the recipes!). Here is my interpretation of her butter cookies. It's as close as I can get to the original, and when I bake them it brings back many wonderful memories. There are suggestions for many varieties from the one basic recipe, which makes for a lot of fun in the kitchen.

1/2 pound (2 sticks) unsalted butter
1/4 pound (1 stick) margarine (not low-fat)
scant 1 cup sugar
2 large egg yolks
1 teaspoon pure vanilla extract
1/2 teaspoon almond extract
2 1/2 cups all-purpose flour

Variations: quartered and drained maraschino cherries,
    jelly, nuts, coconut, colorings, cocoa, etc.

1. Preheat oven to 325°F.

2. In an electric mixer cream butter, margarine and sugar. Add the egg yolks, vanilla and almond extracts and mix well.

3. Add flour and mix only until incorporated. Can chill dough at this point for up to 2 days, or freeze, well wrapped, or proceed to bake right away.

4. Roll into small balls and place on ungreased baking sheets. Make a thumbprint in center of each. Fill with one quarter of a cherry or a dollop of jelly.

5. Bake in preheated oven 12 to 16 minutes or until just golden. Let rest on sheets a few minutes, then carefully transfer to racks. These cookies are fragile.

NOTE: For variety with this basic dough, mix half the completed dough with 1 cup of toasted coconut and the other half with toasted chopped walnuts or pecans, form into logs, wrap and chill, then slice and bake. Or divide dough in half and mix 3 tablespoons unsweetened cocoa into one half, leaving the other vanilla, chill the dough, then roll each half into a rectangle, place one on top of the other and roll into a log, then slice and make marble swirls. Or tint some of the dough red, some green, etc. and combine to make layered squares.

BETTY ANN'S ROGLACH
MAKES 4 DOZEN

No matter how many varieties of cookies I bake, this is the one most requested! It has become a staple at all our family gatherings, and I usually quadruple the recipe.

Pastry:

1 cup unsalted butter (2 sticks) room temperature
6 ounces cream cheese (not diet-type), room
    temperature
2 cups all purpose flour

Filling:

1 cup each chopped walnuts and sugar
1 1/2 teaspoons cinnamon
melted unsalted butter (about 1/2 cup or 1 stick)

Glaze:

1 cup confectioners' sugar, sifted
1 to 2 tablespoons milk
1/2 teaspoon pure vanilla extract

1. Make pastry: In a large bowl mix the butter, cream cheese and flour with your hands or a fork to form a dough. Divide into 4 equal balls and flatten each and wrap in plastic wrap. Refrigerate at least one hour or up to 2 days.

2. Make filling: Combine all ingredients in a medium bowl. Reserve.

3. To make roglach: Roll out one ball at a time very thinly on a lightly floured wooden board to a 12-inch circle. Brush with melted butter and spread with 1/2 cup of the filling. Cut into 12 wedges, like a pie. Roll each wedge into a crescent shape, starting from the outer wide edge. Place on ungreased baking sheets and bake in a preheated oven for about 20 minutes, or until golden brown. Remove to wire racks to cool. Continue with the other 3 balls of dough, making 4 dozen roglach in all.

4. Make glaze: In a medium bowl combine the confectioners' sugar, milk and vanilla until a smooth consistency that drips easily from a spoon.

5. When roglach are cool, drizzle with glaze. When glaze sets up you can package the cookies. These freeze very well.

SWISS APPLE PIE—SERVES 8

This simple recipe is from my mother-in-law, Ruth Litvak. It is especially easy to make for those who suffer from "fear of rolling out dough".

Crisco solid shortening, to grease pan
2 large eggs, lightly beaten
1 1/4 cup sugar
1 cup all-purpose flour
2 teaspoons baking powder
1/4 teaspoon each cinnamon and salt
1/8 teaspoon nutmeg
2 cups Granny Smith, Jonathan or Golden Delicious
    apples, peeled, cored and chopped
1 cup walnuts, chopped
2 tablespoons unsalted butter, cut into small cubes

Optional: whipped cream or vanilla ice cream

1. Preheat oven to 350°F. Grease a 10-inch round pie plate or quiche pan with solid Crisco.

2. Mix all ingredients except the butter by hand in a large bowl. Spoon into prepared pan (mixture will be thick) and dot with the butter.

3. Bake in preheated oven for 25 to 30 minutes. Cut into wedges and serve warm plain, or with whipped cream or vanilla ice cream.

HELENE'S FRENCH APPLE CREAM PIE
MAKES 1 PIE 👨‍🍳 👨‍🍳

My sister Helene is a wonderful baker, and this classic French pie is just one example of her talent.

Crust:

2 cups sifted all-purpose flour
1 teaspoon salt
2/3 cup shortening (Crisco), cut into small cubes and
    refrigerated
6 to 7 tablespoons ice water

Filling:

5 cups pared, sliced Granny Smith apples
3/4 to 1 cup sugar (depending on sweetness of apples
    and your taste)
2 tablespoons flour
1/2 teaspoon each cinnamon and freshly grated nutmeg
1 teaspoon finely grated lemon rind
2 tablespoons butter, diced

sugar to sprinkle on top of crust before baking

Cream Sauce:

2 large eggs, slightly beaten
1/2 cup sugar
1 tablespoon freshly squeezed lemon juice
3 ounce package cream cheese, softened to room
    temperature
1/2 cup sour cream, room temperature

1. Preheat oven to 425°F.

2. Make Crust: Put flour and salt into a mixing bowl.
Cut in the shortening with a pastry blender or a fork
until particles are fine. Sprinkle the cold water over
mixture while stirring lightly with a fork, until dough
holds together. Divide dough in half and roll first half on
floured surface to form a 9-inch crust. Fit into a 9-inch
pie pan.

3. In a large bowl combine the apples, sugar, the 2
tablespoons of flour, cinnamon, nutmeg and lemon rind,
stirring to coat evenly. Turn mixture into the pastry-lined
pie pan and dot with butter.

4. Roll out second crust and cut a 1 1/2-inch to 2-inch
hole in center. Place pastry over filled pie and crimp
edges. Sprinkle with additional sugar.

5. Bake in a preheated oven for 10 minutes, then reduce
heat to 375°F. and continue to cook for 30 to 35 minutes
or until apples are tender.

6. While pie is baking, make Cream Sauce: In a medium
saucepan combine the eggs, sugar and lemon juice.
Cook, stirring constantly, until thickened. Whisk in the
cream cheese and sour cream. Pour this cream sauce
into a liquid measuring cup for ease of pouring. Very
slowly, carefully pour the cream sauce through the center
opening while pie is warm. You can carefully use a thin
knife to lift center of pastry up a bit to help, and you
can also carefully tilt the pie to distribute some of the
sauce. Let some of the mixture sink and get absorbed
before continuing. Be patient, the pie will be able to
accommodate all the sauce. Cool before serving.

RED VELVET CUPCAKES
MAKES 36

Here's a must-have recipe, considering the cupcake mania that has hit the culinary world. They are delicious and freeze beautifully, fully frosted. Just cover the surface of the frosting loosely with plastic wrap and put the cupcakes in an airtight container. If you don't want to make so many, the recipe can easily be halved. I often double the frosting recipe, so that I can put it in a pastry bag with a fluted tip to make these cupcakes look just like ones at the fancy bakeries.

2 1/2 cups all-purpose flour
1/2 cup cocoa powder (<u>not</u> a cocoa mix, which has sugar and other additives)
1 teaspoon baking soda
1/2 teaspoon salt
1 cup (2 sticks) unsalted butter, softened to room temperature
2 cups granulated sugar
4 large eggs
1 cup sour cream
1/2 cup whole milk
1 1-ounce bottle red food coloring
1 teaspoon pure vanilla extract

Buttercream Frosting:

2 cups whole milk
4 tablespoons all purpose flour
1 pound (4 sticks) room temperature unsalted butter
2 cups confectioners' sugar
<u>2 teaspoons pure vanilla extract</u>

1. Preheat oven to 350°F.

2. In a medium bowl mix the flour, cocoa, baking soda and salt. In another bowl whisk the sour cream, milk, food coloring and vanilla. In the bowl of an electric mixer beat the butter and sugar on medium speed 5 minutes or until light and fluffy. Beat in the eggs, one at a time. On low speed gradually beat the flour mixture and the sour cream mixture into the butter-sugar mixture <u>alternately</u>, starting and ending with the flour mixture, as this makes a better texture and structure for the cupcakes.

3. Line cupcake pans with paper liners. Fill each cup 2/3 full. You can use a small ice cream scoop for a neater job. Bake in preheated oven for 25 to 30 minutes. Cool in pans 5 minutes, then remove from pans and cool completely.

4. <u>Meanwhile, make the frosting</u>: In a small saucepan place the milk and whisk in the flour. Bring to a simmer over medium heat and simmer until thickened, about 5 minutes. In an electric mixer, cream the butter, sugar and vanilla until light and fluffy. Mix in the cooled thickened milk and mix until smooth. When the cupcakes are cool, use an offset spatula to frost the tops.

OLD-FASHIONED CARROT CAKE—MAKES ONE LARGE CAKE

3 cups plus 2 teaspoons all-purpose flour
2 teaspoons <u>each</u> baking powder, baking soda and cinnamon
1/2 teaspoon salt
1 cup <u>each</u> chopped walnuts and golden raisins
5 large eggs, room temperature
1 3/4 cups granulated sugar
1 cup vegetable oil
1 pound carrots, peeled and grated

Topping:

1/3 cup dry white wine or dry vermouth
1 cup confectioners' sugar
2 tablespoons buttermilk
<u>1 teaspoon dark rum</u>

1. <u>Bake the cake</u>: Adjust oven rack to middle position. Preheat oven to 325°F. Grease and flour a 12-cup Bundt pan. In a medium bowl whisk the 3 cups flour, baking powder, baking soda, cinnamon and salt. In a small bowl toss the walnuts, raisins and 2 teaspoons flour until well coated.

2. With an electric mixer at medium-high speed beat eggs and sugar until combined. Reduce speed to medium and slowly add oil until incorporated. Increase speed of mixer and beat until mixture is light and creamy. Using a rubber spatula, stir in the flour mixture, the walnuts and raisins, and the carrots until combined. Scrape batter into

the prepared pan and bake until a toothpick inserted in the center comes out clean, 55 to 65 minutes. Cool cake in the pan for 30 minutes, then turn out onto a rack and cool completely, at least 1 hour.

3. <u>Make the topping</u>: Brush the wine or vermouth over the cake until it is absorbed. Whisk the confectioners' sugar, buttermilk and rum in a medium bowl. Drizzle over the cake and serve. Cake can be stored at room temperature for up to 5 days.

CHOCOLATE DECADENCE CAKE—MAKES 8 TO 12 SERVINGS

This is THE ONE for all chocoholics.

1 pound dark sweet chocolate, such as Maillard's or Baker's German Sweet Chocolate
5 ounces (10 tablespoons) unsalted butter
4 large eggs
1 tablespoon granulated sugar
1 tablespoon flour, sifted
2 cups heavy cream
1 tablespoon confectioners' sugar
1 teaspoon pure vanilla
chocolate curls made with a potato peeler, from a bar of sweet chocolate
<u>8 ounces frozen unsweetened raspberries</u>

1. Preheat oven to 425°F.

2. Line an 8-inch cake pan with parchment paper. Do not butter or flour it. Melt the chocolate with the butter in the top of a double boiler. Transfer to a bowl and set aside.

3. Clean double boiler. Combine eggs and sugar in top of double boiler set over gently simmering water. Whisk constantly until sugar dissolves and the mixture is barely warm. Remove from heat and transfer to mixer bowl. Beat at high speed until eggs treble in volume and are the consistency of whipped cream (5 to 10 minutes). Fold in the flour gently. Gently stir 1/3 of egg mixture into the chocolate mixture. Then fold the chocolate mixture into the remaining egg until thoroughly combined. Pour into pan. Tap lightly and place into preheated oven for 15 minutes. Cake will be soft in the center but crusty on top and sides. Cool completely in pan on a rack. Then place it in the freezer overnight or up to one month. This cake must be frozen to obtain the right consistency.

4. Whip 2 cups of heavy cream with the 1 tablespoon confectioners' sugar and the vanilla. Make chocolate curls from the chocolate bar using a potato peeler. Make the raspberry purée: Purée the raspberries in a processor and strain through a fine sieve. Put into a pretty crystal bowl. This purée can be made a day or two ahead and kept refrigerated until serving. Remove chocolate cake from freezer and spin pan <u>momentarily</u> on a burner of stove over high heat. Using hot pads, turn out onto a flat platter. Remove parchment round. Using 2/3 of the whipped cream, cover the cake. Place chocolate curls high in center and then pipe rosettes of whipped cream (using a #6 star tip and pastry bag) around edge of cake, OR for a simpler presentation just spoon mounds of the whipped cream around the outside top edge. Refrigerate. Remove 15 minutes before serving. Pass the raspberry purée separately.

HELENE'S ORANGE CAKE
MAKES 1 CAKE

This moist and flavorful cake is another gift from my sister Helene. This is the favorite cake of a special group of my students—4 generations, from Great Grandmother Kathleen, to great grandson Ethan, who have all attended classes through the years!

vegetable oil and flour to prepare pan
1 cup butter
3 large eggs, separated
1 cup <u>each</u> sugar and sour cream
grated rind of one orange
1 3/4 cup all-purpose flour
1 teaspoon <u>each</u> baking powder and baking soda

Orange syrup:

juice of 2 oranges (about 3/4 cup juice)
juice of 1 lemon (3 tablespoons)
3/4 cup sugar
<u>dash of salt</u>

1. Preheat oven to 325°F. Oil and flour a Bundt pan.

2. In the bowl of an electric mixer, cream the butter and sugar. Add the egg yolks, sour cream and orange rind.

3. Sift together the flour, baking powder and baking soda. Stir into the first mixture. Using a clean rubber spatula, fold in the egg whites, which have been beaten until stiff but not dry. Turn batter into the prepared Bundt pan and bake for 1 hour. Remove from oven and let stand for 10 minutes.

4. <u>Meanwhile, Make Orange Syrup</u>: Combine the orange and lemon juices, sugar and salt in medium saucepan. Bring to a boil and boil 3 to 4 minutes.

5. Loosen cake carefully around edge of pan with thin knife and turn out onto a plate with a rim. Pour hot orange syrup over top of cake <u>slowly</u>, so it will absorb into the cake more easily. Let cool and serve.

LEMON POPPYSEED POUND CAKE
MAKES ONE CAKE

3 tablespoons whole milk
3 large eggs
1 1/2 teaspoons vanilla
1 1/2 cups sifted cake flour (measured after sifting)
3/4 cup sugar
3/4 teaspoon baking powder
1/4 teaspoon salt
grated zest of one lemon
3 tablespoons (1 ounce) poppy seeds
13 tablespoons (6 1/2 ounces) unsalted butter, softened
   to room temperature
1/4 cup freshly squeezed lemon juice
<u>1/4 cup plus 2 tablespoons sugar</u>

1. Preheat oven to 350°F. Grease and flour an 8" x 4" loaf pan.

2. In a medium bowl, combine the milk, eggs and vanilla gently.

3. In the large bowl of an electric mixer combine the dry ingredients, flour, sugar, baking powder, salt and poppy seeds, with the lemon zest, and mix on low speed 30 seconds to blend. Add the softened butter and half the egg mixture. Mix on low speed until dry ingredients are moistened. Increase to medium speed and beat for one minute to aerate and develop the cake's structure. Add rest of egg mixture.

4. Scrape batter into the prepared pan and smooth the top with a spatula. Bake 45 minutes, or until a cake tester inserted in the center comes out clean. You can cover top of cake loosely with foil during last few minutes of baking if cake is browning too quickly.

5. When cake is almost done, <u>Prepare the Lemon Syrup</u>: In a small saucepan over medium heat stir the 1/4 cup plus 2 tablespoons sugar with the 1/4 cup lemon juice until dissolved. As soon as the cake comes out of the oven, place the pan on a rack. Poke the cake all over with a skewer or wire cake tester, and brush it with 1/2 the syrup. Cool in the pan 10 minutes. Loosen the sides with a spatula and invert it onto a greased wire rack. Brush the sides with the remaining syrup and allow to cool before wrapping airtight. Store for 24 hours before serving, to

give the syrup a chance to distribute evenly. This cake will keep fresh for several days, if you can keep the family from eating it!

PRALINE NUT ROLL
MAKES ONE LARGE ROLL

This is a special occasion cake with wonderful flavor notes of hazelnut and vanilla. It takes time and attention, but is well worth it!

Praline Powder

1 cup <u>each</u> hazelnuts (also called filberts) and sugar
1/4 cup water
1/4 teaspoon cream of tartar

Genoise (French Sponge Cake)

5 large eggs, separated
3/4 cup granulated sugar, <u>divided</u> into 1/2 cup and 1/4 cup
1 cup ground toasted hazelnuts, <u>skins removed</u> (see Step #1)
3 tablespoons sifted flour
1 teaspoon <u>each</u> baking powder and vanilla
pinch salt
1/2 teaspoon cream of tartar
1/3 cup praline powder (recipe above)

Praline Filling:

1 cup heavy cream
2 tablespoons confectioners' sugar, sifted
1 teaspoon vanilla
1/4 cup crushed praline powder

Praline Frosting:

1/2 cup firmly packed brown sugar
1/4 cup heavy cream
3 tablespoons unsalted butter
<u>7 tablespoons powdered sugar</u>

1. <u>Make Praline Powder</u>: Preheat oven to 350°F. and spread shelled hazelnuts in a baking pan. Roast for 15 to 20 minutes, or until lightly browned. Rub off the skins in a towel while still warm. Prepare a marble slab with softened butter, OR butter a shallow cookie sheet. Combine sugar, water and 1/4 teaspoon cream of tartar in a large saucepan. Bring to a boil watching carefully. Wipe down sides of pan with a pastry brush dipped in cold water to remove any undissolved sugar crystals. Lower heat and continue to cook <u>without stirring</u> until mixture is a light caramel color. BE CAREFUL WITH THIS MIXTURE, as a sugar burn is very painful! Add hazelnuts. Pour mixture onto the buttered marble slab or buttered shallow cookie sheet and let cool. When cool, break up and put into processor, and process until it becomes a fine powder. (There will be some extra powder—this freezes well and is enough for at least another cake.)

2. <u>Make Genoise</u>: Preheat oven to 350°F. Butter a 15" x 10"x 1" jelly roll pan, line with parchment paper or waxed paper. Butter and lightly flour the paper.

3. In the bowl of an electric mixer, beat egg yolks until frothy, then add the 1/2 cup sugar slowly. Continue to beat until mixture is thick and light colored. Fold in the ground hazelnuts, 1/3 cup praline powder, flour, baking powder and vanilla until blended. Transfer to a large bowl and reserve.

4. In the <u>clean bowl of mixer</u> beat whites with salt and cream of tartar until foamy. Gradually beat in the remaining 1/4 cup sugar until meringue forms <u>soft</u> peaks. Add 1/4 of the meringue to reserved egg yolk mixture, folding in until blended with a clean spatula. Fold in remaining meringue until no streaks of white remain. Pour batter into prepared pan, spreading evenly with spatula. Bake 15 to 20 minutes or until top of cake springs back when lightly touch with fingertips. Loosen edges of cake with a thin knife and turn cake out onto a hand towel which has been sprinkled with powdered sugar. Trim any hard edges about 1/4 inch all around the cake, for easier rolling. Peel off paper and roll cake and towel together tightly. Cool on wire rack.

5. <u>Make Praline Filling</u>: Beat cream in chilled medium bowl until stiff. Beat in powdered sugar and vanilla. Fold in 1/4 cup praline powder. Carefully unroll cake and spread with filling. Reroll gently and transfer rolled cake to a serving tray, using a large spatula.

6. <u>Make Frosting</u>: Combine brown sugar, cream and

butter in a small saucepan. Bring to a boil, stirring, and then lower heat. Cook, stirring constantly, for 2 minutes. Remove from heat and cool to lukewarm. Beat in the powdered sugar until the mixture is smooth. Spread roll with frosting and garnish with a sprinkling of remaining praline. Refrigerate until serving time.

COOK'S TIP

One of the joys of cooking is being creative and putting your own stamp on a recipe. But in *baking*, you really need to follow the instructions and keep the amounts of the ingredients exactly as the recipe states, as changes can affect the texture, balance and taste of the final product. Always be mindful that baking is an exact science. I always use large eggs and unsalted butter when I cook, as large eggs are the standard size for baking, and I use unsalted butter, which allows the cook to control the amount of salt in each recipe, and ensures that the butter is fresh, since salt is a preservative and can mask rancidity. Use glass liquid measures for liquids, and metal or plastic measures for dry ingredients. Aerate flour before measuring it, by shaking it in a covered plastic container, and measure it by spooning it into the measuring cup, rather than using the scoop and sweep method, which results in too much flour in the recipe. Another important technique when baking is knowing how to *cream,* which refers to mixing the butter or other fat with the sugar in an electric mixer until it is fluffy and no longer gritty. Of course you can choose your favorite nuts, fruits and flavorings, remembering to keep the *quantities* the same as in the original recipe. Express your creativity by decorating your baked goods according to your own unique style.

12

GIFTS FROM YOUR KITCHEN

To me, caring means sharing, and there is no better way to show your family and friends how much you care than by offering them homemade gifts. Whether as a "bread and butter gift" for a visit, a show of appreciation for some kindness, a holiday present or an offering of sympathy at sad times, something you take the time to make is always appreciated, especially in our busy world, where this custom is sadly becoming rare. Here are twenty one special gifts, seven savory and fourteen sweet, that I have used over the years to share with friends and family. I package these treats in glass jars or colorful plastic bags, add bows and include directions for making the recipe. Friends always look forward to these special presents, and many are make-ahead mixes that you can prepare in large quantities and have on hand whenever you need them. I hope you and yours will embrace this tradition, also. I have divided these gifts into those that you package and the receiver finishes, and those that you have already made and are ready to eat.

Giant Double Chocolate-Double Nut Cookie Mix (page 202)

SAVORIES:

FRENCH MARKET BEAN SOUP MIX
MAKES 6 GIFTS

Find the dried beans in the bulk food section of your grocery store.

Dried Bean Mix:

1 pound <u>each</u> dried kidney beans, dried yellow lentils, green split peas, dried black beans and dried black-eyed peas

Spice Mixture:

6 teaspoons <u>each</u> salt, dried basil, dried rosemary and dried marjoram
2 teaspoons black pepper
1 teaspoon crushed red pepper
<u>6 dried bay leaves</u>

<u>Additional soup ingredients</u> recipient will need to make 1 batch of soup from the packet of dried bean mix and packet of spice mix:

12 cups (4 quarts) water, <u>DIVIDED</u>
1 Honeybaked hambone
2 large onions, peeled, left whole
<u>1 14-ounce can diced tomatoes, undrained</u>

1. <u>Make dried bean mix</u>: In a large bowl combine first 5 ingredients. Divide this bean mixture into 6 equal portions of *2 cups each*, and place in 6 airtight containers, such as mason jars.

2. <u>Prepare Spice Mix</u>: Combine the salt, basil, rosemary, marjoram, black pepper, red pepper and bay leaves in a bowl. Divide spice mix into 6 equal portions of *4 1/2 teaspoons each* and place into small plastic bags. Put one in each mason jar with the dried beans.

3. <u>Directions to prepare the soup</u>: (Printed on a card attached to the soup mix and spice mix.) "Wash the dried-bean mix from the jar in a strainer in cold water, and place it and <u>one</u> of the onions in a large Dutch oven or stockpot. Cover with 4 cups of the water and bring to a boil, then turn off the heat. Cover pot and let sit one hour or up to overnight (refrigerate if overnight). Then drain and rinse beans, discarding onion.

4. Combine the drained bean mixture, the other 8 cups water, the second onion and the hambone in a large stockpot and bring to a boil, then lower heat to simmer and cook, covered, for 1 hour or until beans are tender. Add the packet of spice mix and the can of tomatoes with their juice, and bring to a boil again. Reduce heat and simmer 30 minutes more uncovered. Discard onion and bay leaf. Remove hambone from soup and shred meat from bone with 2 forks, discarding bone and fat. Return meat to soup. Adjust seasoning and serve. This soup freezes well."

HERBED OLIVES—MAKES 8 PINT JARS

2 pounds <u>each</u> Kalamata and green Greek olives
4 teaspoons <u>each</u> dried Greek oregano, marjoram and thyme or rosemary
12 2-inch strips of orange zest (white part removed as it is bitter), from 2 to 3 oranges
sprigs of dried oregano or thyme
<u>extra virgin olive oil to cover the olives</u>

1. Drain olives and blot them between layers of paper towels, to remove most of the brine they are packed in.

2. Place 8 4-ounce canning jelly jars, their lids and tongs in a large pot of water and bring to a boil. Boil 5 minutes and turn off heat.

3. In a very large bowl, mix together the olives, dried herbs and orange zest. With clean hands use clean tongs to remove canning jars from warm water onto a clean towel on a work surface. Use tongs to put the lids on the towel as well. Loosely pack olives into the jars, making sure your hands are very clean. Lay herb sprigs on top and add olive oil to cover the olives. Cover tightly with lids and store for from 1 day to up to 2 weeks at room temperature.

OLIVE OIL AND HERB MARINATED GOAT CHEESE—MAKES 1 LOG

Multiply this recipe to make as many jars as you want to give as gifts.

6-ounce log top-quality goat cheese (chèvre)

Marinade:

1 tablespoon fresh basil leaves, snipped, or 1 teaspoon dried basil
1/2 teaspoon dried thyme
4 cloves fresh garlic, crushed
freshly grated black pepper to taste
1/2 cup basil oil or other good flavored olive oil

1. Slice log into 1/2-inch rounds and place them in a shallow glass container.

2. Make marinade: Mix the rest of the ingredients together and pour over cheese slices. Spoon marinade over all the slices to coat well. Cover the container and refrigerate at least overnight to let flavors permeate the cheese.

3. Place slices in clean (see recipe above) pint jars and cover completely with the olive oil, adding more oil as needed so that the slices are completely covered. This treat will keep for 2 weeks or more in the refrigerator.

4. Print out copies of suggestions for using this cheese for each gift: "Take a thin crust premade pizza shell, or tortillas or pita bread cut into 2 rounds, and crisp in a preheated 375°F. oven. Crumble some of the cheese on top and add slices of ripe Roma tomatoes. Drizzle entire surface with some of the oil marinade. Broil for a few minutes until bubbly, then cut into wedges. For an even faster snack, toast good wheat bread, spread a slice of cheese on it, add a few sliced kalamata olives and some slivered sun-dried tomatoes and put it into the microwave until melted, about 20 seconds. Or crumble the marinated slices into salads with "designer greens" and a few toasted walnuts, using the marinade as a dressing. This is a wonderful treat to have on hand in your refrigerator!"

ZESTY PRETZEL NUGGETS MAKES 1 POUND

Irresistible…hide them until you need them!

2 tablespoons Hidden Valley Ranch Original dry dressing
1 teaspoon lemon pepper
1 1/2 teaspoons garlic powder
1 pound sourdough pretzel nuggets
3/4 cup vegetable oil

1. Preheat oven to 375°F.

2. In a medium bowl, mix the Hidden Valley Ranch dressing, lemon pepper and garlic powder. Reserve.

3. Line 2 baking sheets with foil. Spread pretzel nuggets in one layer on sheets. Sprinkle with the spice mixture, then pour the oil over top and mix well with spoon.

4. Bake for 25 minutes, stirring about every 8 minutes, until golden brown. Drain on paper towels, then cool and package in plastic bags. YUM!

WILD MUSHROOM PÂTÉ
MAKES ONE LARGE LOAF—

Since this makes such a large loaf, consider cutting it into two or three pieces and wrapping as separate gifts.

1/2 cup walnuts

1 3/4 pound assorted fresh mushrooms, such as cremini, shiitake, portobello, white button mushrooms, etc. cleaned, about 8 to 10 cups total
6 tablespoons unsalted butter, <u>DIVIDED</u>
6 scallions, white and pale green parts, cut into small dice,
OR 3 shallots, finely chopped
1 tablespoon fresh thyme leaves, plus sprigs of thyme for garnish
1 1/2 teaspoons sea salt, or to taste
1 teaspoon freshly ground black pepper
1/3 cup Madeira or dry sherry

1/4 cup finely chopped flatleaf (Italian) parsley
1 teaspoon freshly squeezed lemon juice
dash Tabasco sauce
<u>1 8-ounce package cream cheese, room temperature</u>

1. Heat oven to 350°F. Place walnuts on foil-lined baking sheet and bake until fragrant, about 7 minutes. Cool. Chop finely and reserve.

2. Chop the 1 3/4 pounds assorted mushrooms <u>coarsely</u> in food processor in several batches, or dice by hand. In large heavy skillet over medium-high heat melt 4 tablespoons butter. Add mushrooms, scallions and thyme and cook on High, stirring occasionally, until liquid has been released and then absorbed, about 5 to 8 minutes. Stir in salt, pepper and Madeira or sherry. Cook until skillet is almost dry, about 10 minutes more. Remove from heat, transfer mushrooms to a bowl and let cool.

3. In a large bowl, combine mushroom mixture with reserved walnuts, parsley, lemon juice, Tabasco and cream cheese. Taste and adjust seasoning.

4. Line a 3-cup rectangular mold with plastic wrap, allowing a 4-inch overhang on all sides. Spoon the mushroom mixture into the pan, smoothing top. Cover with plastic overhang and firmly press down all over

terrine with hands, smoothing mixture as evenly as possible. Refrigerate at least 8 hours, or overnight. Remove from mold. At this point you may want to divide it into portions and wrap in plastic wrap. Overwrap each loaf with colored cellophane and tie with a ribbon.

5. <u>Attach recipe and suggestions for serving</u>: "Unwrap chilled loaf and invert it onto a serving platter. Surround with fresh thyme sprigs if desired. Serve with optional toast points made with good dense white bread, crusts removed after toasting, buttered and cut into quarters to accompany the pâté."

TANGY HONEY MUSTARD
MAKES 8 4-OUNCE JARS

An unusual and versatile gift. Buy the dry mustard in the bulk foods section at your supermarket.

2 cups <u>each</u> dry mustard and white or raspberry vinegar
4 large eggs
2 cups sugar
2/3 cup honey
<u>pinch of salt</u>

1. In large screw-top jar mix the mustard and vinegar. Screw on lid and shake well. (Or mix in a large bowl and cover.) Refrigerate overnight.

2. The next day, beat the eggs well and stir into the mustard-vinegar mixture with the sugar and honey. Place in large heavy pot and heat to boiling over medium-high heat, stirring and whisking constantly. Strain through a medium strainer and discard any cooked egg or lumps.

3. Place 8 4-ounce canning jelly jars, their lids and tongs in a large pot of water and bring to a boil. Boil 5 minutes and turn off heat.

4. With clean hands use clean tongs to place jelly jars on a clean towel on a work surface. Fill jars with the warm mustard and cap tightly with lids. Label with the date and refrigerate. Good for at least 3 months refrigerated.

FIRE AND ICE PICKLES
MAKES 6 1-PINT JARS

These are really wonderful and very easy to make.

2 32-ounce jars medium-size whole dill pickles, drained, juice discarded
4 cups granulated sugar
2 tablespoons hot sauce (or less to your taste)
1/2 teaspoon dried crushed red pepper

6 1-pint canning jars
<u>6 cloves garlic, peeled</u>

1. Cut pickles into 1/4-inch thick slices, discarding ends.

2. In a large bowl, combine sugar, hot sauce and red pepper. Mix well. Add pickle slices and stir well. Cover mixture and let stand 2 hours, stirring occasionally. Don't worry if it seems dry, the mixture will exude a good bit of liquid as it sits.

3. Wash pint jars in dishwasher and boil lids and funnel in small pot on stove for 5 minutes.

4. Stir mixture again and then fill jars carefully to the top, adding a garlic clove to each. Cover with lids and tighten with rings. Turn over onto a clean tray lined with a tea towel and refrigerate. After a day you can turn the jars right side up. For best flavor, wait 1 week before eating. Pickles will be good for 4 to 6 weeks, refrigerated.

SWEETS:

GIANT DOUBLE CHOCOLATE-DOUBLE NUT COOKIE MIX
MAKES 8 BATCHES OF ABOUT 10 COOKIES EACH, DEPENDING ON SIZE ☺ 🍥

This has been one of my most popular gifts through the years. It will make a large amount of cookie mix, which you can keep unrefrigerated for about 6 months in an airtight container. Then you and your friends can make up a batch of fresh cookies any time the urge strikes!

Dry ingredients:

9 cups all purpose flour
4 teaspoons baking soda
4 cups solid Crisco shortening (Do not substitute other shortening)
2 teaspoons salt
3 cups granulated sugar
3 cups packed brown sugar
2 cups each broken pecan halves and coarsely chopped walnuts (or you can use all of either nut, 4 cups total
2 12-ounce packages. each chocolate chunks and semi-sweet chocolate chips (or all of either) 4 packages total

To complete one batch of cookies:

3 1/2 cups of the cookie mix
1 large egg, beaten
1/2 teaspoon pure vanilla extract
1 to 2 teaspoons cold water

1. Make the cookie mix: In very large bowl combine the first six ingredients, breaking up the shortening and mixing very well. Stir in the nuts and chocolate. Put into one or two large airtight containers and store in a dry cool place. Makes about 28 cups of dry mix, which you can package into 8 Mason jars, 3 1/2 cups mix per jar.

2. Attach directions on how to make a batch of cookies to each package: "In a large bowl combine the 3 1/2 cups of dry cookie mix with one slightly beaten large egg, the vanilla and enough water to make the mixture into a dough, about 1 to 2 teaspoons. Using a 1/4 cup measure, shape cookies by hand and place on parchment-lined or Silpat-lined cookie sheets. Bake in a preheated 375°F. oven at least one inch apart, as these cookies spread. Do not crowd the baking sheets. Bake for 10 to 12 minutes or until golden and fairly firm. Let cool on cookie sheet 5 minutes, then carefully transfer them with a spatula to racks to cool completely. If you need to reuse the baking sheets, cool them down completely first (you can use ice cubes) or the next batch of cookies will spread too much. These also freeze well."

OATMEAL RAISIN COOKIES IN A JAR—MAKES 1 BATCH OF 3 DOZEN COOKIES

Multiply the ingredients by the number of 1-quart Mason jars you want to make. Layer the ingredients in the order listed, tamping down each layer with a spoon.

Flour-Spice Mixture:

1 cup flour
1 teaspoon cinnamon
1 teaspoon baking soda
1/2 teaspoon nutmeg
1/2 teaspoon salt

3/4 cup firmly packed brown sugar
1/2 cup white sugar
3/4 cup raisins
2 cups old-fashioned oatmeal

Additional ingredients to make cookies:

1 large egg
1 1/2 cups softened unsalted butter (3 sticks)
1 teaspoon pure vanilla

1. Make flour-spice mix: In a large bowl combine the flour, cinnamon, baking soda, nutmeg and salt. Reserve.

2. In a 1-quart mason jar, layer the brown sugar, tamping it down, then the white sugar, tamping it down, the raisins, tamping them down and then the oatmeal. Add the reserved flour-spice mixture on top, tamp down and cover the jar.

3. For each gift: Put the 3 1/2 cups of the cookie mix in a mason jar or plastic bag. Attach directions on how to make the cookies: "In a big bowl combine the ingredients in the jar, one slightly beaten egg, the 1 1/2 cups softened butter and the 1 teaspoon vanilla. Mix until completely blended, using your hands at the end. Shape into balls the size of walnuts, place 2 inches apart on greased baking sheets, or you can line sheets with parchment paper. Bake in a 350°F. oven for 11 to 13 minutes. Cool 5 minutes on sheet, then remove cookies to a rack to finish cooling."

HOT COCOA MIX MAKES ABOUT 10 SERVINGS

Adjust strength and sweetness to your individual taste by adding more or less of the mix per cup. Package this in a clean glass jar and attach a plastic bag of miniature marshmallows. You can increase the recipe as many times as you want to make more gifts.

1 cup nonfat dry milk
1 cup dry creamer
1/2 cup unsweetened cocoa
3/4 to 1 cup powdered sugar, to your taste

1. Place a sieve over a large bowl and sift all ingredients, to eliminate lumps.

2. Mix ingredients well and place into pint jars or other containers of your choice.

3. Attach directions to make one serving to each gift: "To make one 8-ounce mug of hot cocoa, put 3 to 4 tablespoons of the mixture into a mug, then fill with boiling water. Serve with miniature marshmallows if desired.

WHITE CHOCOLATE SNACK MIX
MAKES ABOUT 10 CUPS

A whimsical, fun gift to give. From my dear friend Marcia Gantz, who embodies the spirit of giving in all she does!

2 cups Cheerios
2 cups <u>each</u> Rice Chex and Corn Chex
1 1/2 cups unsalted peanuts
1 cup dried cranberries
1 1/2 cups mini pretzels
2 cups M & Ms

12 ounces Ghirardelli or other quality white chocolate, chopped in food processor
1 tablespoon chopped paraffin (find in the canning aisle at the supermarket)
<u>1 teaspoon pure vanilla extract</u>

1. Place Cheerios, Rice and Corn Chex, peanuts, cranberries, mini pretzels and M & Ms on a large cookie sheet.

2. In a double boiler melt the white chocolate and paraffin over simmering water, stirring until melted and smooth. Stir in the vanilla.

3. Pour this mixture over the cereal mixture and gently fold to coat the mixture completely. Then place in large bowl and mix well. Spread mixture onto parchment paper or waxed paper to set up and dry. Divide into 10 1-cup packages and store in airtight containers, then give to lucky friends, with the recipe attached.

COFFEE CAN PUMPKIN NUT LOAVES
MAKES 5 LOAVES

Save your empty coffee cans from year to year, as they can be reused to make more gifts.

Crisco shortening to grease cans
5 1-pound coffee cans

3 cups white sugar
1 cup light brown sugar
1 1/2 cups vegetable oil (such as Wesson or Crisco)
5 large eggs, well beaten

5 cups flour
1 3/4 teaspoons salt
1 tablespoon baking soda
1 1/2 teaspoon <u>each</u> nutmeg and cinnamon

1 29-ounce can plain pumpkin (NOT pumpkin pie mix)
<u>3 cups or more walnuts, broken into large pieces</u>

1. Preheat oven to 350°F. Grease 5 1-pound coffee cans very well with Crisco. Reserve.

2. In large bowl of the electric mixer, combine sugars, oil and eggs. Beat well together.

3. In another bowl combine flour, salt, soda and spices and add to mixer bowl, stirring to combine well. Add pumpkin and mix well. Stir in walnuts.

4. Fill greased coffee cans equally, about 1/2 full. Place on cookie sheet to stabilize them.

5. Bake in preheated oven for about 1 hour to one hour and 15 minutes, or until a cake tester comes out clean when inserted all the way down the center of the loaves.

6. Cool on racks before removing from cans. The cans are reusable. These loaves freeze very well. Wrap them in plastic wrap, then cellophane if you wish, tie with a bow and present to friends!

GINGERBREAD BOYS AND GIRLS
MAKES ABOUT 32 COOKIES

I like to bake these cookies and package them with a gingerbread boy or girl cookie cutter, along with the recipe printed on red or green paper, cut in the shape of a gingerbread person and laminated. The dough should be divided into four portions and kept in the refrigerator as you roll one portion at a time, as it gets very soft and can be a bit tricky to roll, but it makes great cookies!

2 cups sugar
1 cup solid Crisco
2 large eggs
1/4 cup <u>each</u> molasses and water

4 cups all-purpose flour
1 teaspoon baking soda
1 teaspoon <u>each</u> ginger, cloves and nutmeg
2 teaspoons cinnamon
1/4 teaspoon salt

<u>Optional decorations: raisins for eyes and buttons and red hots for mouth</u>

1. In an electric mixer cream the sugar and Crisco well. Add the eggs, molasses and water.

2. In a large bowl sift the flour, baking soda, spices and salt. Add to the creamed mixture and mix well.

3. Divide dough into 4 pieces, flattening each into a round disk and wrapping each in plastic wrap. Refrigerate for several hours or overnight, as it will be too soft to work with right away. This dough also freezes well.

4. Roll out one disk at a time to 1/8-inch thickness on a well-floured board, keeping the other dough refrigerated. Cut with a gingerbread boy or girl cookie cutter and place on ungreased cookie sheets. Decorate with raisins for eyes and buttons and red hots for a mouth if you want.

5. Bake in a preheated 325°F. oven for 10 to 12 minutes. Carefully transfer to racks to cool.

DRUNKEN APRICOTS—MAKES 30

An elegant treat to finish a festive meal, or anytime your sweet tooth calls.

1/2 pound apricots, best quality available
1 cup apricot brandy

12 ounces best quality bittersweet or semisweet chocolate
<u>30 candy cups</u>

1. Place apricots and brandy in a 9" x 13" rectangular glass casserole. Cover with plastic wrap and microwave on high for 2 to 3 minutes, or until brandy just comes to a boil. Watch carefully. Alternately you can place apricots and brandy in a saucepan and bring to a boil, then transfer to a casserole, cover with plastic wrap. Let apricots and brandy cool at room temperature at least 2 hours or overnight.

2. Chop chocolate into small pieces and place in a glass bowl. Put bowl into a skillet of simmering water and melt, watching carefully. As soon as the chocolate is melted, remove and stir until smooth.

3. Drain apricots on absorbent paper. Dip 1/2 of each apricot in the chocolate and let excess chocolate drip off.

4. Put a piece of parchment or waxed paper on a baking sheet and spray with cooking spray. Lay each dipped apricot on the sheet as you coat them. Put into refrigerator for 15 minutes or until the chocolate sets up. Remove from refrigerator and place each dipped apricot in a foil candy cup. Store at room temperature.

SUE'S APRICOT BALLS
MAKES ABOUT 4 DOZEN ⏱ 👨‍🍳

I make these delicious treats every year in memory of my dear friend Sue Barton, who left us far too early.

8 ounces dried apricots, chopped (the processor does a good job)
1 14-ounce can sweetened condensed milk
2 1/2 cups unsweetened coconut

<u>2 cups or more pecans, chopped</u>

1. In a large bowl mix the apricots, sweetened condensed milk and coconut. Using rubber gloves, shape into small balls, as it is hard to resist licking your fingers.

2. Place the chopped pecans in a pie pan or on a large piece of parchment paper. Roll the balls in the nuts, coating well. Place on waxed or parchment paper and refrigerate an hour or more to set up. These freeze well, but it's best to make them when the family isn't home and hide them, if you want any left to give as gifts!

MAPLE SYRUP GRANOLA
MAKES 14 CUPS ⏱ 👨‍🍳

This mixture is delicious sprinkled over yogurt or ice cream, cereal, fresh fruit, or as a topping on baked fruit cobblers.

cooking spray
1/2 cup <u>each</u> vegetable oil, pure maple syrup and light brown sugar, lightly packed

6 cups quick-cooking or old-fashioned oats (not instant)
2 cups coarsely chopped walnuts

1 cup <u>each</u> wheat germ and sweetened shredded coconut,
<u>1 cup each raisins, dried cranberries or other dried berries</u>

1. <u>Make the maple syrup mixture</u>: In a 2-quart microwave-safe bowl combine the oil, maple syrup and brown sugar and microwave, uncovered, on High for 3 minutes. Remove from microwave and whisk until any lumps disappear.

2. In a large bowl combine the wheat germ and coconut. Stir in the maple syrup mixture well.

3. Spray two 11" x 17" cookie sheets with cooking spray and spread mixture evenly over both pans. Bake in a preheated 350°F. oven on two racks for 10 minutes, switching racks after 5 minutes, then remove from oven and stir well. Rotate pans from top to bottom and bake another 10 minutes. Stir in the raisins and dried cranberries or other dried berries of your choice.

4. Cool on racks in the pans for one hour, then divide into 14 1-cup packages, to share with friends. Keeps well in airtight containers for one month.

SUGAR PLUMS—MAKES 64 PIECES

An old-fashioned treat that's worth revisiting.

4 ounces almond paste
2 tablespoons light corn syrup
1/2 cup or more confectioners' sugar, as needed

food coloring (optional)

1 pound pitted dried dates
1/2 cup superfine sugar, or if you can't find it, whirl
    regular sugar in a blender to make it finer
paper candy cups

1. Make the almond paste filling: In a medium bowl
mix the almond paste, corn syrup and confectioners'
(powdered) sugar. Divide the mixture into as many
parts as you wish different colors, such as red and green
for Christmas, pastel colors for Easter, etc. Color each
portion with a few drops of food coloring. You may need
to add a bit more powdered sugar if the paste gets too
sticky by the addition of liquid food colors.

2. Shape tinted paste into small cones slightly longer than
the dates. You may need to coat your hands with some
powdered sugar as you work.

3. Slit open each date lengthwise with a small sharp
knife and place a small almond paste cone in each slit,
reclosing and reshaping the date so that a small part of
the tinted paste is visible at the open side.

4. Place the superfine sugar in a small bowl and roll each
filled date in it gently to coat. Place finished dates in small
paper candy cups if desired. Store in an airtight container
for up to two weeks.

MICROWAVE PECAN BRITTLE
MAKES 1 POUND

*After cooking a batch of the candy, always let the glass
measure cool to room temperature before cleaning or it
may crack. Then fill it with warm water and heat on High
in microwave until water boils. Sugar will soften and wash
off easily.*

1/2 cup light Karo corn syrup
1 cup sugar
1/8 teaspoon salt

2 cups pecan halves or cashews
1 teaspoon each unsalted butter and pure vanilla
1/2 teaspoon cinnamon

1 teaspoon baking soda

1. Spray a cookie sheet with nonstick spray. Reserve.

2. Spray a 2-quart (8-cup) glass measuring cup or Pyrex
bowl with cooking spray. Add the corn syrup, sugar
and salt, stir, then microwave on High 2 minutes, until
boiling, then cook on High 4 minutes more. Carefully stir
in the nuts, butter, vanilla and cinnamon. Cook 2 minutes
more on High. Immediately stir in the baking soda with a
wooden spoon or heatproof spatula until mixture is light
and foamy. Be careful, as mixture is hot!

3. Quickly pour out onto the prepared cookie sheet
sprayed with cooking spray, using a wooden spoon or
heatproof spatula—DO NOT touch mixture or you can
get burned. Remember that hot sugar is liquid napalm!
Let cool and then break into pieces. Store in an airtight
container.

MILLION-DOLLAR FUDGE
MAKES 48 1-INCH SQUARES

This recipe is attributed to First Lady Mamie Eisenhower. It is one of the richest and most unctuous textured fudges you will ever taste, but just be sure to follow the directions exactly to get the best results.

softened butter to butter pan

4 1/2 cups sugar
pinch of salt
2 tablespoons unsalted butter
1 12-ounce can evaporated milk

1 12-ounce package chocolate chips
3 4-ounce bars Baker's German Sweet Chocolate, chopped in processor
1 7-ounce jar marshmallow cream

Optional: 2 cups coarsely chopped walnuts

paper candy cups

1. Butter a metal or glass 9" x 13" pan.

2. In a large heavy saucepan, combine the sugar, salt, butter and milk. Bring to a boil over medium heat, stirring constantly. Boil, stirring constantly, for 6 minutes or until a candy thermometer registers 225°F. Turn off heat, stir in the chocolate chips, sweet chocolate and marshmallow cream, beating until the chocolate is melted and marshmallow cream is incorporated, putting back on low fire if necessary to melt chocolate. Stir in the optional nuts, and immediately pour into the buttered pan.

3. Let stand a few hours at room temperature, or refrigerate one hour, before cutting into squares. I like to put the squares into paper or foil candy cups for an elegant presentation.

CHOCOLATE BARK WITH DRIED CHERRIES, WALNUTS AND CHOPPED PRETZELS
MAKES ONE PAN, NUMBER OF PIECES DEPENDS ON HOW BIG YOU CUT THEM

I found this killer recipe on a Nell Newman organic chocolate bar. The daughter of actor Paul Newman has earned kudos for her commitment to organic food.

1 13 1/2-ounce bar dark chocolate, chopped in processor or by hand
1 cup each coarsely chopped dried cherries, chopped walnuts and chopped pretzels

1. Prepare an 8" x 12" or 8" x 13" cookie sheet with Release foil or other foil. Reserve.

2. In a double boiler melt the chocolate over medium heat. Put into a large bowl and add the cherries and walnuts. Spread evenly in prepared pan with an offset spatula. Sprinkle with the pretzels. Refrigerate for 1 to 2 hours or until firm.

3. Remove from foil and cut into squares, or break into uneven shards. Put into candy cups. Store in the refrigerator.

WHITE AND DARK CHOCOLATE ALMOND BARK—MAKES 1 1/4 POUNDS

This is a favorite at our house and among our friends. At Christmas use 3/4 cup finely ground peppermint candy, (ground in a spice blender or coffee grinder—just don't use the grinder again to grind coffee unless you like spiced coffee) in place of the almonds. I couldn't leave this recipe out without a revolt from my "posse."

3/4 pound best quality white chocolate, chopped in food processor or by hand
2 to 3 tablespoons Crisco solid shortening

3/4 cup almonds, toasted at 350°F. 8 to 10 minutes until golden, then coarsely chopped. OR 3/4 cup finely ground peppermint candy

1/4 pound best quality bittersweet or semisweet chocolate, chopped in food processor or by hand

<u>foil or paper candy cups</u>

1. Line a 10" x 15" jellyroll baking sheet with heavy duty foil and set it aside.

2. In a large bowl over a pan of barely simmering water, heat the white chocolate and Crisco, stirring constantly until melted and smooth. Be especially careful not to overheat, as white chocolate separates when heated on too high a heat. I have found the addition of the Crisco to be a lifesaver when chocolate "seizes" if any water gets in it when it's being melted also. Stir in the toasted almonds or ground peppermint. Quickly pour this mixture on the prepared baking sheet and spread to about a 3/8-inch thickness, using an offset spatula.

3. In the top of a double boiler heat the dark chocolate over barely simmering water, stirring constantly until melted and smooth. Remove from heat.

4. Drizzle the melted dark chocolate over the top of the white chocolate mixture. With a small knife make a zigzag motion through the two layers to create a swirled effect.

5. Let the candy stand several hours until firm, or refrigerate it about 30 minutes. Use the foil to lift the candy from the baking sheet and break it into uneven pieces. Fill candy cups and package for gifts. Can store tightly covered at room temperature, or in the refrigerator for up to two weeks.

COOK'S TIP

If you've gotten this far in the book, you, too, are a foodie, and I encourage you to try these new recipes and share the wealth with your friends. As I said before, Food is Love, and I wish you many hours of joy both in the kitchen and around the table. Don't just eat to live, but LIVE to EAT well!

INDEX

CPSIA information can be obtained at www.ICGtesting.com
Printed in the USA
BVOW100533100613

322772BV00004B/4/P